We Don't Die

A SKEPTIC'S DISCOVERY

OF

LIFE AFTER DEATH

Praise for *We Don't Die*

"Change the way you look at death and as a result you will change the way you choose to live. Sandra gives you the tools to lead an incredible life. No longer live in fear, no longer will you have to be stuck in grief. Imagine the joy of feeling free to have extraordinary relationships and produce amazing results." —Dov Baron, Author, Leading Authority on Authentic Leadership, Host & Executive Producer of *The Accidental Guru Show*

"Thank you, Sandra, for having the courage to publish your discovery. It's also comforting to know that your declaration is substantiated in the Bible (I Corinthians 15:26) with 'The last enemy that shall be destroyed is death.' Your research is sound and the time is NOW for us to collectively explore this subject." —Jessie Barth, Author of *B: A Capital Tale*

"Physical and mental training as well as practice is necessary to win. *We Don't Die* provides you with the strategies you need to achieve great victories in your life." —David Brabham, International Sports Car Racing Champion

"The journey of discovery is always a challenge, as long-held beliefs do not easily surrender to new understanding. Sandra makes perhaps your most important journey of discovery easy with *We Don't Die*. Sandra's story and her homework for you are designed to make that journey as enjoyable and fruitful as possible." —Tom and Lisa Butler, Authors of *There is No Death and There Are No Dead*, Directors of Association TransCommunication

"As an investigator and expert on detecting deception, the evidence in this book is clear. I've also witnessed suffering and pain my entire career. This book is a must read for those who wish to visualize how to handle grief before they experience it." —Michael A. Coller, Private Investigator and Author of *Seven Signs of Lying*

"Have you ever wondered how you fit into the cosmos—what life holds in store for you? *We Don't Die* provides an entertaining and thought-provoking glimpse into where we come from and how we can make our stay in this lifetime as fulfilling as it can be." —Jacques Dallaire, PhD. Author of *Performance Thinking*

"*We Don't Die* gives you the gift of discovery, hope and healing. This beautifully written book will bring you so much peace. You are never alone and always deeply loved." —Tamara Green LCSW, Love Mentor,® Relationship Coach, Speaker

"Sandra offers immense freedom, joy and possibility for the future of your life and those you love. She has created a gift for millions of people that will impact one of life's most dire circumstances, the death of a loved one." —Greg Hartmann, Cultural Architect, and Author of *Do Due Diligence*

"As a skeptic, I resisted reading this book. However, *We Don't Die* took me on an incredible journey that opened my eyes and heart to the possibility of reconnecting with the love of my life, my mother. Thank you, Sandra." —Travis Lane Jenkins, Renegade Millionaire, Business & Marketing Coach

"Sandra has written a most extraordinary book, one that gently removes the veil between what we've been taught about not only death, but life as well. It is an amazing story that shows the reader just how incredible our existence is, and how to make it even more amazing." —Jim Morack, Speaker, Coach, and Author of *Learning from Life*

"Sandra has managed to tackle some of the most difficult issues of death . . . and life. Page after page offers insight, wisdom, and hope." —Dr. Karen Sherman, Psychologist, Speaker, and Author of *Mindfulness and The Art of Choice*

"There is no need to go into the waters of sorrow alone; take Ms. Champlain's hand, and she will guide you through to the other side, a better, happier person." —Ellen Snortland, Actor, Activist, and Author of *Beauty Bites Beast*

"The continuum of consciousness has implications for all once it is truly understood. *We Don't Die* is a foundational piece to bringing the continuum principal to the fore." —K. Paul Stoller, MD, Author of *Oxytocin: The Hormone of Healing and Hope*, Founder of GriefSOS.com

"We all have a voice in our head that either makes us successful or leads us to failure. *We Don't Die* brings you in alignment with that voice and allows you to change from the inside out." —Woody Woodward, Filmmaker, Author, and Success Strategist

We Don't Die

A SKEPTIC'S DISCOVERY

OF

LIFE AFTER DEATH

SANDRA CHAMPLAIN

Imbue Press

We Don't Die
A Skeptic's Discovery of Life After Death

ISBN 9781614483823 paperback
ISBN 9781614483830 eBook
Library of Congress Control Number: 2012948203

Cover design by:
Kathi Dunn
dunn-design.com

Imbue Press an imprint of Morgan James Publishing
Morgan James Publishing
The Entrepreneurial Publisher
5 Penn Plaza, 23rd Floor,
New York City, New York 10001
www.MorganJamesPublishing.com

Interior design by:
Dorie McClelland
springbookdesign.com

In an effort to support local communities, raise awareness and funds, Morgan James Publishing donates a percentage of all book sales for the life of each book to Habitat for Humanity Peninsula and Greater Williamsburg. Get involved today, visit www.MorganJamesBuilds.com.

Get involved today, visit
www.MorganJamesBuilds.com.

Habitat
for Humanity®
Peninsula and
Greater Williamsburg
Building Partner

Dedicated to my mother, Marion Champlain.

You taught me to work hard, play hard,
and never give up on my dreams.

Thank you for always believing in me. I love you, Mom.

Contents

Foreword by Bernie Siegel, MD   *xi*

Introduction   *1*

1   The Reason for Living Life on Earth   *13*

2   Becoming a Skeptic Is Easy   *29*

3   The Reality of Life After Death   *37*

4   Trusting the World's Greatest Minds   *61*

5   Religious Agreement for Life After Death   *91*

6   Life … The Grand Illusion   *99*

7   Heaven Is Closer than You Think   *111*

8   Seeing with Your Eyes Closed   *129*

9   Reconnecting with Those You Have Loved and Lost   *155*

10   Surviving Grief   *169*

11   The Genius of the Human Body   *195*

12   Riding the Emotional Roller Coaster   *219*

13   It Is All in Your Mind   *235*

14   10 Daily Habits to Super Charge Your Life   *255*

Epilogue   *275*

Acknowledgments   *279*

Recommended Reading   *283*

Foreword

Bernie Siegel, MD

First of all, I would like to say that I agree with Sandra when she says we don't die, but I think it is important to define what the we is that doesn't die. We consist of more than one thing. We are mind, body, and spirit. I compare us to a satellite dish, remote control, and television or computer screen. There are many channels of consciousness available to us and our mind, like a remote control selects the channel to tune into that then defines how we act and demonstrates which program and what Lord we are tuned into. So components may die or become nonfunctioning but the source remains alive and vital and still sends out messages to all living things.

I know from personal experience that consciousness never ends. It does not require the physical body to exist. Blind people see when they have a near-death experience and I learned the same lesson as a four-year-old when I left my body while choking on a toy I had aspirated. I was able to think and see while never wondering how I could accomplish that if I were no longer in my body. When the child on the bed had a seizure and vomited, dislodging the toy parts, I felt sucked back into his body as if by a vacuum. Consciousness never ends, and time does not exist when we leave our bodies. Those were hard things for me to accept and understand, but my experience has opened my mind to the truth.

I have also learned that when a loved one dies that grief can be appropriate but it must not take over your life and be all that you think about. What taught me that lesson was the experience I had with the Angel of Death. After one of my young patients died following surgery, I couldn't accept what had happened and how God could make a world where children died of cancer. The Angel took me to Heaven to see the parade of all the children who had died that week. They were all looking beautiful, wearing white robes and carrying a glowing white candle. When I noticed a child coming, carrying a dark candle, the Angel told me to go and light it. As I approached the child I could see it was my patient, Tony. I asked him why no one had lit his candle. He answered, "They keep lighting it, but your tears keep putting it out." I now understand that we are here to live and learn and that by learning we create a better future for all those who will follow us as we are creating a more enlightened consciousness for them to exist in. So, when our bodies can no longer function and demonstrate the message of our life, then it is time to leave and become perfect again, and either enter a new body with which to demonstrate what the school of life has taught us or communicate via consciousness until that event occurs.

I hear voices and know when they are coming from the collective consciousness. The Voice has helped me to experience a much more meaningful life. I have written about some of the events. Messages that helped my father to die laughing and helped me to adopt a dog named Buddy after writing my book, *Buddy's Candle*. I have also had mystics bring me messages from my dead patients and family members and they mentioned their names and spoke with words as that person had. One quickie: When my parents died, my mystic friend, who does not know them, called me and said my parents were together again and were being shown around by someone who likes cigarettes and chocolate. Before I could answer she said, "Oh, it's Elisabeth Kübler-Ross." Yes, Elisabeth was a close friend and mentor of mine. No coincidence.

I also had another unexpected experience when a friend, while talking to me on the phone, heard how busy I was and said, "Why are you living this life?" She wanted me to slow down and do less but I went into a trance and had a past-life experience. I will share that I realized I had become a surgeon because I had killed with a sword in my past life due to a lack of faith in my Lord, like being tuned into the wrong channel and voice, and I now wanted to heal and cure with a knife. I also learned that *wordswordswords* can become *swordsword-swords* and kill or cure also. I want people to understand that to me, a past life experience does not mean I literally lived the experience but that I am impregnated with the consciousness of someone whose life preceded mine. I think this also accounts for the talent we sometimes see in children that we can't explain. So the body dies but *we* do not.

I also have had experiences with animal communication and, when animal intuitive Amelia Kinkade, while sitting in Los Angeles, told me where to find a missing cat in Connecticut in incredible detail while seeing through the cat's eyes, I became a believer and have since communicated with our pets. The key to this and all consciousness communication is the quiet mind. Similar to the symbolism of the still pond, which then allows us to see the truth reflected back to us. When your life is filled with turbulence, you cannot experience what we are sharing with you.

We have to be open to our potential and not close our minds based upon beliefs, but learn to accept based upon our experience. As Ernest Holmes shared in *Science of Mind*, what if Jesus was the only normal person who ever lived? My definition of God is loving, intelligent, conscious energy. Therefore we are immortal through our love and consciousness and capable of altering the physical world through our consciousness and energy by creating the future we desire. When we choose what is life enhancing for every living thing, we make miracles possible. Our bodies are the tools we use, but cannot last forever as our love, energy, and consciousness can and do.

I can think of so many stories in which messages from the dead have been shared with me by their loved ones. In one case, a murdered young woman loved birds and at her sister's outdoor wedding, a bird interrupted the wedding by making so much noise that everyone's reaction was that it was her sister. As the mother was telling this story, a bird flew in the open window of the room where we were meeting. Never had that ever happened in all the years we met there.

Your son loved seagulls and one winter's day a seagull lands on the highway. In your mind, you hear him say, "Mom slow down." You do and as you drive around the bend you see a pile up of cars caused by a sheet of ice on the road, which you avoid. Your son loved butterflies and after his death, a butterfly follows you while out walking in Connecticut. When his dad got home he looked up the butterfly in his son's book and it was a species only found in South America.

I have photographs of a butterfly that stayed with my wife and me for a day and a half, after my wife rescued it from a store by offering it her hand, as we did an outdoor workshop on the Hawaiian island of Kauai where my patient had died. When we were ready to go to sleep, my wife went out and brushed the butterfly off her shoulder and it came back into our apartment sitting on her other shoulder. It finally flew off when the workshop ended.

Remember, we can be thrown off the Earth when our bodies die but we are still riding the horse of life. When we are ready to leave our bodies and are free of conflict, we can decide to leave with no difficulties. As my father put it in giving his advice to seniors, "Tell them to just fall up." The night he was tired of his body, he told us no dinner or vitamins, and fell up that evening at age 97.

I have worked with people who have been brain dead for years but where legal issues prevent the family from ending their tube feedings. I simply shared with one woman who had been in that state for two years, because we can hear while in coma, under anesthesia, and asleep, that her love would stay with us and if she needed to go, it was alright. She died within fifteen minutes of my speaking to her. I have also had people respond, "I'm not going anywhere."

I had a man "die" during emergency surgery for a perforated intestine and the anesthesiologist was leaving the room to get help to transport the body. I figured, due to my exposure to Kübler-Ross, I had little to lose if his spirit was still around, so I said his name and, "It's not your time yet. Come on back." His heart started beating and he recovered. The anesthesiologist was quite impressed.

So accept your life as an experience, and know that the only thing of permanence is our love and expressing it through our consciousness, as we live and learn through our experience.

THE GREAT TEACHER

Death what a great teacher you are
Yet few of us elect to take your class
And learn about life
That is the essence of death's teaching
Death is not an elective
We must all take the class
The wise students audit the class in their early years
And find enlightenment
They are prepared when graduation day comes
It is your commencement

FROM A DISTANCE

They sang, "God is watching us from a distance"
I don't agree
I know God and it is a short trip to God
If you'd like me to introduce you
To yourself someday let me know
When I was a child
I thought God was way up there
A long way off
Now I know God is here

Those who understand know
That if you can't see God
It's because you can't stoop low enough
Or think you have to be tall enough to see in a mirror
Be still, bend forward, and get close to yourself
And water will reflect your Godliness too

INTRODUCTION

*Don't be dismayed at goodbyes, a farewell is necessary before
you can meet again and meeting again, after moments or
lifetimes, is certain for those who are friends.*

~ Richard Bach, writer, b. 1936

Saturday, October 22, 2005, Omega Institute, Rhinebeck, NY

Heavy raindrops fall on the roof of my cabin, tucked amongst the trees behind the retreat center. The air is cold and damp, my hair and clothes are wet from the walk in the rain and my only warmth is coming from a small heater in the corner of my room. I put on my pajamas and crawl under the covers. The roommate that the retreat center has assigned to me is still out to dinner with her friends.

I sit on my bed and question if I am completely crazy. I clearly feel that I have been led on a path to figure out if life after death is real. The cab driver who brought me here could not believe the class I was here to take even existed. I told him I was taking a course called *Electronic Voice Phenomena*, which promised that it was possible to hear messages from our deceased friends and family, by using tape recorders. Although the cab driver thought I was a little weird, he gave me his email address and made me promise to tell him what happened.

On one hand, I want it to be real, but on another, I think the idea is insane. Is it possible that our deceased loved ones are still nearby and that they talk to us by putting their voices on a tape recorder? The course instructors, Tom and Lisa Butler, have been doing these recordings for 17 years. Why would people waste their time if this weren't possible?

I put all of those thoughts out of my mind and pull out my Sony digital recorder, which had been recommended by people effective at getting *EVPs*. I am always a good student who does her homework and I want to get this recording done before my roommate comes back. When we met yesterday, I lied to her and told her that I was in a writers' workshop, as I didn't want her to know that I was really trying to communicate with the dead. I didn't even tell my family what I was doing this weekend. Only the cab driver knows the real reason I am at the retreat center.

Cuddled under the covers holding my tape recorder, I close my eyes and try to imagine myself sitting in the center of a high-energy field, as our energy is supposedly used by the *other side* to put these voices on the recorder. I imagine my grandmother, grandfather, aunt, and uncle standing around the foot of my bed and press the *record* button. I begin to talk. "Alright, my dear friends, I'm going to do one more recording. Try to speak as loud as you can. If I am supposed to help people believe in life after death, I have to hear you, so please try to talk loud. I will be quiet for about a minute and then I'll say goodnight and I won't bug you anymore." (Earlier in the day I had been talking to the same four *imaginary* people, unsuccessfully trying to hear any voices.)

I stop talking to allow the recording of the raindrops on the roof of the cabin. The dead must manipulate *white noise* so I figured the sound of the rain might be okay. I wait, and after about a minute I say "Goodnight" to my imaginary or invisible friends and press the *stop* button. I put on my earphones, press the *rewind* button and begin to listen.

Not expecting this time to be any different from the other attempts that I have made to listen to the deceased, I press the *play* button on my digital voice recorder. Convinced that I will hear nothing, I wait and listen.

Then, I hear something. A sharp chill runs through my body and my skin is covered with goosebumps. I press *rewind* to hear it again and again and again. My mind is in a state of shock because I should not be hearing the words that I am hearing; I should only be hearing raindrops.

Loudly and clearly, I hear a man saying, "Goodnight Sandra," in what sounds like a computer-generated voice. Then, two faint women's voices say, "Goodnight, goodnight," followed by another male voice saying, "Goodnight."

I am suddenly stunned and afraid. I don't know what to think and I feel sick to my stomach. What I am experiencing is unreal, like nothing I could have ever imagined. "Are these people really here with me? Are people *always* with me?" I become upset with myself for even coming to this retreat center. I find myself wanting to talk to someone human, but it is too late at night and there is no one around. I replay the recording over and over and over. Finally, I am mentally exhausted and just before I fall asleep I have visions of my grandparents and aunt and uncle hovering over me. "Are you really here?" I think to myself and go to sleep very certain that my life will *never* be the same again.

Dear Reader,

Thank you for opening this book today. The story I just shared with you is true. I have spent many years with this information and many more incredible stories, as you will soon discover.

I want to apologize to you for not sharing this information with you sooner. You might have thought that I should have *shouted from the rooftops*, "I, Sandra Champlain, have proven there is life after death." You may have told me back in 2005 that I had enough credible evidence between the EVPs and the other studies I had done to make a profound difference in the lives of people who had lost someone close to them. However, my own fear of being called crazy, weird, being laughed at, or people not wanting to be involved with me stopped me from sharing this information with you until now.

My wonderful grandmother died, followed by my dad's death from cancer, and, just weeks later, we had to put to sleep our beloved cat, Ozzie. My grief during that time was the most painful thing I have ever experienced. It opened my eyes to a suffering that I could not have previously imagined.

Writing this today, I don't care what people think. If they think I'm crazy or weird or choose to laugh at me . . . that is fine. If they choose not to be associated with me, that is okay too.

You see, my friend, I must share my journey with you now. I have the answers that will offer you comfort that there is, in fact, life after death. I will give you evidence that your loved ones have gone on to a great place, and you and I will go there too. I will teach you how you may communicate with them and realize that you are never alone. You will begin to look at who you *really* are, apart from the skin and bones you are made of. I intend for you to be excited about your life, knowing that living on Earth is just a short part of your overall existence. I plan on you having a new, powerful relationship with fear, so that you may realize some of your long forgotten dreams and have new access to results you cannot imagine right now.

How is your life going for you right now? Would the information in this book make a difference in how you would live your life? My guess is that you may be a lot like me; you are someone who works hard, does the best you can, but in the back of your mind you wonder, "Is this all there is? Is there a reason I am here and a purpose to my life?"

Life can be fantastic, but it can really suck sometimes, can't it? We can all think back to good times, when we were very, very happy. Then there are other times of pain and struggle, and frustrations and failure.

There are also those times that life just is neutral: nothing bad, nothing good, we simply just exist.

No matter where you are, I do believe that part of being human is to experience a full range of emotions. You may have realized that life can be very tough and not easy whatsoever. Guess what? I believe life is not meant to be easy.

You may be in one of the following places right now:

You have suffered a terrible loss and miss someone dearly.
You may have been told that you or someone close to you may
    be dying.
You may have a fear of dying.
You may be looking for meaning in your life.
You may be in a depressed state and not know where to turn.
You may desire access to new, incredible results.
You may be intrigued by the title of this book and simply be
    curious.

Whichever place you are in, or in a place I haven't listed, I promise that *We Don't Die* will make a difference for you. It contains necessary information to guide you through life, help you through the pain of grief, and ultimately get you living your life with incredible joy. You, my friend, deserve it.

Where are you in your life now? If you had to tell me on a scale of 1 to 10 (1 being a lousy, sad, depressed existence, and 10 being fabulous, you couldn't be happier) how would you rate your life? You might want to grab a pen and write your answer next to this paragraph.

I am committed, by the way, that your life become much, much better by the time you are finished reading *We Don't Die*. No, forget that, how about your life is much better by the time you finish reading a few chapters? By the time you get to the end of this book, I promise you will be much happier than when you started reading. Months from now you may glance back at this page and realize you are happier than you could have ever imagined yourself to be. Do you want to play that game with me? I hope so.

You may not believe this is possible and I understand. You may be experiencing tremendous loss and pain. I will help you understand why you are feeling the pain, give you some tools to help release it, and get you back into life.

You may be a person who is curious about this book. Your life is absolutely fine and you have no problems, life seems to be wonderful. While that sounds good and you feel good right now, you probably cannot imagine what I am about to say. *Your life can be even better.*

This is not a book to read only. It is a book that will require you to go on a journey of looking at yourself, your beliefs, your relationships, your wants, and your dreams. There will be no test at the end and I will not be calling you to see if you followed the instructions. You are old enough to know that you will only get results if you take action.

Certainly, you will hear about my journey and you will learn some incredible facts. You will hear some opinions from me and other teachers. You will be asked to look at your own opinions. I have had an interesting life and there are parts of this book that will certainly entertain you, and that's okay. Books are also meant for entertainment.

However, my real goal in writing *We Don't Die* is for you to have a great life. For you to learn who you *really* are. For you to understand that there is nothing wrong with you, that you are perfectly fine just the way you are. For you to realize that those things you really want in your life are not only possible, but I want to give you the tools to make those things happen. By the way, in case you haven't heard this lately, *you are special, there is no one like you, and you deserve to have it all.*

There are some very specific things I expect you to get by the time you are finished reading, *We Don't Die: A Skeptic's Discovery of Life After Death.* Of course, I will give you every bit of the supporting facts, figures, and information, so that this information is real to you:

1. *You* survive physical death. Your body disappears but *you* will still exist.
2. Your friends and relatives that have died are still around and you can connect with them.
3. You will feel that you are not alone, ever. You have love around you even if you cannot see it.
4. You will understand *grief*, what it is, why we must feel it, and how to lessen your pain.
5. You will experience *remote viewing*, an extra sensory perception technique that may leave you speechless and understanding that you are much more than the physical body you know yourself to be.
6. You will no longer fear death, and will instead know that death is a natural progression to something better.
7. You will no longer fear life, and will realize that you can accomplish incredible results for yourself.
8. You will have a new relationship with *fear*, have better relationships, and be able to achieve your dreams, realizing that you can never fail.

There is more to life than meets the eye,
and there is more to you than you know.

If you are ready to have the results that I listed above, I invite you to continue reading. Again, I won't be looking over your shoulder to make sure you do the homework.

What I am interested in is just that one thing: I am interested in you having a great life.

What does a great life look like to you? What is it that you want? Only you will be able to answer those questions. I put some blank pages in the back of the book or grab a notebook to write down your dream life now. Take a few minutes and answer the following question:

If you woke up tomorrow and were living your dream life,
what would it look like?

I will wait right here while you answer this question. If you don't choose to answer and figure you'll do it another time, you are only cheating yourself. Even if you don't write it down, take a minute and put down the book long enough to envision your dream life.

This book will show you the direction to get there. If you were to go on a long journey, you would need to know where you were going, right? You'd have to put the address of your destination into your GPS, or at least have a map with you and have planned your route from point A to point B. By having you clarify your dreams, we are simply doing that now, identifying your destination. As *We Don't Die* unfolds, everything you learn will lead you closer and closer to your dream destination.

Let me ask you again, "If you woke up tomorrow and were living the life of your dreams, what would it look like? What would it feel like?"

Make sure you write down everything you can imagine about your dream life, including where you live, who you live with, the level of health you have, the relationships you have, your level of success, perhaps your job, and even what your home looks like and what cars or pets you may have.

Now take it one step further. "If you have all of those things you just listed, and all those dreams were fulfilled, how would your life feel to you? What words would express the joy of living your dream life?"

Write down those answers. Write them down in detail. Only you know the words of what you want your life to be like. For me, things like "Excited to wake up every day, life is an adventure, experiencing a ton of fun, laughter, being with the people I love, doing what I love" are on my list. What is on your list? Can you imagine what it would be like to experience those things?

Those are just some of the results for you to get out of not just reading, but fully participating in, *We Don't Die: A Skeptic's Discovery of Life After Death.*

Let's now get to the most important subject, *you.* What if *you* could never die? Now, I know that our bodies die, that is not what I am talking about. I am talking about *you,* the personality, the mind, the soul. The *you* who dreams, who loves, who creates, who loves to laugh. What if that *you* never died? What if, at the moment your heart stops beating, you simply open your eyes and find yourself in another place?

Have you ever awakened from a dream that seemed so real? But, when you woke up, you realized it was just a dream. That reminds me of a nursery rhyme from the 1800s that many of us know:

> *Row, row, row your boat,*
> *Gently down the stream.*
> *Merrily, merrily, merrily, merrily,*
> *Life is but a dream.*

"Life is but a dream . . ." Could this be? What if, when your body dies, the new place in which you find yourself is so incredibly real that it makes your life on Earth seem like just a dream? What if you looked back on your life (your boat) and got to see how well you rowed down the stream? Did you row gently and merrily, or did you go against the current and try to fight your way upstream?

Be forewarned, *We Don't Die* contains some startling new information that may shake you up a little. You may find yourself saying, "No way is that possible," or, "She has to be making this up." I assure you, all of this information is shared simply for one purpose: for you to realize that you are not who you think you are. You are really a being capable of a whole lot more than what you have experienced so far in your life, and I will share with you some things that will prove that.

I have a question for you: at the end of reading this book, if you got all the proof you needed to believe that *you* could never die and that your deceased loved ones are still near, how would you live your life? Would you take more chances? Would you go after your dreams? Would you say things to people that you normally wouldn't say? Would you have more courage in your life? Would you have better results? Would you love more fully? Would you have an incredible life and be able to look back on it with pride? Would you be able to open your eyes in that other dimension and powerfully say, "Yes, I went merrily down the stream!"

Welcome to a brand new opportunity. Peace, joy, love, success, courage, abundance, and happiness are just some of the results that you can have by reading this book. I do realize that because we are human, things cannot always be merry, and so we will begin that discussion in the very first chapter.

If you are someone who is currently experiencing the pain of grief, I want you to know there will be a lot of comfort and advice for you within these pages. I have experienced that it is possible for you to transform grief into something so much more. As much as I hated the pain associated with grief from my dad's death, I am also grateful for experiencing it. Had the events in my life been different, *We Don't Die* would not have been created. My goal for you is that you find *that thing* that gives you life, that thing that makes you want to jump out of bed each morning with enthusiasm.

Today, I will begin to share my journey with you and give you all the *proof* that I have uncovered that *We Don't Die*. You will read stories about some of the greatest minds in history and why they believed in life after death. You will learn about the many men and woman who are currently communicating with the deceased by using audio and visual tools, as well as those using mental abilities. You will discover how blind people can accurately *see* using the power of their minds. You will learn about a man who wrote a *fictional* novel about the *Titan*, a ship that hit an iceberg on its maiden voyage, fourteen years before the *Titanic* sank. You will learn some amazing things about the world and its inhabitants that may leave you in disbelief, but they are so very real.

The best part about all of this is that you don't have to believe me! You will, however, believe yourself when you have experiences that you cannot explain logically. I have some great, simple exercises for you to do later in *We Don't Die* that will leave you in awe. You will be left wondering, "How did I do that, did that really happen?" I believe that when you can have such profound experiences, you will not only have *faith* but you will have a *belief* of who you *really* are and what you are really capable of. That, my friend, is the main ingredient for you to have a powerful life.

Skeptics, pessimists, disbelievers, and those intrigued, buckle up! Imagine you just sat down on a roller coaster. *We Don't Die* is like a roller coaster: you may feel that it is going in an easy direction and that you already know some of this material. Some of the information might not seem to make any sense, and you may question why the material is necessary. The material is necessary for support, just like the coaster needs solid ground and lots of strength beneath it to keep you safe. There will be some scary parts of this book, similar to climbing steep hills on the roller coaster. Before you know it, you may be happy and smiling as the roller coaster gives you a thrill. There may even be a loop or two that will leave you exhilarated. My intention is that you leave this ride with a big smile on your face.

What is the one rule you must always abide by while riding a roller coaster? *Keep your seatbelt fastened* so you can stay on the ride until the end. If you do, I promise that your life will never be the same and, by the end of this ride, you will realize that *you can never die.*

Sandra Champlain

Chapter 1

Choosing to Visit Planet Earth

Adventure is not outside man; it is within.

~ George Eliot, English Victorian novelist, b. 1856

guide·book, *noun*

A handbook of directions, advice, and information, especially for travelers or tourists.

What would it be like to know who you really are and what purpose your life is serving? What if you knew what lessons you were here to learn and that there is a very special reason you are here on Earth? What if you had a guidebook to refer to, to remind you of who you really are, what you are capable of, and whether you are on track or not? I would like you to do a little imagining with me right now. Are you open to trying something?

Let us imagine what it would be like to be living in a place called *Heaven*. Even if you do not believe in such an idea, I ask you to play along with me. Imagine a place full of clouds, full of joy, full of love, full of angels and lovely music, full of beauty, wisdom, and all good things. Imagine you are a spirit or a soul, with a transparent body, simply floating around from cloud to cloud, enjoying this wonderful existence.

Imagine being perched on your fluffy, soft, white, cozy cloud, and you are awakening to another perfect day. Perfect in just every way. You are supremely wise, and only experience pure joy. Your daily activities consist of floating around the universe to visit the nicest places. You regularly share conversations with the nicest souls. Every wish is granted, all you have to do is think a thought and, *voila*, your thought immediately takes form. It is simple: you wish for a hot fudge sundae, or a waterfall. or a rainbow, or living in a mansion, and it appears instantly before your eyes! Life is good, there is no exercising to be done, no calories to count, nothing to be responsible for, nothing to do but enjoy the peace, love, and tranquility.

Sounds great, doesn't it? However, when you are honest with yourself, you realize that you've been floating in these clouds as long as you can remember, and all of these nice things have become extremely *boring*. Everything so good and wonderful all of the time is boring. You begin your daily activity of hovering around the tops of the clouds, searching for something unique, something special, something different, something new, something to spice up your existence somehow. You have been on this search before, day after day, and know, deep down, that you will *never* find anything new, but yet you still keep on searching.

However, today, you see something unusual. You notice that off in the distance a big, long line is forming. Almost like the line that forms for a popular ride at an amusement park. There is a big flashing sign overhead that says, "This Way to Planet Earth." You slowly approach, having no idea what this *Planet Earth* is all about.

You make your way to the end of the line and see a man, standing alone, patiently waiting. Casually, you ask, "Excuse me, sir, what is this line for?" This guy can barely get the words out, he is so excited. "Oh my goodness, don't you know? Didn't anybody tell you? Everybody is doing it! It's Earth, Planet Earth! There is excitement to be had, adventures to go on, emotions to feel. Right now all we do is read about those things, but we cannot feel any of them. On Earth we can *feel*, with things called *senses*. Apparently, we each get five of them!

When we get to Earth we will get *to touch, to taste, to hear, to smell, and to see.* Here we only get ideas of those senses; we can imagine those things, but all we get to experience is joy and love. They say on Earth we also get a full range of *emotions*; apparently there are many of them we get to have. I cannot wait to get there, because there is no limit to the experiences we can have. Isn't that exciting? Come on, join me in line, its going to be fabulous!"

Intrigued, but not certain, you join the end of the line. Hundreds and hundreds of souls flock to get in line behind you. Now, although uncertain, you really want to find out what Planet Earth is all about, plus, you certainly are ready to experience something new.

You can see the boarding area of the ride, far off in the distance. Suddenly, a woman shows up and hands you a book. She explains that this is your personal guidebook and warns that you will only have a short amount of time to memorize it, because you cannot bring it with you to Planet Earth. "How difficult can it be?" you think, and skim through the guidebook, not reading, just glancing at the pictures.

The first chapter is called *Why Visit Planet Earth* and discusses the importance of feeling emotions. Apparently, Earth is the only place in all the universe where you can feel a wide range of these emotions. "Cool," you think, happy to believe that this new place won't be boring.

You are given a pencil and must circle the top three emotions that you want to experience the most on Earth. Being such a wise soul that you are, you circle: *Love* (of course, that's a given), *Generosity* (because it feels good to help others), and *Independence* (who wouldn't want that?) Of course, you don't read the fine print that tells you that you will not be *given* these emotions, but you will be given situations in which you will be able to *experience* these emotions.

The next chapter deals with picking your parents and the area where you would like to live. "Hmmm . . ." you think. "I like the idea of an area where the temperature changes and the landscape and beauty will change depending on the time of year. Yes, I think my eyes will really enjoy that," and put a check mark on an area in the northeastern part of North America.

"Parents, what does that matter?" You like the looks of an Air Force fighter pilot and his dynamic young bride. You love to fly in the clouds and think you'll get along great with this guy. You read that this woman's mother had recently been killed in car accident. "I'll start that love and generosity right away," you think. "The moment she takes one look at me, I'm certain she'll be happy again." You are so excited about this adventure that you neglect to read the description of the family life you will experience. What you miss is that this man, now an airline pilot, travels quite a bit and is rarely home. You also miss reading that two other souls had just arrived before your arrival; they are called *twins*.

Being nosy, you glance at the woman to your left. She has put a check mark in the middle of Europe with the words joy, disappointment, and envy circled. "No thanks," you mumble under your breath. The man put his check mark in the western part of Africa, with the words suffering, sadness, and neglect circled. You are curious and ask this man why he would pick such emotions to experience. "Well," he says, "this is not my first time to Planet Earth. I have been there many, many times before. The first time I picked the greatest sounding emotions—love, happiness, and abundance. Each time you go there, you have to pick something new. The whole purpose of visiting Planet Earth is to get smarter. The more times you go, the smarter you get and eventually you get the opportunity to become a Supreme Being of Magnificent Radiance, which I hear is absolutely incredible! That is my real goal, so I have been to Earth many, many times. I have chosen all the other emotions before. Suffering, sadness, and neglect are the last three that I have not experienced, so that is why I picked them. In addition, every time I am on Earth, I seem to end up somewhere cold! Apparently, Africa is warm, with the sun shining. Boy, am I ever ready for that!"

There are some big, bold words written on the bottom of the page with the picture of a stop sign. However, you are so busy meeting your fellow passengers that you fail to read a most important part:

Warning: once you arrive on Planet Earth, you will forget all about this place. You will forget that you chose these emotions to experience and these parents. You will forget that you were given a guidebook; that is why it is critical that you memorize it now. We need you to forget this place so you may experience the fullest range of emotions possible for your soul to grow.

To help you believe that you are a person of Earth, not the eternal soul that you really are, we are giving you a companion for your journey. This companion will be with you at all times. He or she will remember your past experiences and remind you of them. This companion will be a voice that will talk to you inside your mind all the days while you are on Earth.

During your stay, there will be some guides who will appear on your journey, to help you along the way. It is essential to listen to each person you meet, because they might be one of your guides. In case of an emergency, there will be only one way to get help. You will be able to access this guidebook through your thoughts. To achieve this, you must stop the voice inside your mind and quiet your senses. We have put reminders around the Earth in the form of stop signs. These signs will be a reminder to you, to stop The Voice and quiet your mind. Then, you must have the intention of getting an answer to your question, and the answer will come in that stillness.

Of course, you miss reading all of that!

The line moves very quickly and soon you are being instructed to step into an area with five other travelers. You see the tram approaching, and discreetly squeeze past the others, your objective being to get the very best seat on the tram, next to the window. As the gate opens, you slide past the others and take the window seat. "Victory!" you think. A seat belt automatically fastens around you and you hear, *"Five seconds until departure, five . . . four . . . three . . . two . . . one . . . blast off!"* The tram takes off at lighting speed and you travel through the magnificent, vast universe. "This is better than any roller coaster," you think, as you travel past many suns and moons and stars. You see colors you have never seen and galaxies you could never have dreamed of. However, your tram is rapidly heading into a very dark area, something you believe to be a black hole. . . .

Your eyes open, things seem very blurry. Your face is wet from tears. There is also an uncomfortable wetness at the other end of you. You feel a strange ache in your body and a void that needs to be filled. You are not quite sure of who you are or where you are. You remember nothing about your previous existence.

You try to make a sound with your mouth, but the only thing that comes out is a loud a cry. You wait; nothing seems to happen. You decide to scream a little louder along with your cries. This discomfort feels so awful to you. As you squint, you see a change in the light and a figure coming close. You get picked up and held and think, "Ah, this feels incredible." Your tears are quickly dried, your wet cloth is exchanged for a dry one, and a rubber end of a bottle is forced between your lips. Your body does feel better, and the person holding you makes you feel loved and she smells so good. You realize that there is nothing to fear with this person around, until you hear other screams not too far away from you. Quickly, you are placed back in your bed and this warm, loving being is gone, and you feel sad. You see in the distance that there are two others in need of food and comforting as well. However, these two seem bigger than you.

As time goes by, things don't really change. You now know that these others are called your *brother* and your *sister*. You don't bother to cry too much because you know that, when you do, it is the others that seem to get more of Mom's attention. You feel sorry for Mom, and worry that she never gets any rest. You choose to not be a problem and decide to play quietly alone and entertain yourself. "These two need her much more than I do," you think.

Time continues and your body begins to grow bigger. Your brother and sister are growing, too. Mom and Dad are very loving, and always seem to have great adventures to take you on. Your family arrives at a place called Disneyland. Your young eyes are drawn to all the amazing colors. There are giant balloons and flowers everywhere. A friendly giant mouse and a yellow bear named Pooh stop by to say hello. It is a place of pure fun and magic!

Before long you reach up to hold Mom's hand only to find Mom is not there. You look everywhere but realize there is no Mom or Dad, no brother or sister. Filled with a new emotion called *fear,* you begin to cry. Your soul gets the first experience of being alone and it hurts really bad. It is not long before your parents find you and you are happy again; however, you are unaware that something is beginning to develop in you called *The Voice.* You won't realize it until many years later, but in that first horrible experience, *The Voice* began talking inside your head. It started telling you that you are not loved as much as your brother or sister. Sometimes, *The Voice* tells you that you are not really loved at all. Being *unlovable* may not be the truth, however *The Voice* tells you it is. So you will eventually grow up being independent, on your own, but deep down, longing to be loved.

Although you are not aware of it, *The Voice* continues to grow along with you. It makes decisions about every event that happens and tells you what you need to do to protect yourself in the future.

On one occasion you visit a doctor for a check up, only to hear him tell your mom, "She is too big, if she can stay this weight as she grows another few inches taller, she will be just fine." "Something is wrong with you," *The Voice* says, but it sounds like your voice and you believe *it*. When you get home from the doctor, you ask for a snack. Your brother and sister each receive a cupcake and you get an apple. "Life is not fair," *The Voice* tells you, "you are different from others, you are certainly not loved and you cannot have any of the good stuff."

The Voice gets louder and louder and becomes a constant companion talking to you in your mind forever more. With every opportunity, it shares how unlovable and different you are. It reminds you that you are not supposed to have any of the good stuff. *The Voice* now convinces you that you deserve anything you want and, when no one is watching, you can sneak some candy out of the cupboard or some ice cream out of the freezer.

As you continue to grow older you find yourself playing the game *kickball* with a group of other kids. Not knowing that your vision is bad, you cannot kick the ball no matter how hard you try. The kids make fun of you and laugh at you.

The Voice is quick to tell you, "Sports are not for you. You are clumsy, you are different, and nobody wants you on their team." Eventually, your parents figure out that you have a vision problem and you get your first pair of glasses. Unfortunately, the message about how different and unwanted you are gets ingrained in your mind and *The Voice* continually reminds you of that truth.

The other kids now make even more fun of you and start calling you names. "Four eyes . . . Sandra . . . dandruff." I guess dandruff was the best word that they thought rhymed with Sandra. It hurts so bad that the other kids don't like you, but you want to be liked so you start bringing candy and goodies for the other kids to eat. It doesn't take long for *The Voice* to convince you, "The only way to get people to like you is to give them things and do things for them."

Dear reader, you are probably aware by now that the soul waiting in heaven and the person it became was me, Sandra Champlain. Can you look at your own life and see how your story could have been created?

Do I believe this story is the truth and is exactly what happened to me? Am I the way I am today because of my past and my experiences? Am I really that different from other people? Am I unlovable, and cannot have the *good stuff* that other people get in life? I am going to answer that by simply saying, "*Maybe.*"

As much as I wish to entertain you with my story, the real point of this book is to empower you in the life you are now living. We all want results, we all want success, we all want love, we all want abundance.

One of the ways I can give this to you is by asking you to *try on* some of these ideas like they are the truth. Imagine yourself in a clothing store. You want to buy yourself a new jacket. You try on many jackets to see which one looks the best on you, which one fits correctly, and which one you feel most comfortable in. After trying many jackets on, hopefully you find one that fits, and you walk out of the store feeling great and looking great. However, if you don't find one you like, you simply take off the jacket and return it to the rack.

This book is meant to be read just like trying on a jacket. I ask that you give it a chance, move around in it, see how you feel in it. After the final chapter, if it's not a *good fit* simply return it to the rack, no harm done. However, if it is a fit, you will have the most stylish, magical jacket that money can buy. You will not only look and feel good, but the jacket will empower you to live a life you could not have previously imagined. Are you ready to step into the fitting room?

There is no doubt in my mind that our past plays a role in who we are today, and you probably agree with that statement. As a kid I grew up feeling very different, separate from my brother and sisters, alone, not good enough, and that there was something very wrong with me. To make matters worse, I have had a constant companion talking to me, every moment of my life. I call it *The Voice*. People call it all kinds of different things: the ego, the identity, the inner voice, the inner critic. We all have one and, if you don't think that you do, just stop reading for a moment. Go ahead and put the book down. Most likely *The Voice* in your head has been talking to you since you picked up this book and chose to read it. It may have said, "Should I buy this? The title is weird. How can anyone make a claim that we don't die? Of course we do," and now it is saying, "Why is she asking me to put down this book? What if I want to keep reading? What is the point of this?"

The Voice never stops talking. One of the classic flaws of all human beings is this: we think *The Voice* is our voice! No, it is not ours. *The Voice* is a complex survival mechanism that takes the information it received in our past and uses it to shape our future so *it* survives. Did you hear me? I said, *it* survives. Most of the time *The Voice* wants you to survive, but not always. I have not been in the mind of a person who is contemplating or succeeds in committing suicide, but I can imagine *The Voice* does a great job at convincing the person that ending his life is the only option he has.

Imagine this: it is late, you have already gone to bed, but your mind is awake. You feel a little hungry and remember that there is a chocolate birthday cake in your refrigerator. Only a few pieces had been eaten and it sits alone in the fridge. You remember the fudge-like frosting and the moist center.

Your tongue begins to salivate as you picture cutting a slice for yourself and sinking your fork into it. That memory, that image, that part of you that really wants that cake is *The Voice*, reminding you just how good you will feel when you take a bite of it. However, another voice chimes in, "You have been good for two days now, you have only eaten lean meats and fruits and veggies, you haven't had any sugar. You've been to the gym twice and your muscles are getting stronger." That is also *The Voice*, reminding you of how good you will look continuing on the path you are on. Then, the first voice comes back with a compromise, "Just one piece of cake won't harm you. You will feel better and will get a good night's sleep. Just do an extra 20 minutes on the treadmill tomorrow."

You know how this story ends, right? You end up consuming more cake than you've ever eaten in one sitting! *The Voice* starts yelling at you about what a failure you are, how you will never lose weight or get in shape. If you are single, *The Voice* might mention how no one will ever love you or find you attractive because you have no self-control. Eventually, you simply eat more cake and it may be months before you step foot in the gym again.

Dr. Richard Schwartz, who earned his PhD in Marriage and Family Therapy from Purdue University, and is coauthor of *Family Therapy: Concepts and Methods*, the most widely used family therapy text in the United States, created *IFS Training*. IFS stands for Internal Family Systems, also known as the *The Voices* inside our heads. His worldwide therapists help patients realize that we all have these voices in our heads, separate from the *Higher Self* that we really are. By using *IFS*, people have had amazing success breaking free of habits, compulsions, negative memories, and addictive behaviors. (See SelfLeadership.org for more information.)

From this point forward, I will use the term *The Voice* when I talk about the little voice that we all have, the one that says the negative words to ourselves. I am also going to introduce you to your *Soul Self*. The *Soul Self* is that part of you that is wise, all-knowing, loving, and compassionate, and the part of you that can listen to *The Voice*. You will notice, when you pay attention, that *The Voice* mostly speaks negative words to you, it convinces you to be afraid and, ultimately, it prevents you from having the results you want in your life. If you listen to *The Voice* right now, what is it saying? I want you to understand that you cannot be *The Voice* if you can listen to *The Voice*. That part of you that is listening is your *Soul Self*, your higher self.

Back to the chocolate cake. Have you had the experience of listening to bad advice coming from inside your own head? Oh, I know it can be frustrating. I want to give you another example and then we'll look at ways to have the results you want, despite what *The Voice* tells you!

I once trained to run a marathon. Unfortunately, I was not in good enough shape to run an entire marathon and canceled my trip to Jacksonville, Florida. However, my *Soul Self* told me I could still succeed and, on a cold winter's day, I headed north out of my driveway and I *walked* 26.2 miles. I had no supportive friends, no one cheering me on, nothing. It was just me on a country road in the middle of winter, with a vision of accomplishing a goal.

I used every mind game I could think of to keep myself motivated: I imagined small gnomes at the side of the road cheering me on. Hearing a familiar siren, I saw Santa Claus drive by on top of a fire truck. (There was a local campaign to collect toys for underprivileged children and Santa was advertising that.) Each time the truck went by and Santa waved, I pretended that he was cheering me on as I walked my marathon. I tried to keep my mind clear, and focused my attention on the sounds of the birds, the look of the road, the shape of the trees. It was a very peaceful walk.

Eventually, I made it back to my house nearly eight hours later. It had already gotten dark outside and my entire body was sore and exhausted. I collapsed on my couch and do you know what *The Voice* said? "Sandra, you are a failure. Everybody knows that you cannot walk a marathon, only run a marathon. Don't bother telling people that you walked or they will just laugh at you." It was in that very moment that I saw how *The Voice* (my ego, the inner critic), that nasty voice, *was not me!* My *Soul Self* lovingly told me that completing 26.2 miles on foot was something that less than 1% of the world's population has done. I began to cry and realized that I have believed *The Voice* my entire life, that what it said was the *truth*. In that moment I was free. In that moment I had *power*.

The development of *The Voice* comes to us in all different ways, as we are different people. You can look back on your own life and see how some of the major events have shaped you into who you are today. There is nothing wrong with having *The Voice*, because it is part of being human, just like having a head or a mouth. Don't waste your time trying to make it wrong or trying to get rid of it; the best thing we can do is to identify and understand it so that you have power to get the results you want in your life.

Unfortunately, *The Voice* helped you create all the qualities you don't like about yourself. Like me, *The Voice* may have been telling you for years now that there is something wrong with you, that you don't matter, that people don't understand you, that you are different, that no matter how hard you try, you will always be a failure.

The good news is that *The Voice* also helped you create all the good things you like about yourself. *The Voice* has told me that I am unlovable, that I am different from others, that I cannot have the good stuff. Out of that, my good qualities were developed: I am generous, loving, and independent. Out of those qualities I have had success in my life.

Let's back up a second. I don't want you to miss this. Did you notice anything about the three words I used a couple of sentences ago? Remember the story about our young soul in Heaven who picked the three emotions to learn in this life? The three emotions picked were *Generosity, Love,* and *Independence.* However, without ever knowing that *The Voice* is at play, it is easy for all of us to not acknowledge our accomplishments and simply focus on the negative. By taking a step back, you can see that you have made incredible advancements in your own life.

HOMEWORK ASSIGNMENT

Go to the Notes section at the back of this book or to your notebook and *try on* the idea that you were once a soul who chose to come down to Earth to learn three main things.

Assignment #1: Write down the negative messages that *The Voice* tells you about yourself. No one has to see this besides you. My voice knows these answers well, because it is quick to remind me of them over and over. "You are ugly, you need to lose weight, you are different from other people, you have no willpower, you are stupid, you are a failure, you don't matter to people, and no one will ever love you." Now, it's your turn. Be real with yourself, what does *The Voice* say about you?

Assignment #2: Ask the people in your life what they think your best qualities are. Those who care deeply for you, ask them what they love about you.

If *The Voice* isn't allowing you to do this exercise, I've got some news for you. *The Voice* isn't interested in you trying new things. It feels safe doing things it knows from the past that don't allow you to take a risk into the unknown. Have your *Soul Self* tell the *The Voice* that this exercise is fun and will feel good!

The more people you talk to, the more you will start hearing some similar words. You might hear things like, "You are so smart," or "You have the best sense of humor," or "You are such a good listener." There may also be words like loving, fun, generous, creative, outgoing, clever, etc. Write down every word people say. If you cannot talk to someone, simply imagine the things you know they would say about you and write those down. As a gift to the other person, tell that person what their best qualities are and what you love about them too!

You'll soon start seeing the same few words repeating themselves; those very well could be the three things your soul circled while waiting in line to visit Planet Earth!

There does seem to be a problem here, have you noticed? How is it possible that you see yourself one way and other people see you another way? *Who are you, really?*

The Voice is not going to like this answer and it is going to fight me on this, just watch what happens. Who you *really* are is *who other people think you are*. If you don't believe me, it's a simple mathematical equation. How many people did you ask? Two, five, twelve, twenty? There is only one person with your view and there may be a dozen people with this fabulous perspective of you. Believe it or not, *they are right*. You are the wonderful person that they described, not the you that *The Voice* defines.

Hmmm. Is the person that your friends and family described worth having their dreams fulfilled? This is a simple *yes* or *no* answer, my friend. If you say *no*, realize that it was *The Voice* that was speaking, not your *Soul Self*. Go back and do the exercise again until you get a *yes*.

> *You are a perfect human being and*
> *you deserve to have the life of your dreams.*

Bonus Assignment: Do you like movies? Albert Brooks did an excellent job dealing with *The Voice* in his head in the movie titled *Defending Your Life*. It is a comedy with Meryl Streep, and you will surely be able to identify with the battle going on in his mind. It is a very funny movie about a soul who was on Earth. Go on and rent it. A little laughter will do you good right about now.

Chapter 2

Becoming a Skeptic Is Easy

All great truths begin as blasphemies.
Every person who has mastered a profession
is a skeptic concerning it.

~ George Bernard Shaw, playwright and co-founder
of the London School of Economics, b. 1956

skep·tic, *noun*

A person who questions the validity or authenticity of something purporting to be factual.

Do you remember your childhood? Can you think back to the time that life was wonderful and magical, and any dream was possible? Maybe you had dreams of being a fireman or a ballerina or even the president. I wanted to be either a veterinarian or airline pilot like my dad.

Imagine for a moment that you were once that little soul in Heaven and were given the opportunity to come to Planet Earth to learn. Do you remember being a kid who just wanted to be outside, explore, and play? We didn't want to take naps, we didn't want to sit quietly, we wanted to be out in the world having fun! And, by no means did we want to go to bed at night, right?

Part of the deal we made with the universe may have been to *forget* who we really are. We have all had experiences in our lives that have taken away the magic of life. We each have *The Voice* in our head constantly telling us not-so-good words about ourselves. Eventually, we grow older and live our lives no longer excited to wake up in the morning, we rarely play, we long to take naps, and we can't wait to go to sleep at night. What happened to the children we used to be? Are you interested in being excited again and having some magic in your life? I know I am.

I don't believe any of us were born as skeptics or pessimists. I believe we all have had a series of events that broke our hearts and shut down those curious and excited parts of ourselves.

As a child, I loved dreaming of magic. My parents were incredible and made sure every holiday was magical for my brother, sisters, and me. The Easter Bunny came once a year and hid colored eggs all around our house and gave me a basket filled with jellybeans and chocolate. Whenever I lost a tooth, the Tooth Fairy would sneak into my room while I was sleeping and I would always find a small toy or a quarter under my pillow. Saint Nick came the night of December 5th. We put plates under our beds and the next morning it would be filled with small toys and candy. I loved life and these times were always so exciting.

Every year, my favorite night of them all was December 24th. Santa Claus would be coming and there are no words to describe just how excited I was! Mom would allow us to open one present from under the tree on Christmas Eve. The gift was usually from Mom and Dad, but sometimes there was something from my grandparents or aunt and uncle. The gifts were always okay, but I knew that the real good presents came the next day, from Santa Claus.

Mom tells me the story of what I was like as a kid. Although Heidi and Steve were just one year older than me, I was the one who could not handle the anticipation of Santa's visit to our house! I remember going to bed at night, being so excited that I couldn't fall asleep. Mom would remind me that Santa would only come down the chimney if we were fast asleep. It took everything I had to quiet my mind enough to fall asleep. I knew that when the clock showed *a.m.*, it was morning and I could get out of bed! So, 4:00 a.m. Christmas Day I would get up and wake up my parents and brother and sister and shout, "Santa has been here, wake up, Santa came to our house!" Mom and Dad would let us open our stockings, but we couldn't open up any of the big presents until they got out of bed. I hated that.

The older I got, the sneakier I got. My fun, older brother, Steve, would take me upstairs in the attic and I had to promise not to tell anyone what we found. He would show me the far corner of the attic, where he found a black garbage bag. Then, very slowly, he would open the bag and it was full of presents! Looking at the gift tags, these were Christmas gifts that my grandparents and aunt and uncle would send from Massachusetts. We lived in Connecticut. We knew that we shouldn't be snooping, but it was so much fun! Steve and I got very sneaky too; we could slightly unwrap the present, just to see what was inside and then tape the package back up.

The following year I ventured out on my own as I discreetly snuck into my mom's closet. I found the black garbage bag there and, again, it had presents inside. There were two identical boxes and I opened one of them, like my brother had shown me, to see what was inside. I found a white jewelry box. Knowing there were two of them, I figured out that these would be gifts from Mom and Dad, one for me and one for my sister Heidi.

Christmas Day came and I woke everyone up as I normally did at 4:00 a.m. We waited for my parents to get out of bed as we sat on the couch and looked at the contents of our stockings. Finally, Mom and

Dad got up, brewed their coffee, and we were allowed to tear into the pile of presents that Santa Claus brought.

Then I saw it, a box and the wrapping paper I had seen before. However, it did not say, *To: Sandra, From: Mom & Dad*. You know what it said? *To: Sandra, From: Santa Claus.*

That was one of the worst moments of my life and I can still remember it today as I write this. I was devastated. Santa Claus wasn't real. My brother apparently knew this already and he was happy to point out that "There is no Easter Bunny, no Tooth Fairy, and no Saint Nick either, Sandra!"

In that moment my magical world disappeared and my new world of trusting no one began. I became a skeptic. My parents had lied to me.

My mom did give me the perfect present when I was five years old. She gave me my little sister, Karen. I can still remember the day Mom announced that she was pregnant. I started dancing around near the bottom of our staircase and singing "Goody, goody gumdrops . . . Mom's going to have a baby!" She was born September 19, 1971, and, although we were too young to go to the hospital, Dad, Heidi, Steve, and I looked up from the parking lot and saw Mom holding the baby in the window. This was going to be my special person and I felt like Karen was born just for me.

Nobody seemed to understand me, but little Karen did. I could share with her that world of play and excitement and make believe, because she was so much younger. I could have magic again in my life by sharing Santa Claus, the Easter Bunny, and the Tooth Fairy with her.

When I wasn't playing big sister to her, I spent a lot of time alone. I felt different from other kids and it was obvious that I was different. I was uncoordinated and couldn't throw a ball or swing a bat. I had glasses and the other kids always made fun of me. *The Voice* in my head was quick to remind me how awful I was and how different I was from other kids.

At some point, I discovered baking. I taught myself how to bake breads and cakes and entered them in the Bridgewater Fair's cooking competition. I loved baking.

At the age of 14, I entered an adult cooking contest hosted by the local newspaper. I won the grand prize and got $100 (that was a lot of money in 1980) and my picture in the paper. What did I enter? My famous chocolate cake with mocha buttercream frosting.

Until now, I have not told you about who I am or why I wrote this book. Although you and I are different people, I want you imagine that we all came into this world the same way: we lived our first few years believing that anything was possible for us. As you can see in my story, I got shut down rather quickly. I got lost in an amusement park and felt alone, I couldn't have the cupcake my brother and sister got, I found out there was no Santa Claus or any magic in life.

The Voice in my head became my constant companion reminding me that I am different, I'm unlovable, that I don't matter to other people, that I can trust no one, and that I'm never going to get the good stuff.

As I go on with my story, I want you think about you and your life. You, like me, started life excited. Somehow, as events started happening in your life, *The Voice* started telling you things about yourself that became the truth to you. As humans, we begin this battle with ourselves to prove that we are good enough, lovable, that we matter, and that we definitely deserve the good stuff! To prove I was good enough, I excelled in almost everything I touched: I learned to fly airplanes and got my Solo Pilot's License at the age of 16. I was the top graduate in my college class, and led the largest Weight Watchers meeting in New England with over 300 people attending my weekly class. I have held a position of authority in every job I have ever had. I have created and maintained two successful businesses.

Perhaps you got the hint when I mentioned Weight Watchers? The *good stuff* I keep referring to is food. It is no coincidence that my early years of dieting led me to believe that I could not have the delicious treats that others were allowed to have. Have you ever attempted to tell yourself that you cannot have something you really want? Have you ever told yourself that you cannot eat a donut only to later consume a dozen of them?

Yours truly has made her lifetime about food. I didn't just bake cakes and breads growing up. I became a chef after attending The Culinary Institute of America in Hyde Park, New York, the best cooking school in the world! Even though I graduated top in my class, I still felt I wasn't good enough.

After college, I went to work in the hotel and restaurant management industry with dreams of someday owning my own restaurant. In 1991, I opened a coffee and chocolate store in Connecticut. Chocolates were always my true love, and this store gave me the perfect place to create scrumptious hand-dipped chocolates and truffles and serve the finest of coffees and teas. There was only one major problem. I still had *The Voice* telling me I could not eat chocolate. This led to many days of unhappiness, frustration, weight gain and weight loss, and weight gain again. I ended up hating the business I had loved, because I could no longer deal with the pain of feeling that I was overweight, out of control with food, and, ultimately, I felt like a failure.

As you can see by my story so far, the inquisitive, excited child was now gone. What happened in your life? Can you see that there were many events that happened in your past that made you live life with a lot less joy and excitement and that shaped you into being the person you are today?

1996 brought excitement to my life again. I had the opportunity to start another business. One that promised excitement, travel, and even a bit of glamour!

Back up to 1987, just before graduation day at The Culinary Institute of America, I had been asked to cook for race car teams at the Daytona International Speedway in Florida. My mom, Marion, introduced me to automobile racing. She had owned her own travel agency and did travel arrangements for many race car drivers and crew members in the IMSA series. The last weekend in January, there is a race called *The 24 Hours of Daytona*, where teams from all over the world compete to see whose car will have the most endurance and survive a 24-hour road race.

This race required not only cars of endurance, but drivers and teams of endurance. Each team had three drivers who would take turns driving the race car over the 24-hour period. However, the mechanics and crew members would patiently stay awake those 24 hours for any pit stops, refueling, or to fix problems the car had.

For this 24-hour battle in 1987, one team owner got the idea that it would be beneficial to have a chef cook for the crew rather than having them eat hamburgers, hotdogs, and donuts. My loving mom, Marion, volunteered me to cook for the team.

Over almost a ten-year period, I cooked for that team at that race in Daytona. Then, in 1996, I attended a race, just for fun, in Connecticut. The team I had cooked for at Daytona was racing and I joined my mom for a day of fun. The actor, Craig T. Nelson, from the television series *Coach*, was also a race car driver at the time. A large tent was set up, with chefs and a buffet for this celebrity and his team. However, when I took a look at the food, I realized the quality was horrible! Brown, wilted lettuce in the salad, the chefs using their hands to touch lunch meat, no gloves, no tongs, nothing sanitary—it was awful. After asking a few questions, I found out that the race team was paying a huge amount of money to have this poor quality food and service.

Then the words seemed to slip out of my mouth. My need to be the best had me say to the team owners, "I bet I could do much better than this and double the quality of the food." Craig T. Nelson and team owner Rob Dyson, said, "Yes," and our new business, *Marion's Hospitality* (named after my mother), was born.

This new business allowed me some excitement in life again. I could see the United States and Canada, and it allowed me an opportunity to make good money, work hard, and make a difference with some of the most famous race car drivers and race teams in the world and, it got me away from chocolate.

However, I don't believe I was really happy. I couldn't see then what I can see now. My life was certainly very busy and very full, but it wasn't enough. Do you know what I mean? Your life may be full of things to do and people you see on a daily basis who love you, but there is still something missing, isn't there?

HOMEWORK ASSIGNMENT

Remember when you were a kid. What did you love to do? What dreams did you have? Who were your friends? What did you want to be when you grew up? Please take some time to walk down *Memory Lane* and remember as much as you can about your childhood dreams.

Chapter 3

Life After Death Is Real

Physical death is a transitional step in the total life process. The soul, which does not die, having finished with the Earthly body, moves to a higher level of life, where it grows under greatly enhanced circumstances.

~ Norman Vincent Peale, writer and clergyman, b. 1898

1996 was not only the year I started my new career as a chef for the race car teams, but it brought with it a tremendous fear of dying, although I was never certain of why. By that time I had experienced some loss—I had a grandfather die when I was 14 years old and quite a few pets over the years. Nothing happened to provoke that insatiable fear and the unending question that persisted, "What happens after we die?"

You know, now that I think about it, when I was 14 my dad was diagnosed with cancer and was told by the doctors that he only had a few months to live. My dad had lymphoma, and my grandfather had leukemia. My grandfather did not make it, and I still remember being in the back seat of the car when Mom told us kids that Grampy had died. I wanted to burst out in tears, but felt I could not, we had other kids in the car whom we had been taking home after school. I loved my grandfather; he taught me how to fish and I have wonderful memories of playing the card game *Gin Rummy* with him. The pain of losing him was almost unbearable.

Dad was sick at the very same time and, like I said, he had been given only a few months to live. As a 14-year-old, I didn't believe it. I told Dad that he wasn't going anywhere, that it was not his time to die. I really believed it. Somehow, Dad must have believed it too, because he started working with Dr. Bernie Siegel.

Bernie (as he prefers to be called) had created *ECaP*, which stands for Exceptional Cancer Patients, and has helped hundreds of thousands of people with their mind-and-body connection. My dad, previously given only three months to live, went into remission as the cancerous tumor disappeared from his body. Bernie went on to write *Love, Medicine & Miracles* and has given his entire life to empowering people. There is no doubt in my mind that my father got to live almost another 30 full years because of Dr. Bernie Siegel. (For more information about Bernie visit BernieSiegelMD.com.)

Back to my story of living with the fear of dying. As an adult, whenever the thought came to mind, I tried to distract myself and avoid thinking about death and dying. My life was so busy that it was easy to become occupied with life, and I was not able to think of anything else besides running my coffee and chocolate store from afar and preparing food for the race car teams. However, when my mind was quiet, the fear of dying would sneak in, leaving me again faced with this awful fear.

Before long I found myself beginning a long journey to find some answers. I did not think I would find *the* answer, but rather *an* answer for me personally. I wanted something to believe in, anything that would give me hope. Ideally, I wanted some *proof* that would calm the ever-nagging voice, desperately wondering what happens after we die.

I started out by researching the religion I was most familiar with, Roman Catholicism. I was clear that I believed in many of the teachings of Jesus Christ and the Christian ways to live a good life, but there was no proof of *never-ending life*, just teachings of faith.

From there I studied Judaism, Hinduism, Buddhism, and more. What I found was an amazing belief system in each, filled with values and faith, but lacking the proof I so desperately wanted. *The Tibetan Book of Living and Dying*, by Sogyal Rinpoche, gave me an eye opening possibility that we may be eternal creatures who have been here on Earth many times. This book fascinated me, and I began to devour books that had credible stories of reincarnation. I liked the idea of it, after all, we live in a time of recycling! Why not recycle our souls? It did not make sense to me to get one chance at life and then disappear to vast nothingness after we die.

We humans have been questioning whether there is life beyond death since the beginning of time. It dawned on me that my search was probably a normal part of the human experience. Ancient philosophers Plato and Socrates searched for answers around 400 BC, as did chef and chocolate maker Sandra Champlain two thousand years later.

The answers did not come through this method of exploration. I decided to give up my journey, or so I thought. "There are no answers," I tried to convince myself. "Do the best you can, Sandra, be a good person, be generous and kind to others, and surely, you will have nothing to fear."

Although I did not produce any evidence about life beyond death, I found myself interested in a new field of study: the human mind. Incredible evidence seemed to be appearing about what our minds can do when focused on results. Athletes who used *visual imagery* and practiced their events in their minds before a competition, did far better than those who did not. My dad would tell stories of visual imagery, imagining the character from the game *PAC-MAN* traveling throughout his body eating up all the cancer cells.

In college, I went to see a hypnotist perform, and saw how crazily my friends behaved on the stage. It was a great show and so funny! My one friend ran to the stage and spoke in a made-up foreign language, another friend had to recall his favorite TV show as a kid and become the main star. The 22-year-old man became the cartoon character, *Speed Racer,* before my eyes. It was great! When they returned to the audience, they were certain that *something* made them act like they did, and that they did not choose their crazy behaviors themselves.

My mind could not believe that was possible. My *inner skeptic* quickly appeared, telling me hypnosis was impossible. However, my friends seemed pretty convinced that they didn't choose to do those goofy things on stage, that the hypnotist had some power over them. I don't think I would normally have chosen to investigate hypnosis; however, I read an article about *Hypnosis and Weight Loss.* Me, the girl constantly trying to lose weight, may have a new thing to try!

I was happy that my fear of dying was put on hold because now I was excited to investigate this new world called *hypnosis.* I really wanted to see if I could be hypnotized. The problem I had, though, was that *The Voice* kept telling me, "Hypnosis is not real. It is a scam. There is no such thing. Don't waste your money."

The skeptic in me got involved and came to an agreement with *The Voice.* Instead of simply scheduling an appointment with a hypnotherapist for weight loss, I chose to buy an airplane ticket, fly to California, and take a course to become a hypnotist!

I learned that weekend that hypnosis *is real.* Under a specific set of circumstances (a relaxed body and mind), the brain can be told information that will allow the body to produce amazing results! I do want to mention something very important here: *no one can make a person do anything that they would not normally do.* My friends who were on stage with the hypnotist would normally have done crazy things.

Hypnosis, visual imagery, and Neuro-linguistic programming (NLP) all take place when our minds are in a very relaxed state. There is nothing to fear with these techniques because we are *always* listening to the commands and will simply open our eyes if we are told to do something that we don't want to do. When I was hypnotized at the school in California, the instructor gave me a cue, that when I heard the word *green,* I would have the urge to join him on stage. I heard the man tell me that and remember thinking, "This guy is handsome, of course I'll join him on stage." However, I don't remember him ever saying the word *green.* Without knowing it, I felt I somehow appeared on stage without remembering how I got there. That was cool. Another time, he gave me the cue that I would think of my favorite singer and when I heard the word *blue,* I would rush to the stage and sing my favorite song. I clearly remember opening my eyes and saying, "No way, I don't sing." You see, no one can make you do something you don't want to do. But if there is something you want, hypnosis can make it very easy for you to achieve it.

I became a Certified Hypnotherapist that year and went on to work with dozens of people, to help them lose weight, quit smoking, be better athletes, and get good grades. I regressed people to childhood and found that people retained detailed memories from when they were children.

I told one of the race car drivers that I took the course on hypnosis. He told me about a bad crash he had the previous year that left his legs in pain and his mind in fear of driving around a certain type of corner. He asked me if I thought hypnosis would help alleviate the pain and help him have confidence to go around that corner without fear. Truthfully, I had no idea. I always believe that it is worth taking a chance, so we decided to go for it.

In the back of a motor home, parked in the middle of a racetrack,

I hypnotized him. At the same time, Alyson, the race team's massage therapist, massaged his muscles. It was an hour-and-a-half session, where I had him visualize himself successfully driving around the corner he feared, and completing this race as well as races in the future. I gave him the *cue* that when he put his gloves and helmet on, the pain would disappear.

He felt happy and confident after the session with me. Although he did not win the race, he reported that he drove pain free for the very first time since the accident, and he drove fearlessly around that corner, maintaining high speed. It was a victory for him.

The next race he drove was the Indy 500. I sat in my mom's living room and watched the 500-mile race. He started in 16th position and quickly moved his way up to being in the lead. I watched with so much excitement, knowing he was probably driving fearlessly and pain free. He would have won the race if not for blowing a tire towards the end. I believed the hypnosis session had something to do with his outcome.

Looking back, it is amazing how skeptical I was about hypnosis. I was so opinionated and right about everything. I didn't trust and I didn't have faith. The only way I would know if something was real was if I could prove it.

Do you feel that way? Have you lived your life believing certain things are real and other things are not? Gosh, I have even believed people are a certain way, and I knew I was right about them. As a teenager, I was certain my mom had no understanding of the way the world really was! Did you think you knew more than your parents, like I did?

I would like to compare our minds to a glass. We come into this world fresh and excited, where every possibility exists. Our glass is completely empty and can be filled with anything. However, events happen and our glass quickly gets filled with our memories, judgements, thoughts, and decisions about *how life really is*. Also, we have *The Voice* inside our head that is filling the glass, telling us negative things about ourselves and how scary the world is.

So then we try to learn something new, read a book with a new idea, or meet a new person who seems interesting. There is one problem: our glass is already full and there is no room for a new idea or a new relationship. Our minds compare the new thing to all it already knows in the full glass. We not only become skeptical, but we can really be closed-minded and often give up on the dreams we had in the past because the full glass tells us our reality. Sad, isn't it?

Here is another example, while we are on the subject of glasses. This time, having to do with reading glasses. We, as humans, learn something in every event or interaction we have in our lives. Imagine that for each experience we have we put on a pair of glasses. For example, as a youngster I got lost at Disneyland. The glasses I put on? *I'm unlovable, I don't matter, I am on my own.* I find out Santa Claus is not real; the glasses I put on? *People lie and you can't trust them.* The kids make fun of me at the playground; the glasses I put on? *There is something wrong with me, the only way people will like me is if I do nice things for them.* My first love breaks my heart and dates my best friend; the glasses I put on? *I'm not good enough, I will never be loved, I cannot have friends because they will hurt me.*

Can you imagine me with all those pairs of glasses on my face? Yes, I know I would look ridiculous. But in my experience, I don't realize I was wearing all those pairs of glasses. I think the view that I have of the world is *real*. I know you are picturing me with those glasses, but I am picturing you wearing many, many pairs of glasses too! You have had your own opinions in life, even your own opinions about what I am saying now!

Shall we both move forward and get to the good stuff here? There is only one move we can make if we look at the water glass filled with water or the dozens of pairs of glasses on our faces. Yes, we must either dump the water from the glass or remove all the glasses from our faces so we can see something new. We must identify that we filled the glasses or made these decisions so we can be the ones to let the past go. Not to worry, you will never forget about the past, but it no longer has to stop you or me from achieving what we want to achieve in our lives.

I first learned that my glass was full and that I was wearing a fine array of invisible glasses in 2002. Since starting the racetrack catering business with my mom six years earlier, I found myself exhausted, no longer excited about life, and desperate to take a vacation. I got an opportunity to travel to London and remembered I had a business card from a gentleman I had met on the dance floor during a tropical vacation to the Club Med resort in the Turks and Caicos Islands where I had traveled years before. Gratefully, I was able to reconnect with this dancing partner over a casual dinner.

Looking at my friend, he appeared different from how I remembered him. He had lost a great amount of weight, quit smoking, gave up heavy drinking, was now in a romantic relationship with the woman of his dreams, and had opened several lucrative businesses. I wanted to know what happened to this man. I wanted the results that he had! I was sick and tired of the same kind of life happening to me over and over—a life filled with fear, doubts, questions, and never feeling good enough or loved. "Two words," he said, "Landmark Forum." Little did I know that I was about to have the most eye-opening experience of my life, during this weekend seminar! (LandmarkEducation.com)

Remember how our little soul in Heaven was told that certain guides would come into his life from time to time and get him back on track? That he should listen to the people he met just in case they were one of these guides? I have no doubt that Jonathan was put in my life so I could begin to discover who I *really* am.

To continue, two weeks later I was sitting in my chair at the Landmark Forum. In the matter of three days I learned what it was to be human, more specifically, how our minds work. The course is led in many different languages worldwide and there are common denominators to how every human's mind works. Identifying these *ways of being* leads people to realize that their particular circumstances (i.e., the problems and struggles they are facing in their lives) are similar to what everyone else on the planet is experiencing. From our strengths and weaknesses, to our views of the world, to *The Voice* in our head, to our survival instinct, we are all products of our past.

However, through intensely studying these *distinctions* and applying them to our own lives, several new opportunities open up and new thinking occurs. With new thinking comes new results. I will save my experiences in the Landmark Forum for another book, however I can tell you that I left that weekend course with less *baggage* than I started with. The many pairs of glasses came off, the glass was emptied and I knew who I was as a person, what I wanted in life, why I was stopped so many times in the past, and how I could continually move forward. Three important relationships in my life were healed, I became courageous, and a whole slew of amazing results began to happen. I even started dating again. What a ridiculous idea, to think I couldn't find love in my life with almost seven billion people on the planet. I felt like I was a kid again, any dream was possible for me and my life was good!

I did many advanced courses that Landmark Education offered, to polish my skills in self-expression and leadership. Then, one day, I met *Nance*.

Nance was fun! She was positive, high-spirited, creative, smart, and, bottom line, this woman made me laugh! I predicted that, in a very short time, we would become the best of friends. Nance had so many great qualities that I could deal with the one characteristic of her that I did not quite care for. She was one of those strange people I called *new age*. She believed in angels, spirits, mediums, and psychics, and the world of the *unseen*.

Believe it or not, my skepticism did not go away after doing the Landmark Forum. I never had believed in any mystical stuff and Nance was certainly not going to convince me that I should. I believed that there was a whole world of desperate people looking for answers and that the psychics, mediums, tarot card readers and the like were all out just to con people out of their hard-earned money. I remember going to a bookstore and seeing shelves that were full of these new-age books. "These poor people who read these books," I remember thinking, "should really get a life!"

Although I didn't believe in the stuff Nance believed in, I adored her. Her stories of angels and *how the universe really works* kept me entertained. Nance had a deck of *angel cards* and occasionally she would give me a *reading* of what my angels wanted me to know. The messages were all good, all the time, and my logical mind told me that I could find a message specific to a part of my life in any of the cards. There was no way that Nance could convince me that the angels had anything to do with what cards were drawn and what message they said!

During the spring of 2004, Nance gave me a deck of these Angel Cards as a gift. The cards were created by Doreen Virtue, PhD, who is known throughout the world as the *Angel Lady*. I was packing for my upcoming race in Sebring, Florida, and tossed the deck of angel cards into my suitcase.

When I arrived in Florida, I envisioned the nine days ahead of me, standing and cooking 14 to 16 hours per day in the hot, humid temperature, and I felt discouraged. Instinctively, I pulled out the deck of angel cards to look for some entertainment. I pulled the *Music* card from the deck and read the description in the guidebook that accompanied it. Music, it seems, is good for the soul. The instructions were to keep music playing in the background. I was not a person who normally played music at work, but chose to plug in the old radio for entertainment. "Maybe it would make the week go by faster," I thought. As it turned out, the music was a great idea. "Thank you angels!" I was happier at work as I sang along with the music from the 1980s.

I decided to pull out an angel card for inspiration the following eight days. For fun, I followed the instructions in the book: I shuffled the 52 cards while asking the angels what specific message I needed that day. Every day, except one, I pulled out the same card! What card was it? It continued to be the *Music* card, day after day after day. I remember thinking how weird that was. What are the chances of pulling the same exact card eight out of nine days?

Over the days that passed, I kept the music on in the background while cooking at the racetrack. Remarkably, the words really spoke to me and seemed to describe what was going on in my life. There was also another coincidence that regularly began happening. I would think about a particular song, and a minute or two later that song would play on the radio.

That was my very first awareness that some psychic abilities might be possible. The problem was *The Voice* in my head refused to believe in such a thing! I had proudly stated that those occurrences were not possible and anyone who claims to have psychic abilities should "get a life." The battle in my mind began. I became convinced that the disc jockey must have told the listeners the titles of the upcoming songs and the seed was planted in my mind, expecting that song to play. That explanation did not last long after I began to experiment. With the radio off, not hearing the coming attractions, I predicted the songs that would be played on the radio. When I turned the radio on, those songs were being played.

When the race ended, I headed home and did a little research on Doreen Virtue, the *Angel Lady*. Trained and licensed as a psychologist, Doreen began to hear *voices* in her head claiming to be spirits, guides, and angels. Thinking she was crazy and that normally she prescribes medication for those people with those voices, she chose not to listen to them. One day, they warned her of a carjacking that would happen to her. Again, choosing not to listen, the event took place, just as she had been previously shown in her mind's eye by these guides.

Over the years, Doreen had become one of the world's most credible psychic mediums. She has dozens of best selling books and many different decks of angel cards.

To my surprise, Doreen Virtue was speaking the following month at the Omega Institute retreat center in Rhinebeck, New York, only an hour-and-a-half drive from my chocolate shop. I called Nance, filled her in on the course and said, "You got me into this, you are coming with me!"

The weekend seminar surprised me. I thought there would be some kind of scam going on, some hidden way for fortunetellers to get money from people. This did not happen. Doreen gave several lectures about angels, spirit guides, and other interesting topics. However, what fascinated me the most was not what Doreen would teach. Rather, when someone would raise their hand, Doreen would answer their question, but would also tell them the name and details of their deceased loved one she saw appearing by their side. The person who received the message would start to cry and report that they did have a grandmother named Ruth who lived in North Dakota who would teach her how to quilt every summer when she was young.

Skeptic me was looking for the scam behind it all. "These people must be plants or part of the show, but why?" The retreat was reasonably priced and they were not selling anything. With my fear of dying still hovering in the background of my mind, I had to do more research.

When I returned home, I found that Doreen Virtue offered a three-day course called "Medium Mentorship." Her promise was that in three days I would effectively be able to see the deceased people around others. "IMPOSSIBLE," I thought . . . so I registered for the course.

Several months and several thousand dollars later I was in Laguna Beach, California, at the Medium Mentorship course. I felt completely out of place in our small group of twenty people. I had my khaki pants on with a polo shirt and the rest of the crowd looked like gypsies in their angel dresses.

After we introduced ourselves, we went right to work. We were told to each pick a partner, and our coaching was to connect psychically, heart to heart, with that partner. Then, we were to lovingly ask their deceased relatives for permission to show themselves to us and to tell our partner what we saw. I remember hearing Doreen say that this was just a practice session, and I was to create a person in my imagination. This took all the pressure off me, because deep inside as I wanted this so much to be real, *The Voice* kept telling me that I had been conned out of thousands of dollars and that I should just go home.

I picked a partner, a woman I had never met before, held her hands, closed my eyes, took a deep breath, and began imagining. As I created this fictitious person in my mind, I told my partner the story of who I saw. I began, "I see a blonde man named Jan. He was a fisherman in Denmark with really bad, red, ruddy skin and a gap between his front teeth. I believe he is your grandfather on your mother's side." I also told her that I got the impression that he died from lung cancer. What followed was a personal message that she was to tell her mother from her grandfather.

When I opened my eyes, I could see that my partner was crying. She soon told me that I got every detail correct about her mom's father, Jan, from Denmark, who looked the way I described him, and who died of lung cancer! The message was also very specific and my partner understood just what it meant.

It was now my turn to get the reading. My partner, who had never met me before and knew nothing about me, began to tell me all about my grandfather, whom I called Grampy. She knew his name was John and that he walked with a cane, and she saw a big German shepherd standing by his side. This was *Champa*, Grampy's faithful companion.

Three days of Doreen Virtue's Medium Mentorship course proved to be miraculous. I was not correct all the time, for apparently our imagination looks just like how the deceased loved ones present themselves, making it difficult to know who is real. It did not matter to me; I got the experience I was looking for my entire life. I, Sandra Champlain, now had proof for myself that *We Don't Die*.

Why did I not choose to start writing this book in 2005? Well, here I was, the gal who had badmouthed all the psychics and mediums on the planet, as well as the clients who paid them for their services. There was no way I was going to tell anybody that I got certified as a medium by the world famous Doreen Virtue, PhD. I told no one and stayed quiet about it.

The more people I talk to, the more I realize that many people have had weird things happen to them that cannot be explained. Have you had any of those experiences?

Over the months that followed I had many strange experiences. I started just *knowing* things about people. I knew people's names before they introduced themselves, I'd know the name of a telemarketer before the phone rang, I knew the names of people's deceased friends and relatives without them telling me. I knew the cab driver's name and his wife's name before he told me. What was happening to me? *The Voice* had been doing a great job of convincing me that what I learned in California was not real and that I made up all the experiences.

However, I wanted to figure this out. Why was I accurate only sometimes? Is there a way to perfect this skill? In the back of my mind I knew how many people suffer from grief when a loved one dies and I knew that telling people what I knew could help them.

I went to a local bookstore. Have you ever had the experience of a book *jumping off the shelf*? Well, I had it when I noticed a bright orange book titled *The Idiot's Guide to Communicating with Spirits*, by Reverend Rita Berkowitz, a minister of Spiritualism. This was the book for me! Clearly written by someone with a sense of humor!

Rita is a minister, a medium, and an artist. For over 30 years she has *seen* deceased people around her clients and can draw pictures of them. Throughout her book were actual photographs of people as they lived and Rita's drawings of these deceased folks. Amazingly, the portrait she drew matched the photograph in every example. (To see her amazing portraits visit TheSpiritArtist.com.)

I learned a lot from that book, including that Sir Arthur Conan Doyle, who wrote *Sherlock Holmes* and President Abraham Lincoln were both involved with Spiritualism. Spiritualist church services seemed similar to the Sunday services I was accustomed to, yet at the end of a Spiritualist service, the ministers tell the congregation who the deceased people are in the room!

I knew that I had to find a Spiritualist church. I turned to the back of the book and found that Reverend Rita and her church were located in Quincy, Massachusetts, about forty-five minutes from where I live! It gave me goosebumps. "Was this a coincidence or am I being led on a path?"

I chose to meet Rita and attend her Sunday church service. The service was beautiful and felt quite normal. I was fascinated at the end when she did the medium part. I could tell by the look on peoples' faces that Rita had accurately described their deceased friends.

After the service, I joined the parishioners for morning tea. When I met Reverend Rita and introduced myself, she smiled. She told me that I had an incredible bright, white light of energy surrounding me, that I am meant to be a teacher and a healer and that I ought to get busy! She invited me to attend the service the following Sunday, as she was going to have guest lecturers that she felt I would enjoy.

I sat in the pew at the First Spiritualist Church in Quincy, Massachusetts, the following Sunday. There was a pleasant-looking couple sitting up front. Clearly, the wife was the minister and she did the church service. Instead of the usual medium readings at the end of the service, her husband began to speak. He shared that although his wife believed in life after death, he could not believe, unless he found some kind of scientific proof. In the front of the congregation, he told us he now had that proof.

He then talked about *Electronic Voice Phenomena*. How it is possible to record random sounds and when the recording gets played back, voices from deceased people would show up. To me, this was crazy!

I remember, as a teenager, trying to hear messages from the dead by spinning an album backward on a turntable. However, this man sounded convinced, so I listened.

He told the story that he and his wife were now each on their second marriage, and that they both had children die in their first marriages. He then shared that he had a fan blowing in the background for *white noise* and left a tape recorder on their bed for 20 minutes. He and his wife left their house and, when they returned, there was a clear message from their deceased children. He played the recording and a weird sounding voice said, "Daddy, don't be scared, we are still here with you," followed by another voice giggling.

That moment scared and excited me at the same time! As much as my mind was telling me that this could not be true, the other part of me said that this is the kind of proof that I needed. That if I could do these recordings and hear voices myself, people wouldn't think I was crazy and I could help people with all the knowledge and experience I have.

The man talked about a book to buy if we were interested in trying to record *Electronic Voice Phenomena* (EVPs) ourselves. The book is called, *There Is No Death and There Are No Dead*, by Tom and Lisa Butler. Tom and Lisa served as the EVP experts and taught Universal Studios about their recording technique for the movie *White Noise*. The EVP community was very upset when a horror movie was created. Since their first recording in 1982, all of the EVPs have only been loving or humorous messages.

I went home and ordered the book *There Is No Death and There Are No Dead* and a digital tape recorder. I still remember sitting on my living room floor recording the white noise coming from a station on my television. When I hit the play button, a thought occurred to me, "If somebody starts talking to me on this thing, it is going to scare the heck out of me. I am not ready for this, this is something that I should not be playing with," and I buried the book and the recording device in my drawer and vowed to not touch it again.

Several months passed by and I had the urge to go back to the Omega Center in Rhinebeck. I had been overeating again and knew that the vegetarian cuisine and the nature walks would do me good. I only had one weekend free, the weekend before Halloween, and began looking at the Omega website to find a course that interested me.

That is when I saw it: "Tom and Lisa Butler, *Electronic Voice Phenomena*," on the only weekend I had available. These occurrences were no longer coincidences. I felt I was somehow being guided to the Omega Center to work with this couple.

I have to be honest, I was scared to death to attend this course. It was one thing to see visions in my mind, but I could easily convince myself that it was my imagination. Now, I had the possibility of hearing voices. I was not quite sure I wanted to do this!

Friday night I entered the classroom at the Omega Center. There were only five students plus Tom and Lisa. My classmates had all either lost a spouse or a child and were desperate to reach them. There was nobody I needed to hear from, that's for sure! Tom and Lisa Butler were nice, normal, not the mystical type I expected. We learned all about EVPs and how they were first recorded. Thomas Edison even devised a recorder in the 1800s, hoping to hear a voice from beyond.

I thoroughly enjoyed the course. Everyday we recorded sounds and then would download them onto Tom's computer and play them back. Tom and Lisa seemed to frequently hear messages from my recorder, specific ones that mentioned the name of my mom, her father, and my grandmother. I was a little upset because now I was ready to hear them too. They explained that they have been listening to these recordings for 17 years and they have become accustomed to hearing the *whispers of voices* within the background sounds.

I returned to my little cabin Saturday night after class. I wanted so desperately to hear something. Alone in my cabin, in the middle of the woods with only a small light on and the flicker of the gas heater in the corner, I chose to try to record an EVP. Outside was pouring rain, and my sense told me that rain would be a good background sound for my recording.

As I sat on my bed, I questioned whether I was completely crazy or not. I thought I had done the right thing by following my instincts and registering for this course. I began to question whether it is possible that our deceased loved ones are still nearby and if they can use this technology to communicate with us. As much as I wanted it to be true, it really did sound crazy. I chose to do the homework and pressed the *record* button on my digital tape recorder. I imagined my deceased grandmother and grandfather as well as an aunt and uncle by the foot of my bed. I began to speak to these imaginary people and said, "All right my dear friends, I'm going to do one more recording. Try to speak as loud as you can. If I am supposed to help people to believe in life after death, I have to hear you, so please try to talk loud. I will be quiet for about a minute and then I'll say goodnight and I won't bug you anymore." I had been trying repeatedly to get something on the recorder earlier, with no results.

I continued to record the sounds of the raindrops outside. After a minute, I said, "Goodnight," just before pressing the *stop* button. Not expecting this time to be any different from the last several attempts, I pressed *play* on the digital recorder. I snuggled under my blanket with my big headphones around my ears. Convinced that I would hear nothing, I waited and listened.

Then, I heard it. A sharp chill ran through my body, flooding my skin with goosebumps. I pressed rewind to hear it again. There it was, a message for me starting at the 46-second mark on the recorder. It said, "Goodnight Sandra," in a man's voice, followed by two women each saying, "Goodnight," and a final man's voice saying, "Goodnight."

Immediately I felt nauseous. I was stunned, scared, and all alone in this cabin. Suddenly the fun of trying to connect to the other side was no fun at all. What I experienced was so real, like nothing I could have imagined. I began to worry, "Are they still here watching me? Are dead people always with me? Don't I have any privacy?" and I got very scared. I really wanted to talk to someone human, but there was no one. I would have to wait until class the next day.

I replayed the recording over and over and over. Finally, when I was mentally exhausted and emotionally overwhelmed I laid my head on the pillow. "I must try to sleep," I thought. I closed my eyes with visions of my deceased grandparents looking over me. "Are you really here?" I whispered to the air, and realized that my life would never be the same.

The next day in class I played my recording for Tom and Lisa. Sure enough, I recorded a class-A EVP. Class As are the most rare, but are the loudest and most clear. My classmates were delighted, as hearing my recording convinced them that their loved ones were still near.

It was easy to be in this group of warm, loving people and talk about contacting deceased people by recording EVPs. I got wonderful words of encouragement, that love is all around, and that I should never fear death. I will be describing *Electronic Voice Phenomena* more in another chapter, but want you to know that I finally was able to rest my fearful mind and believe that there is life after death.

When I got home from the class, I continued to experiment with recording EVPs. As time went on, I could hear many more voices come through, often just whispers in the background noise and, after some practice, I found it was easier to hear what the people were saying.

I heard messages for my grandmother from my grandfather, the bark of Champa, my grandfather's dog, with his voice saying, "That's Champa." I met relatives that I hadn't known existed. Then, I kept hearing, "It is Joka." Someone had a message for my grandmother, but I could not understand the name. My aunt then told me that my grandmother had a brother who was nicknamed "Joker," but with the strong, Massachusetts accent, Grammy called him "Joka."

My aunt wanted to hear the recordings and she was able to hear them. At Christmas, I decided to tell other family members about the recordings and they asked if we could do a recording around the dinner table. For *white noise*, I turned on the faucet on the kitchen sink and recorded the sound of the water running. When we replayed the message, there were several "I love you's" and "Merry Christmas" was said with different family members' names spoken by the those we could not see.

I met a woman at a seminar who confided in me that her father had passed away while she was in prison and she was unable to let go of her guilt for disappointing him and never saying goodbye to him. I shared my journey with her and she asked if we could do a recording to try to reach her father. I brought the woman to my hotel room during a break, and began my normal practice: I held her hands and envisioned the two of us being circled in a whirlwind of increasing energy, almost a tornado-like force field around us. Whether I believed it or not, I was taught that the deceased need a high amount of energy to do EVPs and that we could increase our energy field. It always seemed to work for me, so I did it. Then, I turned on the shower in the bathroom for background sound. My instinct was that the sound of water could be easily manipulated into voices as my first recording of raindrops seemed to work.

A clear message did come through for this woman. He said her name and said, "I love you. I am proud of you." He then followed with, "So easy to talk now, easy to breathe." She then told me that her dad had a tracheotomy, and lived for several years without the use of his voice. He had a device that he would hold to his throat in to speak artificially. This woman then released her guilt and knew for sure that her dad was proud and loved her.

On a trip to Atlanta, I met a young man in the shuttle bus from the airport to the hotel. He shared with me that his younger sister had passed away and he missed her terribly. Courageously, I told this man of my journey and about EVPs. Within the hour, the shower was on and we attempted to contact his sister! That was the first time

I saw an image of a person during the recording. I saw a brown-haired, brown-eyed girl with a braid on either side of her head. She must have been only eight or nine years old. I shared this information with the man and he said, "That's her." The recording produced, "I love you, Billy. Remember the game we used to play? Remember *Clue*?" My new friend, Bill, told me that he and his little sister (who died at the age of nine) played the game *Clue* very often.

There was one person I was afraid to tell about my recordings and that was my dad. Although he was a cancer survivor who believed in miracles, I was scared to tell him that I was recording voices of the deceased. On one visit to Florida I couldn't stand the fear anymore and said, "Dad, I have something to tell you, but I'm worried what you might think." Dad was so great, he told me that I could tell him anything, and so I did. I told him about my journey, starting from the angel cards all the way to doing the recordings. His eyes were big as he couldn't believe what he was hearing. All he said was, "Okay," not quite knowing how to respond to the story I told him.

But then I had something happen. In my mind's eye I saw an airplane. It was a yellow Piper J-3 Cub, with black lettering on the side. I imagined a man laughing and felt the uncontrollable need to tell Dad about this airplane. This laughing man said in my mind, "John, I did get to bring my toys with me." Dad began to cry. He had known a man with cancer and had been trying to help the man with visual imagery, so he would beat cancer as my dad had years before. My dad kept telling him that he couldn't die, because he could not bring his toys with him. This man owned a yellow Piper J-3 Cub with black lettering on the side.

To this day I have recorded hundreds of messages, both for myself and for people I have met on my journey. Most messages are whispers. I, like Tom and Lisa Butler, have trained my ears to hear these whispers. Only occasionally is there a loud, clear message.

I will discuss more about how to record EVPs in another chapter, if that is something you should choose to do. There are also many men and women around the world who will help you record an EVP if you wish to connect with a deceased loved one.

Electronic Voice Phenomena messages are not to be feared. The messages are usually messages of love, a shared memory, or occasionally something humorous (it seems we get to keep our sense of humor in the hereafter). People often want to hear specific messages about certain events to confirm that it really is their loved one. Sometimes those messages appear, but often it is an "I love you." If you were to pass away and finally get an opportunity to say something to someone you haven't spoken to in a very long time, what would you say? I think, "I love you" is the perfect thing to hear.

After my weekend with Tom and Lisa Butler, I was introduced to many other pioneers in proving there is life after death, and continued my journey to gain more evidence of our souls' survival.

Unfortunately, I have been fighting a battle with an enemy who has not let me share this information until now. That enemy is myself. That enemy is *The Voice* inside my head.

Remember the story of the soul in Heaven who gets to come to Planet Earth? We were told we would forget who we *really* are. One way to assure that we'd forget is that *The Voice* would be with us. It has taken me seven years of gathering *proof* to finally come forward with this information and *The Voice* is fighting me every step of the way.

The Voice we each have in our heads has a job to do. It will take the greatest things that could happen to us and make them seem like they are *no big deal* and redirect our attention to the things that are bad or wrong in our lives. For instance, I proved that *life after death is real* and my voice seemed more concerned with looking for the next diet to go on. Ridiculous, isn't it?

Pay attention to what *The Voice* is saying in your head right now. Have you gone into disbelief? Have you gotten distracted and are choosing to stop reading for a little while? Are you wearing the many pairs of glasses and it is telling you that this cannot possibly be true?

The Voice also never likes to be *wrong*. It will fight for its truth, even if it means that you have a terrible life. Have you ever been in an argument with someone and, no matter what, you feel like you are right and you won't even listen to the other person's side of the story? It is not really *you* arguing with them, it is *The Voice*, desperately trying to win.

Pay attention to what *The Voice* is saying to you right now. If it is excited, ready to read more, congratulations. However, if it is fighting you and is very judgmental, it has no interest in you living an extraordinary life. It wants you to forget who you really are.

I encourage you to let your *Soul Self* (the part of you that can listen to *The Voice*) watch the inner workings of your mind, and turn the page to the next chapter.

No homework assignment after this one. I do want to thank you for being willing to take off the glasses and empty the glass.

I have a special *Thank You* gift for making it this far. Please visit: WeDontDie.com/SurpriseGift.html.

Let's move on, there is an exciting, new world of opportunity that is waiting for you.

Chapter 4

What the World's Greatest Minds Say

I am confident that there truly is such a thing as living again, that the living spring from the dead, and that the souls of the dead are in existence.

~ Socrates, ancient Greek philosopher, b. 470 BC

soul, *noun*

The principle of life, feeling, thought, and action in humans, regarded as a distinct entity separate from the body, and commonly held to be separable in existence from the body; the spiritual part of humans as distinct from the physical part.

Our roller coaster just took a turn that perhaps you did not see coming, nor did I when it first happened to me. *Electronic Voice Phenomena*, also known as capturing voices of the deceased, is one of the very real tools that is being used today, around the world. It was first discovered in 1959 and the *American Association for Electronic Voice Phenomena* was founded in 1982. "Why haven't I heard of this before?" you may ask. My answer is the same for much of this new information that I will present to you shortly: *"Because the world was not ready for it."*

One thing we know about human beings is that we do not like change. Let me ask you, "Do you think the world is flat?" Now you may laugh at that and say, "The world is round, not flat!"

However, for hundreds of years, the Earth was thought to be flat and that it was the center of the almighty universe. There is documentation that ancient philosophers knew the Earth was round and that our Sun was in the center of our solar system thousands of years ago. However, the general population did not agree with this, no matter how much proof there was. Poor Galileo spent the last two years of his life in jail under house arrest because of his claim that the Sun, not our Earth, was in the center! Ferdinand Magellan's crew proved that the Earth was round in 1522 after taking three years to circumnavigate the world on their ship.

Human beings don't typically like change and, when change happens, it has to be gradual for it to be believable. Thankfully, when enough people get involved with the same story, a *tipping point* can occur and a conversation can be changed. Malcolm Gladwell's book, *The Tipping Point: How Little Things Can Make a Big Difference,* offers many examples of what it takes for a belief system to change.

I believe that the tipping point about life after death will occur within my lifetime. That before I pass to the next stage of my existence, more people will believe in life after death than do not.

Things have already changed quite a bit. When I was younger, I only remember hearing about a few psychics and mediums. What often followed was the word *hoax, con, scam,* or *weirdo.* Twenty years later, it is quite normal for people to consult with mediums and psychics. There are even many hit TV shows about them, like *Medium, Ghost*

Whisperer, and *Long Island Medium.* Go to a bookstore or do a search on the Internet for *paranormal, mediums* or *psychics* and see just how regular these discussions are around the world. Getting psychic counseling has become fairly regular—people see their doctors, counselors, and healthcare professionals, along with consulting their psychics, angel practitioners, astrologists, and mediums.

How are you doing with this conversation? Ten years ago, I can honestly tell you, I would have been one of those people fighting for the world to be flat! I would be fighting this conversation right now, because *I know better,* psychic abilities are impossible!

You know what I just realized? How much I believed other people. I believed their words that hypnosis isn't real, that psychic ability isn't real, that life after death is impossible. You know how they got their information? They believed other people! I know when I am looking for a correct answer about something, I sometimes do a search on the Internet. The problem with that is there is no guarantee the information there is correct either. There are as many skeptics who make valid points about the impossibility of life after death as there are valid points by people who have credible information.

I will make a deal with you. I will not try to convince you of anything, okay? However, I will give you a few exercises to do that will yield incredible results for you. Your rational mind will not be able to figure out how you could do such amazing things. Then, and only then, will I ask you to consider that *you are much more powerful than you think you are.* I know who you are, I know you are a great person and want the best life possible. I believe that we must all be willing to accept some new ideas to have new results.

What things have changed in your lifetime? Do you realize that just one hundred years ago we did not have a television, telephone, computer, or even a refrigerator in our homes? Could you imagine showing a person who lived in the early 1900s an iPhone or a GPS or a laptop computer? I'm sure they couldn't handle the new technology that fast. New ideas take time to be implemented, but where would we be without change and new technology?

Regarding *Life After Death*, we are living in a *World Is Flat* conversation. Sorry, that is just the way it is. But times are changing quickly. In 1991, *International Social Survey* said that 55% of Americans believe in life after death, as well as 26% from the United Kingdom. In 2009, an amazing 73% of Americans believe in life after death and 53% in the United Kingdom believe. I, like many other people, do have faith in the afterlife; however, I can say there is a whole new level of living when one has proof.

I urge you to be one of the trendsetters by the time you are finished reading *We Don't Die*, and take a stand for a new conversation. By doing so, you will help heal many people. You will give people hope, remove pain, remove fear, lessen grief and suffering, and give people a reason to *live* life and to *love* life. By sharing *We Don't Die*, you may help one person in one of these groups. If you haven't heard this before, there is nothing better in life than helping another person.

Did you know that over one million people commit suicide every year due to grief and depression? Did you know that well over 27 million people take antidepressants every day in the United States? Did you know that there are more than 155,000 deaths every day in the world and over 113 million people experiencing the pain of grief every day? I'm guessing that you, like me, have experienced the pain of losing someone you love. What difference will it make to you when you believe your loved one is still around? Think about it. What kind of affect would that have on the planet if people believed We Don't Die?

Like the ancient people thousands of years ago knew the Earth was round, so did many people know that *We Don't Die*. Let's hear from several of the most brilliant minds of all time, and what they have to say about life after death:

The soul comes from without into the human body, as into a temporary abode, and it goes out of it anew . . . it passes into other habitations, for the soul is immortal. . . . It is the secret of the world that all things subsist and do not die, but only retire a little from sight and afterwards return again. Nothing is dead; men feign themselves dead, and endure mock funerals and there they stand looking out of the window, sound and well, in some strange new disguise.

~ Ralph Waldo Emerson

Live so that thou mayest desire to live again—that is thy duty—for in any case thou wilt live again!

~ Freidrich Nietzsche

I look upon death to be as necessary to the constitution as sleep. We shall rise refreshed in the morning.

~ Benjamin Franklin

I know I am deathless. No doubt I have died myself ten thousand times before. I laugh at what you call dissolution, and I know the amplitude of time.

~ Walt Whitman

So as through a glass and darkly, the age long strife I see, Where I fought in many guises, many names, but always me.

~ General George S. Patton

What happens after death is so unspeakably glorious that our imagination and our feelings do not suffice to form even an approximate conception of it. The dissolution of our time-bound form in eternity brings no loss of meaning.

~ Carl Jung

Why should we be startled by death? Life is a constant putting off of the mortal coil—coat, cuticle, flesh and bones, all old clothes.

~ Henry David Thoreau

I believe there are two sides to the phenomenon known as death, this side where we live, and the other side where we shall continue to live. Eternity does not start with death. We are in eternity now.

~ Normal Vincent Peale

It's so silly. All you do is get the heck out of your body when you die. My gosh, everybody's done it thousands of times. Just because they don't remember, it doesn't mean they haven't done it.

~ J D Salinger

I adopted the theory of reincarnation when I was 26. Genius is experience. Some think to seem that it is a gift or talent, but it is the fruit of long experience in many lives.

~ Henry Ford

Death is nothing else but going home to God, the bond of love will be unbroken for all eternity.

~ Mother Teresa

What the caterpillar calls the end of the world, the master calls a butterfly.

~ Richard Bach

I have absolutely no fear of death. From my near-death research and my personal experiences, death is, in my judgment, simply a transition into another kind of reality.

~ Raymond Moody

I've told my children that when I die, to release balloons in the sky to celebrate that I graduated. For me, death is a graduation.

~ Elisabeth Kubler-Ross

The fear of death follows from the fear of life. A man who lives fully is prepared to die at any time.

~ Mark Twain

Mark Twain (born Samuel Clemens in1835) was greatly interested in the idea of life after death after he had a dream of his younger brother, Henry, being killed in a steamboat explosion. One month after the dream, Henry was killed in an explosion of the steamboat, The Pennsylvania, on June 21, 1858.

About ten days ago, I retired very late. I had been up waiting for important dispatches from the front. I could not have been long in bed when I fell into a slumber, for I was weary. I soon began to dream. There seemed to be a death-like stillness about me. Then I heard subdued sobs, as if a number of people were weeping. I thought I left my bed and wandered downstairs. There the silence was broken by the same pitiful sobbing, but the mourners were invisible. I went from room to room; no living person was in sight, but the same mournful sounds of distress met me as I passed along. It was light in all the rooms; every object was familiar to me; but where were all the people who were grieving as if their hearts would break?

I was puzzled and alarmed. What could be the meaning of all this? Determined to find the cause of a state of things so mysterious and so shocking, I kept on until I arrived at the East Room, which I entered.

There I met with a sickening surprise. Before me was a catafalque, on which rested a corpse wrapped in funeral vestments. Around it were stationed soldiers who were acting as guards; and there was a throng of people, some gazing mournfully upon the corpse, whose face was covered, others weeping pitifully. 'Who is dead in the White House?' I demanded of one of the soldiers 'The President' was his answer; 'he was killed by an assassin!' Then came a loud burst of grief from the crowd, which awoke me from my dream.

~ Abe Lincoln

President Abraham Lincoln saw his assassination in a dream. After his death, his casket was, in fact, put on a platform in the East Room where soldiers were stationed to act as guards. Before his death, President and Mrs. Lincoln invited Spiritualist Mediums into the White House to try to contact their deceased son.

It was very interesting, and really the phenomena that we saw appeared inexplicable as trickery—tables raised from all four legs, movement of objects from a distance, hands that pinch or caress you, luminous apparitions. All in a [setting] prepared by us with a small number of spectators all known to us and without a possible accomplice. The only trick possible is that which could result from an extraordinary facility of the medium as a magician. But how do you explain the phenomena when one is holding her hands and feet and when the light is sufficient so that one can see everything that happens?

~ Pierre Curie

Marie & Pierre Curie, Nobel Prize winners in Physics, were fascinated with mediumistic séances and were part of 43 scientific experiments that were carried out by the Institut Général Psychologique of Paris between 1905 and 1907. They believed that it was possible to discover, in Spiritualism, the source of an unknown energy that would reveal the secret of radioactivity.

Once you eliminate the impossible, whatever remains, no matter how improbable, must be the truth.

~ Sir Arthur Conan Doyle

As a doctor, Arthur Conan Doyle was fascinated by early experiments in thought transference and healing through mesmerism and hypnotism. He became interested in the *Society for Psychical Research* (SPR), established in 1882 to scientifically investigate paranormal phenomena, such as *extra-sensory perception* (ESP).

After holding séances with his wife Jean to get in touch with members of their family killed in the first world war, Conan Doyle came out as a Spiritualist. He claimed to converse with the spirits of the dead. He wrote books on Spiritualism and addressed vast audiences around the world on the subject, giving more attention to those books than to Sherlock Holmes. In North America he was at odds with magician Harry Houdini, who argued that all Spiritualists' tricks could be replicated by a competent magician.

Psychic Mediumship

You begin to understand that there's no such thing as death. Only the body dies. The soul and personality live on. Not only that, but the soul is usually much happier in heaven. If they didn't finish their life's purpose, they'll often act as a spirit guide to the living person, to vicariously fulfill their mission through that living person.

~ Doreen Virtue, PhD

A *Psychic Medium* is a person thought to have the power to communicate with the deceased. I do believe that all people possess the ability to receive information from the deceased; however, like learning any sport or playing any musical instrument, there are people who are extraordinarily gifted. There are thousands of great mediums around the world, but in this section I am only including those who have personally made an impact on me.

Doreen Virtue, PhD

Angeltherapy.com

Doreen, who holds BA, MA, and PhD degrees in counseling psychology, was the founder and former director of WomanKind Psychiatric Hospital at Cumberland Hall Hospital in Nashville, Tennessee. She was also an administrator at Woodside Women's Hospital in the San Francisco Bay Area. Both all-women psychiatric hospitals specialized in treating women's psychological issues. Doreen also directed three outpatient psychiatric centers, including an adolescent drug and alcohol abuse center.

As I described earlier, I had first encountered Doreen when she gave a presentation at the Omega retreat center in Rhinebeck, New York. Although she focused her conversation on *angels*, she also shared accurate information about deceased loved ones whom she *saw* around people in the audience.

I liked Doreen; she shared her incredible journey, which began when she prescribed medication to people who heard voices in their heads, and ended in hearing voices in her own head! These voices claimed to be her angels and gave her a clear vision of her being carjacked. She refused to give in to the image and to the voices, and the carjacking took place just as she imagined in 1995. After that, she chose to sharpen her natural clairvoyance skills and combine them with her clinical psychology background.

Doreen has published over 20 books and conducts experiential workshops on spiritual psychological issues worldwide. Many of her students are medical and psychological professionals, including MDs, RNs, psychologists, and social workers.

I have personally studied with Doreen four times, and each time was amazed at how many of the images that appear to come from my *imagination* were really accurate names, faces, and information from people's deceased loved ones. I have met several hundred participants during her courses and each person was able to see, in their mind's eye, something they should not be able to know.

Reverend Rita Berkowitz

TheSpiritArtist.com

Often, when thinking about a Medium, it's easy to envision a gypsy-like person hovering over a crystal ball. That is not an image of Rita Berkowitz, as she is as normal looking as any well-dressed, middle-aged woman you might see in your travels.

I first learned about Rita at a bookstore, when my eyes were attracted to her bright orange book titled *The Idiot's Guide to Communicating with Spirits.* At that time, I was experiencing many random visions from *the other side,* but was looking for a way to sharpen my skills. What I love most about people is their senses of humor, and I knew by the title that author Rita Berkowitz was a fun lady!

Rita is a *Spirit Artist*, a Medium, as well as a minister in the Spiritualist Church. As a Spirit Artist, she draws portraits of a deceased loved one she sees by your side. She also tells her clients any messages she receives from that person.

I had first met Rita several years ago at her church in Quincy, Massachusetts. I was fascinated that as part of the normal Spiritualist Sunday church service, the minister gives messages from departed loved ones to people sitting in the church. She perfectly described my grandfather and gave me a special message, and gave my friend Bob a message that could have only come from his deceased mother.

In 2011, almost a year after my father had passed, I chose to meet with Reverend Rita as a client. Grief is tough. Even though I believed that my father's spirit was still around me, I missed him terribly and wanted evidence.

Rita is a lovely, warm, compassionate woman. She immediately *saw* and described my little grandmother *Betsy* who had passed away two years before. She saw my grandfather, complete with his light blue shirt, grey pants, a cane in his hand, and his German shepherd dog by his side. I hadn't spoken a word either. Then she said, "Dad is here."

Rita picked up her pencils and began to sketch an image. His brown eyes came first, followed by the rest of his face. She drew a picture of my dad in his younger days that looked very close to a photograph I have of him while he was in the US Air Force in the 1960s. Apparently, when we pass from this life to the next place, we can be any age we want to be.

Rita also told me specific information regarding the last year of my dad's life. It seemed as if Dad were telling her the story and she was just conveying the message. She knew the month he first had pain in his back, she described the tumor that was in his spine, she told of him going in the hospital, the hospice, and the nursing home. Then she pointed to her abdomen and said that Dad described his pain as, "It feels tight," which is exactly how Dad described it to me so many times. She then demonstrated how Dad would lift himself out of a chair, which was very difficult for him to do with the damage to his spine. He would lean far over, put his hands as far back on the seat of the chair as possible and push himself up. She knew that I had an older brother and sister and a younger sister. There was no question in my mind that Dad, Grammy, and Grampy were in that room with Rita and me.

A big question I had for Dad was why, even at the end of his life, he kept on fighting to live. As his adult children, we all knew there may not be too much time left in his life, although Dad kept speaking of treatment to beat his cancer right up to the end. I often wondered, was Dad afraid to die? Rita smiled and said, "Oh no. Your dad knew he was going to pass, he wanted to make sure you kids knew to never give up on anything."

John Holland

JohnHolland.com

I had the wonderful opportunity of meeting and speaking to John Holland after a demonstration of mediumship that he did during an event called *Soul Survival* in New York. John is one of the most authentic, respected, and accurate mediums who regularly speak on stage to comfort people. He also has a great sense of humor and makes the audience feel very comfortable.

John was born with an inner sense of knowing—knowing that he was the different one in his family. As a naturally-gifted psychic medium, he's studied metaphysics all his life, spending over two intensive years in England, training and working with some of the top psychic mediums. He received confirmation of his special psychic abilities after a near-fatal accident when he was 30 years old, when his unique skills were amplified and brought to the surface.

When he contacts the Spirit World, one of his most familiar sayings is, "They want to talk to you as much as you want to talk to them!"

If you witness John on stage, you will find he loves to educate as much as be a medium, and explains the actual mechanics of mediumship— how he's linking with a spirit and the different forms of communication, both in words and images, that spirit uses to send messages through him.

John believes that his job as a psychic medium is not only to help those to connect with their loved ones but, just as importantly, to empower everyone to follow their own spiritual journey. Often, for those who lose a loved one, it can cause them to question their own beliefs about life after death and, as a spiritual teacher, John helps people tap into their psychic abilities and help them discover and recognize the signs and symbols associated with their loved ones who have passed on.

John says, "If I can help people connect with someone on the Other Side—by linking with the Spirit World—to bring peace, comfort, and perhaps some closure, or, if I can help you understand and tap into your own inner-guidance for answers, then I'll be satisfied that I've done my job!"

James Van Praagh

VanPraagh.com

James Van Praagh is a warm, kind-hearted medium who has had much attention due to his extraordinary talent in delivering messages from the deceased. He has appeared on *Oprah, Larry King Live, Dr. Phil, A&E Biography, Maury Povich, 20/20,* and *48 Hours.* His books have been featured on the *The New York Times* Bestseller list and he was the co-producer of the TV series *Ghost Whisperer.*

During his early days, James was invited to attend a session with a medium in Los Angeles, although he didn't even know what a medium was. Given that, he was understandably doubtful when the medium informed James that he would be doing the same work within two years. James says, "My first reaction was, I have enough trouble dealing with the living, why do I want to talk to the dead?"

As James' sensitivity increased, he began doing psychic readings for friends. During these readings, he began receiving detailed messages from the beyond. Though at first this seemed bizarre, the more he learned, the more he could not deny the fact that he had the gift to reach beyond the familiar plane of existence we call life. Today, James is recognized as one of the foremost mediums in the world.

Naturally, there remain skeptics about his abilities. James, however, is the first to say that he welcomes healthy skepticism, declaring, in fact, that he is a skeptic himself.

What I love about James is that he is also a teacher. To search James Van Praagh, you will also find one of the many courses he offers on how to learn mediumship. James feels extremely fortunate to be a conduit of comfort, healing and, most importantly, love. "As a medium, I have never experienced anything but love and compassion and healing in my work. It is the love bond between people that allows me to make the connection between the living and the dead."

Maureen Hancock

MaureenHancock.com

I had the unique experience of attending one of Maureen Hancock's *Postcards from Heaven* presentations in Massachusetts. I had heard stories of Maureen, but it wasn't until I witnessed her first hand that I saw how incredible and accurate she is with her medium skills.

Her presentation was held in a small gift shop south of Boston and nearly 50 chairs were in the room. Maureen is not only beautiful and compassionate, but she is funny! Literally, she is a trained comedian and delivers extraordinary messages from the deceased along with her crazy sense of humor. Her presentations are sold out months in advance because she is so accurate. She is fast, she quickly works her way through the audience to give as many people as possible the messages from their deceased loved ones. I was amazed that she continued almost 45 minutes past the ending time of the presentation because there were more people that she had to give messages to.

Maureen does her stage shows during weekends and evenings to provide her income to support her family, so she can do the things most important to her. She is cofounder of two non-profits: *Seeds of Hope*, holistic care for cancer patients and support for parents who have lost children; and *Mission for the Missing*, providing assistance and equipment in missing children and adult cases.

I was very moved by Maureen's message to me. In just a few seconds she told me my dad's first name, correctly stated that I had two sisters and a brother, and told me that Dad was proud of me for something I recorded (I had just recorded a CD called *The Law of Chocolate*). She went on to see my grandmother and grandfather, along with their

German shepherd dog, and I was to wish someone a "Happy Birthday" whose birthday had something to do with Christmas. Their daughter (my Aunt Donna, whom I live with) was born on December 26th, the day after Christmas. She mentioned a few other personal things to me, then quickly went to talk to the next person.

Instrumental Trans Communication

Tom and Lisa Butler

ATransC.org

Tom and Lisa Butler are the current directors of the *Association Trans-Communication* (ATransC), which has been recording voices from the hereafter since 1982. There are voices that come through on tape recorders as well as pictures of the deceased that appear on videos or photographs. Tom and Lisa are the authors of the book *There Is No Death and There Are No Dead,* which explains their journey and gives readers instruction how to do these extraordinary recordings.

Studying with them gave me my first auditory evidence of our survival after physical death when I recorded only the sound of raindrops on my digital recorder and heard, "Goodnight Sandra," when I played the message back. This evidence is called *Electronic Voice Phenomena,* also referred to as *EVP.* It is believed that the deceased manipulate the sound waves that have previously been recorded on a device. This means that the sound of a fan or raindrops can be changed into the sound of spoken words. Most of these voices sound like whispers but, on occasion, a loud, clear word or message can be heard.

There are several thousand members worldwide of the ATransC, many of whom work with others to prove that their loved ones are still around. Although it is easy to learn how to record EVPs, it does take some practice listening for these whispers on the recordings. One thing is clear to me, every person who heard a voice from a deceased loved one shortened their grieving time dramatically and had a new excitement for their own life.

For instructions on recording EVPs please go to WeDontDie.com/EVP.html.

Mark Macy

SpiritFaces.com

I met Mark at a conference called "Life After Death, The Evidence." Mark, an atheist, began his personal journey in 1988 when he was diagnosed with cancer. Like myself, his fear of dying led him to prove that there is life after death. In 1991, he heard claims that people in Europe were receiving photographs from the deceased on videos and began his research on Instrumental Trans Communication (ITC).

Mark founded the *International Network for Instrumental Transcommunication* (INIT) in England in 1995, along with a dozen other researchers from eight countries. Their intent was to open a contact bridge between Heaven and Earth, or more precisely, between our world and the finer worlds of spirit, using technology as the medium. Over five years, the group received dozens of phone calls and TV images from the hereafter.

When I met Mark, he had created a device called a *luminator*. This device somehow rearranges the subtle energy field around a person, so that when they are photographed using a Polaroid camera, often a second face will appear in the image. Although I had experienced a lot, I was skeptical about this.

Each one of us at the conference had our photograph taken by Mark. Although my picture only developed into a picture of myself, the woman sitting to my right had a different result. My new friend's teenage daughter had died several years before. She fell off a building to her death and they never had any idea if it was an accident or suicide. Earlier at the conference, this tall, slender-faced older woman with her hair pulled back, had shown me a picture of her daughter.

Her daughter had lots of hair, a round face, and a beautiful smile. When her picture developed, you could clearly see two faces within the one picture. One was the mother, with hair pulled back, no smile, and a slender face, the other looked just like the photograph I had seen of her daughter, with all the hair, the round face, and the big smile. If I had not seen that Polaroid picture develop in front of my very eyes, I would never have believed it.

Mark Macy has written a book called *Spirit Faces*, and has been featured on television documentaries, aiming to share my very same message, that *We Don't Die*.

Induced After-Death Communication

Allan L. Botkin, PsyD

Induced-ADC.com

Clinical Psychologist Dr. Allan Botkin, who worked for 20 years treating combat veterans in a VA hospital, founded *Induced After Death Communication* (IADC) purely by accident. He had been using a well-known technique called Eye-Movement Desensitization and Reprocessing (EMDR) to aid patients who had Post Traumatic Stress Disorder. PTSD is a severe anxiety disorder that can develop after exposure to any event that results in psychological trauma.

During a scheduled appointment, Dr. Botkin administered a series of eye movements to a patient that not only relieved the person of the anxiety but also caused this person to see images of the deceased! Dr. Botkin had not previously been involved with life after death studies, nor did he have an opinion of the afterlife. However, when regularly administering this new pattern of eye movements to his clients, he found increasingly, people were able to clearly see and receive images from the deceased. Many times the person was not even aware of the deceased person; however, the visions and experiences of the people they saw proved to be accurate.

Dr. Botkin perfected this method and founded IADC. Deep sadness and grief are often immediately eliminated with IADC regardless of people's personal beliefs. He is the author of *Induced After-Death Communication: A New Therapy for Healing Grief and Trauma* and has trained over 70 psychotherapists worldwide to use IADC therapy to help patients overcome deep grief and sadness, by connecting them to the deceased.

Near-Death Experiences

Raymond Moody, BA, MA, MD, PhD

LifeAfterLife.com

Dr. Raymond Moody is the leading authority on the near-death experience—a phrase he coined in the late seventies. Dr. Moody's research into the phenomenon of near-death experience had its start in the 1960s. *The New York Times* calls him "the father of the near-death experience."

Dr. Moody is the author of twelve books including *Life After Life*, which has sold over 13 million copies worldwide. Dr. Moody continues to capture enormous public interest and generate controversy with his work on near-death experience and what happens when we die. He also trains hospice workers, clergy, psychologists, nurses, doctors and other medical professionals on matters of grief recovery and dying.

There is so much speculation about near-death experiences, and it is easy for skeptics to believe that our brains normally have these experiences as part of the dying process. Common to near-death experiences are: hearing sounds such as buzzing, having a feeling of peace and painlessness, having an out-of-body experience, a feeling of traveling through a tunnel, a feeling of rising into the heavens, seeing people (often dead relatives), meeting a spiritual being such as God, seeing a review of one's life, and feeling a reluctance to return to life.

Dr. Moody has personally spoken with thousands of people who have had such experiences in his over 30-year career. While certainly some of these experiences may be part of the normal, physiological processes of dying, there are far too many examples of people seeing things that they should not normally be able to see.

As one woman explained to Dr. Moody:

"When I woke up after the accident, my father was there and I didn't even want to know what sort of shape I was in, or how I was, or how the doctors thought I would be. All I wanted to talk about was the experience I had been through. I told my father who the person was that had dragged my body out of the building. I even knew what color clothes the person had on and how they got me out. I even knew about all the conversation that had been going on in the area. And my father said, 'Well, yes, these things were true.' Yet my body was physically out this whole time and there was no way I could have seen or heard these things without being outside of my body."

Kenneth Ring, PhD

Near-Death.com

In 1977, Kenneth Ring, a young professor of psychology at the University of Connecticut, read Dr. Moody's book, *Life After Life*, and was inspired by it. He felt that a more scientifically structured study would strengthen Moody's findings. He sought out 102 near-death survivors for his research.

Dr. Ring is the author of five books, including *Life at Death: A Scientific Investigation of the Near-death Experience* and *Mindsight: Near-Death and Out-of-Body Experiences in the Blind*.

Dr. Ring and Sharon Cooper studied 31 blind people, who either experienced a near-death experience or out-of-body experience.

Half of these people had been blind since birth, yet each one of these people was able to see accurate information of the doctors operating on them, the people who came to visit, the colors they were wearing and often visions of angelic figures and deceased relatives.

> *Death is no more than passing from one room into another.*
> *But there's a difference for me, you know. Because in that*
> *other room I shall be able to see.*
>
> ~ Helen Keller

Dr. Ring shares many of his findings on his website, *near-death.com*, and these are his conclusions from the more than 35 years of research on near-death experiences:

1. In the cases in which the people came closest to death, or were clinically dead, just as Dr. Moody's cases reported, they told of being outside of their bodies, of moving through a void or dark tunnel toward a luminous light, of meeting with departed relatives and friends, of having a feeling of great comfort and bliss and of being surrounded by compassionate love, a feeling so beautiful they longed to remain and when they returned to the Earthly realm, they were affected by this feeling the rest of their lives.

2. No one type of person was especially likely to have this experience. It cut across race, gender, age, education, marital status, and social class.

3. Religious orientation was not a factor affecting either the likelihood or the depth of the NDE. An atheist was as likely to have one as was a devoutly religious person.

4. Regardless of their prior attitudes—whether skeptical or deeply religious—and regardless of the many variations in religious beliefs and degrees of skepticism from tolerant disbelief to outspoken atheism—most of these people were convinced that they had been in the presence of some supreme and loving power and had a glimpse of a life yet to come.

5. Drugs, anesthesia and medication did not seem to be a factor in inducing these impressions and exquisite feelings of a NDE. In fact, drugs and anesthesia seemed to be more likely to cause a person to forget memories of a NDE.

6. Dr. Ring definitively concluded that NDEs are not hallucinations, because hallucinations are rambling, unconnected, often unintelligible and vary widely, whereas NDEs tend to have similar elements of a clear, connected pattern.

7. Based on the information of those who had reported such incidents, the moment of death was often one of unparalleled beauty, peace and comfort, a feeling of total love and total acceptance. This was possible even for those involved in horrible accidents in which they suffered very serious injuries. Dr. Ring found there was a tremendous comfort potential in this information for people who were facing death.

8. After going through an NDE, people reported a loss of fear of death as well as a greater appreciation of life. They also reported stronger feelings of self-acceptance and a greater concern and sense of caring for other people. They had less interest in material things for their own sake. Many tended to become more spiritual, though not necessarily more involved in organized religion.

9. Almost all subjects who experienced an NDE found their lives transformed and experienced a change in their attitudes and values, as well as in their inclination to love and help others. Dr. Ring was convinced that these were absolutely authentic experiences and noted that since returning, many of them had occasion to think about "what might have been." And their subsequent lives were powerful testimony to our common ability to live more deeply, more appreciatively, more lovingly and more spiritually.

Other Pioneers

Brian L. Weiss, MD

BrianWeiss.com

As a traditional psychotherapist, Dr. Brian Weiss was astonished and skeptical when one of his patients began recalling past-life traumas that seemed to hold the key to her recurring nightmares and anxiety attacks. His skepticism eroded, however, when she began to channel messages from "the space between lives," which contained remarkable revelations about Dr. Weiss's family and his dead son. Using past-life therapy, he was able to cure the patient and embark on a new, more meaningful phase of his own career.

Since 1980, Dr. Weiss has regressed more than 4,000 patients and is the author of eight books, including *Many Lives, Many Masters*, that includes voices of Master Spirits that came through a patient during a past life regression.

Here are some of the teachings from the Voices of the Master Spirits:

1. "Our task is to learn, to become God-like through knowledge . . . By knowledge we approach God and then we can rest. Then we come back to teach and help others."

2. "There are many gods, for God is in each of us."

3. We have to be on "different planes at different times. Each one is a level of higher consciousness. What plane we go to depends upon how far we've progressed . . ."

4. "We must share our knowledge with other people. We all have abilities far beyond what we use . . . you should check your vices . . . if you do not, you carry them over with you to another life . . . when you decide you are strong enough to master the external problems, then you will no longer have them in your next life."

5. "Everybody's path is basically the same. We all must learn certain

attitudes while we're in physical state . . . charity, hope, faith, love . . . we must all know these things and know them well."

6. "Everything is energy. . . . Humans can only see the outside, but you can go much deeper. . . . To be in physical state is abnormal. When you are in spiritual state that is natural to you. When we are sent back, it's like being sent back to something we do not know. In the spirit world you have to wait and then you are renewed. It's a dimension like the other dimensions. . . ."

7. "The fear of death . . . that no amount of money or power can neutralize" . . . remains within us. "But if people knew that life is endless; so we never die; we were never really born, this fear would dissolve." We have "lived countless times before and would live countless times again . . . and spirits are around us to help while in physical state and after death, in spiritual state." We and our deceased loved ones would join these guardian angels.

8. "Acts of violence and injustices against people do not go unnoted, but is repaid in kind in other lifetimes."

9. "Everything comes when it must come. A life cannot be rushed . . . we must accept what comes to us at a given time . . . life is endless . . . we just pass through different phases. There is no end. Time is not as we see time, but rather in lessons that are learned."

10. After death "we get to the spiritual plane, we keep growing there, too. When we arrive, we're burned out. We have to go through a renewal stage, a learning stage and a stage of decision. We decide when we want to return, where and for what reasons. . . . Our body is just a vehicle for us while we're here. It is our soul and our spirit that last forever. . . ."

I had the opportunity to hear Dr. Weiss lecture about his past and most recent discoveries in 2010. If you are interested, Dr. Weiss conducts national and international seminars and experiential workshops as well as training programs for professionals.

International Association for Near-Death Studies (IANDS)

Iands.org

IANDS was founded in 1978 and is devoted to the study of near-death and similar experiences and their relationship to human consciousness. Included are the pioneering works of psychiatrists. Elisabeth Kübler-Ross, Raymond Moody, and George Ritchie, as well as the findings of Kenneth Ring, PhD, Michael Sabom, MD, Bruce Greyson, MD, and many others.

The members are worldwide, including many prominent health care professionals. Current research, NDE testimonials, education and upcoming conferences are all offered to the public. What is amazing to me is the number of experiences shared by doctors and surgeons, of extraordinary near-death experiences. I encourage you to read some of the stories and watch some of the videos on their website. I was left speechless after watching what some doctors experienced in their operating rooms.

> *Death is simply a shedding of the physical body like the butterfly shedding its cocoon. It is a transition to a higher state of consciousness where you continue to perceive, to understand, to laugh, and to be able to grow.*
>
> ~ Elisabeth Kübler-Ross

Elisabeth Kübler-Ross

EKRfoundation.org

Elisabeth Kübler-Ross was a Swiss-born psychiatrist who worked with terminally ill patients. In 1969 she authored *On Death and Dying*, in which she first discussed the Five Stages (of dying, grieving or any kind of loss): denial, anger, bargaining, depression and acceptance. She found that people experience most of these stages, although in no particular order, after being faced with the reality of their impending death.

She also taught over 125,000 students about death and dying and was greatly involved with the formation of Hospice and Palliative Care for the terminally ill.

After a lifetime of working with the terminally ill, Elisabeth Kübler-Ross heard enough stories of near-death experiences and visions from her patients that she started her own investigation into the afterlife. Although previously a skeptic on life after death, she researched more than 20,000 people who had NDEs, had a near-death experience herself, and authored the book *On Life After Death*, convinced of our continual existence after physical death.

> *Extraordinary skepticism requires extraordinary accuracy.*
> ~ Gary E. Schwartz, PhD

Gary E. Schwartz, PhD

DrGarySchwartz.com

I had the privilege of hearing a lecture by Dr. Schwartz at a conference called "Life After Death: The Evidence." He founded the VERITAS Research Program at the University of Arizona, *Discovering the Truth about the Survival of Consciousness and Continuity of Life*. During his lecture I was amazed to hear about some of the many tests Dr. Schwartz conducted, most very scientific in nature, that certainly had me convinced in the validity of the mediums he studied.

Dr. Schwartz is highly experienced in speaking publicly about health psychology, energy healing and spiritual research. He has been interviewed on major network television shows including *Dateline* and *Good Morning America*, as well as on *MSNBC, Nightline, Anderson Cooper 360* and *The O'Reilly Factor*. His work has been the subject of documentaries and profiles on Discovery, HBO, Arts & Entertainment, Fox, History and the SciFi Channel, among others. He has been interviewed on hundreds of radio shows and his work has been described in various magazines and newspapers including *USA Today*, the *London Times*, and *The New York Times*.

The amazing Dr. Gary Schwartz has published more than 450 scientific papers, including six papers in the journal *Science*, co-edited 11 academic books, and is the author of *The Energy Healing Experiments, The G.O.D. Experiments, The Afterlife Experiments, The Truth about Medium, The Living Energy Universe* and *The Sacred Promise: How Science is Discovering Spirit's Collaboration with Us in Our Daily Lives.*

I am clear that Dr. Schwartz has performed more investigative double-blind and triple-blind tests than anyone, and I am clear that reading his books and listening to his interviews will have you drop any remaining bit of skepticism about life after death. I encourage you to visit DrGarySchwartz.com for details of these findings.

Victor Zammit

VictorZammit.com

Although I have not formally met Australian attorney Victor Zammit, I receive his *Friday Afterlife Report,* which gets delivered to my email address every week with the latest findings about life after death. Victor was previously a skeptic and, through his research, published the book, *A Lawyer Presents the Evidence for the Afterlife.*

His website and his book are translated into many languages, as he is passionate about sharing his findings globally so that people may lead better lives. Each week, he presents such incredible information that it would be nearly impossible to follow his findings every week and *not believe* in the afterlife.

Bob Olson

AfterLifeTV.com

A former private investigator, Bob Olson is an Afterlife Investigator & Psychic Medium Researcher. In his search for evidence of life after death since 1999, Bob has tested hundreds of psychic mediums, spirit artists, past-life regressionists, and other related practitioners to weed out the legitimate from the phonies, frauds, and scam artists.

Bob Olson is the founder and editor of *AfterlifeTV.com, BestPsychicDirectory.com, BestPsychicMediums.com,* and *OfSpirit.com* Magazine.

I personally enjoy watching the videos Bob has on *AfterLifeTV.com.* He regularly talks with authors and experts discussing what he has learned in his investigations of the afterlife.

R. Craig Hogan, PhD

YourEternalSelf.com

Craig Hogan is a writer and trainer of writers with 38 years of experience. He is the director of the *Center for Spiritual Understanding* and on the boards of the *Academy of Spiritual and Paranormal Studies* and *Association for Evaluation and Communication of Evidence for Survival.*

He is the author of *Your Eternal Self,* which I read from cover to cover, leaving me fascinated by near-death experiences, especially how blind people could accurately see and describe what they saw when they became conscious again.

For those of you who need to know research details, *Your Eternal Self* will provide the scientific facts and findings and gives you all the supporting references.

Dr. Hogan is also co-author of *Guided Afterlife Connections,* which contains 26 accounts of people who have had their own afterlife connections through the Guided Afterlife Connections procedure. The book states, "People are having their own connections with loved ones in the afterlife, without mediums. The life-changing connections greatly reduce grief and trauma."

I presented all the pioneers in this chapter so you could get a taste of what kinds of things are currently being studied in the world of *Life After Death*. My list of who is out there and what they are investigating is nowhere near complete. Every week I am learning about a new way someone has effectively been in contact with the deceased, even through things like the computer, text messages, or voicemail. While these things may seem unbelievable, I encourage you to explore them.

Remember, there are two voices inside your head: *The Voice*, which is not just skeptical but can very often tell you this is not the truth, and your *Soul Self*, the wiser part of you that remembers who you really are. If you doubt that, just listen to the voice in your head. Then ask yourself, "Who is the one listening?" That is who you really are. That is your *Soul Self*.

I want to repeat something to you. I am interested in you having a great life. The way to do that is for you to learn new things and take new actions. Stop doing the same things in life. You have been wearing many pairs of glasses and your water glass may have been too full for you to learn some of these new ideas.

Have you ever heard Albert Einstein's definition of insanity?

Insanity is doing the same thing over and over
and expecting different results.

HOMEWORK ASSIGNMENT

Allow yourself to listen to *The Voice* in your head. See what it is telling you about the chapter you just read. Is it telling you that the information is right, wrong, needs further investigation? Thank *The Voice* for its opinion.

Now, do something new. Pick one person, practice, or organization from this chapter, the one that you found the most fascinating and write down that interest. You may write, "Find out more about

Electronic Voice Phenomena," or *"Go to Bob Olson's website."* Then, set a date and time to do that.

We'll discuss *how to achieve results,* later in the book. Right now, you must know that *learning something new* and *taking an action* are needed to have a new result.

Chapter 5

Religious Agreement for Life After Death

A man may be the greatest philosopher in the world but a child in religion. When a man has developed a high state of spirituality he can understand that the kingdom of heaven is within him.

~ Swami Vivekananda, Indian spiritual teacher, b. 1863

When I began to share my journey into life after death, I was confronted with many people who believed I shouldn't be doing this research, because it was against their religious beliefs. Growing up Catholic, I knew that my faith did believe in life after death. After all, "Christ has died, Christ has risen, Christ will come again" is spoken during every mass I have attended. In addition, we regularly prayed for our departed brothers and sisters and that their souls could be seated with the Father in the Kingdom of Heaven.

Remember when I told you the story of when I first wanted to start recording *Electronic Voice Phenomena*? I can still remember that day clearly. I became afraid and the *The Voice* told me, "This is the devil's work, you are a good girl and have no right to play around with this." Clearly, had I grown up as an Athiest or perhaps belonged to another religion, *The Voice* would have said something else.

I have found that it has been difficult to share my journey with those that I believe are very religious. Why? Because of my own fears. I want people to like me. I don't want to get into arguments and I certainly don't want to offend anyone and have them start an argument with me.

This led me to investigate what the top world's religions believe about life after death. Guess what? Most religions believe in life after death and believe that we are spiritual beings.

This chapter will give you a brief summary of the people in this world and their religious beliefs about life after death.

On this day, as this book is being written, there are 7,008,672,042 or 7.009 billion people in the world, according to the US Census Bureau.

The most recent numbers I could find come from *The World Factbook of 2009* which was compiled by the Central Intelligence Agency. Here are the main religious traditions of the world's seven billion inhabitants:

CHRISTIAN: 2.3 billion
(Including Roman Catholic, Protestant, Orthodox, Anglican)
MUSLIM: 1.6 billion
HINDU: 966 million
BUDDHIST: 500 million
SIKH: 25 million
JEWISH: 15 million
BAHA'I: 8 million
CONFUSIANISM: 6.3 million
JAINISM: 4.2 million
SHINTOISM: 4 million
NON-RELIGIOUS: 660 million
ATHEISTS: 143 million

Life After Death Beliefs

Christianity: (Including Roman Catholic, Protestant, Orthodox, Anglican), 2.3 billion
Christian beliefs about the afterlife vary between denominations and individual Christians, but the vast majority of Christians believe in some kind of heaven, in which believers enjoy the presence of God, other believers and freedom from suffering and sin.

Islam: 1.6 billion
Islam teaches the continued existence of the soul and a transformed physical existence after death. Muslims believe there will be a day of judgment when all humans will be divided between the eternal destinations of Paradise and Hell.

Hinduism: 966 million
Hindus believe death is part of the continuing cycle of birth, life, death and rebirth. The soul of the dead transfers to another body after death, known as reincarnation.

Buddhism: 500 million
The death of the physical body is certain, but only a part of an ongoing process of reincarnation until one receives enlightenment. After death, it is believed that the dead person goes through a transformation in which they discover death and prepare for rebirth (if there is one).

Sikhism: 25 million
Samsara, or rebirth, of a person is based on their karma. Human birth is the only chance to escape samsara and attain salvation.

Judaism: 15 million
Traditional Judaism firmly believes that death is not the end of human existence. However, because Judaism is primarily focused on life here and now rather than on the afterlife, Judaism does not have much

dogma about the afterlife and leaves a great deal of room for personal opinion. It is possible for an Orthodox Jew to believe that the souls of the righteous dead go to a place similar to the Christian heaven, or that they are reincarnated through many lifetimes, or that they simply wait until the coming of the Messiah, when they will be resurrected. Likewise, Orthodox Jews can believe that the souls of the wicked are tormented by demons of their own creation, or that wicked souls are simply destroyed at death, ceasing to exist.

Baha'i: 8 million

Baha'is believe in an afterlife in which the soul is separated from the body. At death, according to the Baha'i faith, the soul begins a spiritual journey towards God through many planes of existence.

Progress on this journey toward God is likened to the idea of heaven. If the soul fails to develop, one remains distant from God. This condition of remoteness from God can, in some sense, be understood as hell.

Thus Baha'is do not regard heaven and hell as literal places but as different states of being during one's spiritual journey toward or away from God. Baha'is understand the spiritual world to be a timeless and placeless extension of our own universe and not some physically remote or removed place.

Confucianism: 6.3 million

Confucius regarded Heaven, *T'ien*, as a positive and personal force in the universe. However, he discouraged his students from worrying about the afterlife, as he believed it to be *beyond human comprehension*. Instead, he encouraged them to live in harmony and to help other people through service, teaching, or just being a good family member. Confucius thought that there was great joy to be found in everyday family life, participating in communal activities, enjoying music and spending time with one's friends.

Jainism: 4.2 million

Jains believe that all people are caught in an endless cycle of birth, death and rebirth. It emphasizes *Ahimsa*, non-violence toward both humans and animals. Reincarnation and karma are important beliefs. In Jainism, death leads ultimately to the liberation of the soul into an individual state of total knowledge and bliss, although this process may take several cycles of death and rebirth. The only way to break this vicious cycle is to accumulate good karma or credit for good deeds. So, they place great emphasis on charity, non-violence and benevolence.

Shintoism: 4 million

The word *Shinto* literally means *the way of the Gods*. Shinto is the native religion of Japan and stresses the importance of harmony between humans and nature. It involves the worship of *Kami,* which are many godlike natural or spiritual presences. After death, it is believed that a person becomes a spirit deity, and eventually becomes part of a collective ancestral spirit.

Non-religious: 660 million

Non-religion is also referred to as *irreligion,* meaning lack of religious faith, or indifference toward religion. Some non-religious people have hostility toward religion. Many people who claim to be irreligious believe in life after death, although it may not often be verbalized. President Thomas Jefferson believed in the natural world without a need for religion; however, he believed in life after death. Thomas Paine, one of the founding fathers of the United States, was irreligious, believed in free thinking, yet did believe in life after death.

Atheism: 143 million

Atheists are people who deny the existence of god. That does not mean they deny the existence of an afterlife, it means they don't believe a god is required for one to go on living after death.

New York Times bestselling author and atheist Sam Harris states, "Consider it: every person you have ever met, every person will suffer the loss of his friends and family. All are going to lose everything they love in this world. Why would one want to be anything but kind to them in the meantime?"

Although not believing in a god or religion, he gains inspiration from meditation. Paying attention to the present moment-to-moment, Harris suggests that it is possible to make our sense of self vanish and experience a new state of personal well-being.

This *present moment technique* is the very same as the instructions given to our new young soul traveling to Planet Earth for the first time. Remember what the guidebook said?

> *In case of an emergency, there will be only one way to get help. You will be able to access this guidebook through your thoughts. To achieve this, you must stop The Voice inside your mind and quiet your senses. We have put reminders around the Earth in the form of Stop signs. These signs will be a reminder to you, to stop your thinking and quiet your mind. Then, have the intention of getting an answer to your question, and the answer will come in that stillness.*

I shared that I was writing a book with a heart surgeon recently who has spoken with thousands of people before undergoing heart surgery. Certainly there is fear of the unknown and people realize that they may lose their life during an operation. He told me that 100% of the time, whether a person is religious, irreligious, or atheist, the same three things are shared by all people:

They feel love for their family and those they are closest to.

They have sadness and regret for the things they have not said or done.

They pray and have faith in an afterlife.

EXTRA CREDIT ASSIGNMENT

Are you religious? Do you fit into one of the categories that I listed above? It becomes very easy for us to believe that we are doing something wrong or against our religion by discussing life after death.

Take some time to research your personal faith and specifically find out: What are the beliefs about life after death? You may be very surprised to hear how many people of your faith know about some of the things I have discussed here, or have had an amazing experience being contacted by someone in the afterlife.

Chapter 6

Life . . .
The Grand Illusion

So if you think your life is complete confusion,
because your neighbors got it made. Just remember that
it's a grand illusion, and deep inside we're all the same.

~ Styx, *The Grand Illusion* album, 1977

il·lu·sion, *noun*

**Something, such as a fantastic plan or desire, that
causes an incorrect belief or perception of reality.**

What if the point of being on Planet Earth is to experience emotions,
be able to use our five senses and enjoy the unique atmosphere only
available here? What if we come from some other place to experience
these things in order for our *Soul Self* to grow and mature? What if life
is really a *Grand Illusion,* like the song the band *Styx* sings in the quote
above? This chapter will address the possibility and the probability of
life being a *Grand Illusion.*

We live our day-to-day lives believing we are important individuals, the things we do on a daily basis are important and our relationships are important. What we eat is important, exercise is important, getting an education is important, doing our very best is important, telling the truth is important, having a good job is important, being loving and forgiving is definitely important.

We live our lives filled with emotion, don't we? Think of something you are worried about right now. Could it be your health or your financial situation? Maybe it is a conversation you are afraid to have or you are worried about your son or daughter. How does worry feel? Yeah, it feels awful!

Think of some of the fears that you have. Some of us have fears of flying, others have fear of public speaking, some are afraid of dying, others are afraid of being alone, some have fears much, much worse.

Think of someone you love and I mean really love. Take a moment and feel how good love feels. It can be a person or even a pet. Think of them now and soak up the love that feels so good. You deserve to feel good. Yes, I am talking directly to you, not someone else. You are a wonderful person, you're smart, you're loving, you do your best and you deserve to feel good.

Think of the successes you have had in life. What are you proud of? Is there a job you had in your past in which you excelled, or sometime when you made a big difference for another? Are you a parent of a terrific kid? Have you won any awards in your life?

What do people love about you? What do your friends say? What does your family say? What makes you so different from other people?

Do you feel special right now? Do you feel unique? Well, you should. Out of the seven billion people on Earth right now, you are the only you. If there was one grain of rice for every human on the planet, you would be one grain in one of the 61,000 gallon (231,000 litre) containers filled with rice. That puts in perspective how many of us there are on this planet right now, doesn't it?

Did you know that our Earth has been spinning well over 300,000 years with human beings living on it? In 2011, scholar Carl Haub published the article "How Many People Have Ever Lived on Earth?" The answer is approximately 107,602,707,791 give or take a few! It took me a minute to figure out what that number said! Each one of the one hundred and seven billion of us has felt special and unique in our lifetimes. We have each felt pleasure and pain.

Planet Earth, the Milky Way, and the Almighty Universe

Let's talk about the planet we inhabit, Earth. The Earth is about 4.6 billion years old, but life did not exist on this planet until about 2 billion years ago, when certain kinds of bacteria and algae began to appear. Land plants did not appear until about 430 million years ago; reptiles, 300 million years ago; and modern mammals, 75 million years ago. The first apes appeared about 35 million years ago and the first apelike men, about 10 million years ago. Man only appeared about 300,000 years ago.

If you were to cut the Earth in half, it would be 7,926 miles wide. We already know there are about 7 billion human beings living on it. Every second, four of us are born and every 1.8 seconds, one of us dies.

The Earth's atmosphere is composed mainly of nitrogen (78%), oxygen (21%), argon (.93%) and carbon dioxide (0.03%). We live about 90 million miles away from the sun. The Earth is just the correct mass and has the correct rotation that causes gravity to exist, so that we don't float away into outer space. Lucky for us, the Earth provides everything we need for human life to occur.

However, we are not alone. Life exists here on Earth for 8.7 million others species of plants and animals. 75% of that number lives on the ground and 25% of them live in Earth's waters. That's a lot of life! It is predicted that there are:

7.7 million species of animals, 298,000 species of plants, 611,000 species of fungi (molds, mushrooms), 36,400 species of protozoa (single-cell organisms with animal-like behavior, e.g., movement) and

27,500 species of chromista (e.g., brown algae, diatoms, water molds, of which 13,033 have been described and cataloged).

That is an absolute incredible amount of life on our one planet. Could it be all by chance that we are here on Earth along with 8 million varieties of other life? The point of this chapter, by the way, is to get you to think that perhaps there is a bigger picture to who you are and what your life is for, that you are not just some random, chance creation, that your life is important and that there is meaning to it. You will learn some amazing facts about our bodies, our Earth and the Universe that you probably would not have believed if science had not discovered them. There are so many unseen things that really do exist like radio waves, television signals, GPS systems and wireless Internet signals. Personally, I do believe that our deceased loved ones are in that same invisible place, the space that exists all around us. They no longer have bodies, but they continue to vibrate as energy no different than the music we can hear but we cannot see. They are literally here, after death better known as the Hereafter.

Have you ever looked up at the stars and wondered about the vastness of the universe? Well, when we do look at the stars, we are looking at just a small amount of stars that exist in our galaxy, the Milky Way. Scientists believe that the Milky Way consists of somewhere between 200–400 billion stars. Our sun is just one of these stars. It is believed that at least 10% of these stars have planets in their solar systems, which would mean there are at least 20 billion solar systems just in our galaxy.

That number alone boggles my mind. Scientists believe that there are more than 50 billion planets in our Milky Way and estimate that 500 million of them could be in the habitable zone; meaning, they could have life on them. We live on just one of these planets, one out of 50 billion in our Milky Way galaxy.

How many galaxies are there? This is a difficult number to know for certain, since we can only see a fraction of the universe, even with our most powerful instruments. With the help of the Hubble Telescope the most current estimates guess that there are 100 to 200 billion galaxies in the Universe, each of which has hundreds of billions of stars. A recent German supercomputer simulation put that number even higher: 500 billion. In other words, there could be a galaxy out there for every star in the Milky Way. Amazing, isn't it?

In the universe it is predicted that there are 1,000 stars for every grain of sand we have on our planet. Think about that the next time you are at the beach running your fingers through the sand!

I think you'd find some of the pictures taken from the Hubble Telescope very interesting. There is also an incredible TV show called *Hyperspace* that will give you a perspective of just how small we are in this vast universe. You can see all my space stuff at WeDontDie.com/Universe.html.

Our Inner Universe

As humans, we live our lives like everything is very real. The relationships we have, our job, our home, our clothes—everything seems so real to us. Why do we think they are so real? Because we can *see, touch, smell, taste,* and *hear* them. Our five senses tell us what is real and what is not. Our senses lead us to perceive the reality that we experience.

per·cep·tion, *noun*
The ability to see, hear, or become aware of something through the senses.

So, when we perceive something through our senses, it must be *true*, right? There are a couple problems with that. Our human brains process about 2,000 *bits* of information per second through our senses. While this may seem like a lot, it is not, because every second there are 400 billion bits of information occurring in the world around us. Have you ever noticed that you and a friend witness the exact same event, but her description is not the same as yours? Well, her mind simply did not pick the same 2,000 bits that yours did.

Another factor to consider is that we don't just perceive the bits. Our mind takes the bits and passes them through our past memories of those bits and subconsciously tells us how to think about what we see. For example, what are your thoughts about the ocean? Is it beautiful, vast, blue and inhabits a lot of life? Do you love to go swimming in it? Do you love to go on boats and enjoy the boat bouncing around in the waves? Would you enjoy being miles out in the ocean and jumping into the water to cool down if it is hot outside?

Or, do you look at the ocean with fear? Do you not know how to swim? Have you had the experience or know of someone who drowned or almost drowned? Have you gotten seasick in the past? Have you seen the movie *JAWS* and believe there are too many big fish under the water that can eat you? The ocean remains the same, but our past memories tell us how to feel about it.

This goes for our perceptions of human beings too. Look at a person in your life that you don't particularly care for or someone who hurt you in the past. How do you feel about him? Maybe you believe that he's a jerk, can't be trusted, is selfish and egotistical. Now take a look at someone who loves that person and thinks the world of him. You both are looking at the very same person, but you perceived that person doing or saying things that caused you to store *jerk, can't be trusted, selfish,* and *egotistical,* in your mind. The other person might have stored memories of *loving, generous* and *fun.* Who is right, and who is wrong?

It is a human condition that *The Voice* inside our head needs to be right. Often, though, we cannot see that we don't have love, happiness, or satisfaction in our lives because we have to be so *right* about how a person is! If you have a person in your life whom you judge negatively, or with whom you've had an argument, consider this fortune cookie message I got years ago:

The best place to stand during an argument
is on the other person's side.

I believe all people are generally good people. We all try to do our best in life, but we each have our perception of what is real for us or not. When you can follow the advice of the fortune cookie, you have the opportunity to have incredible relationships, accepting people just as they are, realizing they may be different from you because they have a life different from yours.

EARLY HOMEWORK ASSIGNMENT

Who is a person in your life that you have a negative feeling about? What perception do you have about that person? Notice if you are being right and making that other person wrong. Follow the advice of the fortune cookie and try to see life from the other person's side. Can you have some compassion for who that person is and why they would have said or done the things that they have done? Could the 2,000 bits of information that they have processed and run through their memory banks be responsible for any disagreement? Can you let that resentment go?

To get the most value from this exercise, have a conversation with that person, even if they are dead. Call them on the phone, meet with them face to face, or simply imagine them sitting in a chair in front of you.

Back to our reality. Our five senses tell us what is real and what is not. Sensory perception takes place in our brains. However, our brains cannot accurately tell what is real or not real. Have you ever had a dream that seemed real? Last night I dreamt of the ocean; perhaps that's why I just thought of that example! In the dream, I was swimming from one boat to another. I was very aware of the giant fish that might have been in the water with me and I was afraid. The dream was real, the water was real, the scary fish were real. Then, I woke up.

Your body is like a robot that is controlled by the mind. What the mind tells the robot is real, the robot will experience. So, in my dream, I experienced the cold, wet water and the fear of being eaten by a shark! It wasn't real, but my robot (body) thought it was.

Here is another example. I want you to imagine that there is a lemon sitting in the bottom drawer of your refrigerator. Now imagine that you grab a cutting board and a sharp knife and set it on the counter. Get that cold lemon out of the bottom drawer of the fridge. Can you see the lemon? It's color, it's shape? Can you feel the texture and weight of it? It's a little cold, isn't it? Take the lemon and put it on the cutting board. With the knife, cut the lemon into four equal segments. You can hear the knife as it hits against the cutting board. You can see a little juice running from the lemon wedges onto the cutting board. You can smell the lemon, can't you? Now, take one of those wedges and bring it to your lips. Open your mouth and take a big bite. Is your mouth puckering right now? Are you salivating? Can you taste the lemon?

While reading the words in this book, you became very aware of the lemon, right? It was simply an illusion in your mind, yet you produced the bodily sensations that the lemon was real.

Is a lemon *real* to begin with? Is this book real? Is the chair you are sitting on real? The obvious answer is yes, because we can touch, see, hear, smell and taste things. However, the real answer may be no, because even the things we can sense may have no substance at all.

Have you heard that only energy exists in the universe? Physicists and scientists agree that everything we can touch, see, hear, feel, or taste is all made up of energy.

The lemon is what we call *matter*. Anything we can touch is a form of matter. Matter is made up of *molecules* that are very small parts of all living and non-living things.

I hope that I am not confusing you too much right now, but if I have, sometimes confusion may lead you to experience a headache. So, let me give you an aspirin. Before I give you the aspirin, let us realize that an aspirin is matter. There is a shape and size to it. The aspirin is made up of small chemical compounds called molecules. Molecules are always moving, rapidly *vibrating* and consist of things called *atoms*. Each molecule consists of two to millions of atoms, depending on the complexity of the matter.

An atom is even a smaller piece of matter. Inside the molecules of the pill of aspirin I just gave you, you can find a chain of atoms that scientists call C9-H8-O4. This means that the aspirin molecule contains 9 *carbon atoms*, 8 *hydrogen atoms* and 4 *oxygen atoms*.

In the past, people thought that atoms were unbreakable, so the hydrogen atom was considered the smallest particle. However, at the start of the twentieth century, it was discovered that atoms are made up of protons, neutrons and electrons. The protons and the neutrons make up the center of the atom, called the nucleus and the electrons fly around above the nucleus in a small cloud. The electrons carry a negative charge and the protons carry a positive charge and a neutral charge is held by the neutron.

Today we know that the electron is really indivisible and so fundamental; however, protons and neutrons appear to be built out of much smaller particles called quarks. I am not a quantum physicist, so I'm going to share the next part simply. Quarks are believed to be made of energy, *strings* of light energy. If you can imagine a violin or guitar string vibrating, that might give you a picture of what one of these strings of light inside a quark looks like.

Unfortunately, no human eye has been able to see these strings. In fact, if you put a tiny camera inside an atom, you know what you would see? Nothing. It would be invisible, because all that's in there is vibrating energy. The *Inner Universe* that we all share is as hard to fathom as the outer Universe. The lemon or the aspirin that we see and touch becomes invisible when we break it down to its smallest size. Strings of energy cannot be seen, but we know they exist because we can see things that exist around us.

As hard as it is to understand that things we see are really nothing more than vibrating strings of light, there are things that exist in reality that we do not see, things like radio waves or television signals. Even the wireless connection that your computer uses to connect to the Internet or the cell phone frequencies that you use to connect to your friends halfway around the world, are invisible!

Let's talk about the radio, something we all probably take for granted these days. You climb in your car, buckle your seat belt, put the car into drive and off you go. Sooner or later, you hit the power button on your radio and listen for the news or turn on your favorite station. Music and voices come out of this little box in your dashboard. You know, your forefathers and mothers would have been blown away by the idea of a radio! "Impossible, it cannot be true, words come out of mouths not out of little boxes," is what they'd say.

It wasn't until the 1860s that Scottish physicist James Clerk Maxwell predicted the existence of radio waves; and in 1886, German physicist Heinrich Rudolph Hertz demonstrated that rapid variations of electric current could be projected into space as radio waves similar to those of light and heat.

In 1866, Mahlon Loomis, an American dentist, successfully demonstrated *wireless telegraphy*. Loomis was able to make a meter connected to one kite cause another one to move, marking the first known instance of wireless aerial communication.

An Italian inventor, Guglielmo Marconi, first proved the feasibility of radio communication. He sent and received his first radio signal in Italy in 1895. By 1899, he flashed the first wireless signal across the English Channel and two years later received the letter *S*, telegraphed from England to Newfoundland. This was the first successful transatlantic radiotelegraph message, in 1902. Then came the telegraph, radio transmitter, and eventually, radio as we know it today. What was once *impossible*, is now *possible*.

As humans, our brain does a great job at making *big deals* into *no big deal.* But it is a big deal that we can see a picture, movement, and sound on a television or movie screen. It is a big deal that we may own a GPS that can *talk* us from one place to another in our cars. And the radio, it is a big deal to have music or a voice coming from an invisible source!

We live in an extraordinary world of things that really do exist even though we cannot see them! Things like *radio and television waves, microwaves, infra-red, visible light* (which really isn't visible at all), *ultraviolet light, x-rays,* and *gamma rays* are real. Just as real is the love and communication that we receive from our deceased friends and family members. I believe it is now the time to trust that there really is much more to life than meets than eye.

EXTRA CREDIT ASSIGNMENT

Watch the movie *What the Bleep Do We Know* and the TV show *Hyperspace.* They will amaze you!

Chapter 7

Heaven Is Closer Than You Think

The late Mrs. Thomas A. Edison told me that when her husband was dying he whispered to his physician, "It is very beautiful over there." Edison was a scientist, with a factual cast of mind. He never reported anything as fact until he saw it work. He would never have reported, "It is very beautiful over there," unless, having seen, he knew it to be true.

~ Norman Vincent Peale, writer and clergyman, b. 1898

heav·en, *noun*

The abode of God, the angels, and the spirits of the righteous after death; the place or state of existence of the blessed after the mortal life.

Good heavens, is there a Heaven? If there is, what is Heaven, where is it, and more importantly, am I going to end up there?

I told you the story earlier about the young soul who starts in Heaven and gets the opportunity to come to Planet Earth to live, learn, and experience emotions and senses. Life is a place of education that we only visit for a short while, but Heaven is a reality and is a place of sheer joy.

We humans want desperately to believe that our life on Earth has a purpose, and when it ends there will be something magnificent waiting for us on the *other side.* When someone we love dies, we want to believe that they have gone to a place of peace and wonder. It gives us faith and allows us to live a better life if we believe that there will be a reward at the end of our lifetime.

Heaven Is for Real, Glimpses of Heaven, 90 Minutes in Heaven, Flight to Heaven, Heaven Is Here, and *The Five People You Meet in Heaven* are all best-selling books because of their subject matter. We want so much to believe in this place, if it *is* a place, and believing in its existence will undoubtedly help us calm our fears of living life.

After investigating life after death for over fifteen years, I can tell you: HEAVEN IS REAL.

I don't know if the name *Heaven* is accurate, but I do believe it exists and it is wonderful. Some call this place by other names: The Other Side, the Afterlife, the Hereafter, The Promised Land, Nirvana, Life Everlasting, Kingdom Come, Utopia, and Summerland. I will be using the word *Heaven* when speaking of this place and I encourage you to substitute the word that works best for you.

Throughout time and around the world, there have been hundreds of thousands of people speaking about Heaven. This includes various religious views and doctrines, accounts from mediums who have talked to the dead, and people that have had near-death experiences, those hypnotically regressed to times between lives, past life memories of children, and *Electronic Voice Phenomena.* Throughout my many years of investigating life after death, many common stories about Heaven have emerged. What follows is what I believe happens during the death of our bodies and what happens afterwards.

The Dying Process

The thought of dying is very scary. No matter how much faith we may have in an afterlife, the reality is that our bodies will die. It is normal for us to believe that we are our bodies and death of our bodies seems like a *permanent* end for each of us. Our survival instinct is so strong and we each have *The Voice* that fills our heads with fear, being afraid of the unknown in the moments before physical death. Certainly for those who are suffering, death may be welcomed, a means to be set free from pain.

But the evidence we have seems to show that there is nothing to fear, as death is easy and often described as enjoyable, as in passing from one room to another. What if people knew that death itself does not hurt and the moments that follow are so enjoyable and beautiful, surrounded by a place that resembles Earth, with our family and friends sharing incredible love with us?

However, as humans, we are still convinced of our mortality. In our final moments before our bodies die, we often think about our families, our loved ones and our relationships, both the good relationships and the not so good. We think of things we should have said or shouldn't have said, we think about the regrets that we have and the things we are leaving undone. Regardless of believing in God or not, we become open to believing in a higher power and think about the next level of our existence. For many of us, *The Voice* is with us to the very end and can often be a nuisance, persuading us to be afraid or trying to get us to hang on to life.

A common experience is for people to get *glimpses* of Heaven or *visions* of their deceased loved ones or angels by their bedside before dying. Often times, we get a spurt of energy, just long enough to deliver an important message before we pass.

Arriving in Heaven

The moment then comes when *The Voice* finally stops talking to us. Some of us feel like we are moving through a tunnel to a luminous light, others feel like we are being escorted by those that love us to a new and magnificent place, others of us simply *wake up* in a new and wonderful existence. Often, we hear beautiful music and see colors that we didn't know existed in our current world. We are filled with a feeling of comfort and love and feel totally cared for.

We feel like ourselves, we remember who we are and, although we don't have a physical body, we feel as if we do. We feel strong and healthy and if we were sick before our death, we now feel well. If we had aches and pains, they are gone. If our bodies were damaged in any way, we are whole again. Those who were deaf can hear, those who were blind can see. Those of us who struggled with compulsions and addictions are now free from them. We have perfect health and are any age we wish to be.

We are not alone when we pass. We have our family and friends who have passed before us by our side, making us feel comfortable, so that our transition is easier. The place we are in seems so real and makes us feel like our life on Earth was *just a dream*.

Children who pass from this life to the next grow up in Heaven. They are loved and nurtured by loving relatives and guides and your *Soul Self* will be reunited with them when it is your turn to go. Because there is no such thing as time, you do not feel like you missed any time away from them.

For some, our journey takes us over a bridge to Heaven. There is a beautiful poem called "The Rainbow Bridge" that is shared with many of us who lose our beloved pets. Often, losing a pet that we love can be as painful as losing a person that we love. Fear not, you will be rejoined with your pets in Heaven.

THE RAINBOW BRIDGE

Just this side of heaven is a place called Rainbow Bridge.

When an animal dies that has been especially close to someone here, that pet goes to Rainbow Bridge. There are meadows and hills for all of our special friends so they can run and play together. There is plenty of food, water and sunshine, and our friends are warm and comfortable.

All the animals who had been ill and old are restored to health and vigor. Those who were hurt or maimed are made whole and strong again, just as we remember them in our dreams of days and times gone by. The animals are happy and content, except for one small thing; they each miss someone very special to them, who had to be left behind.

They all run and play together, but the day comes when one suddenly stops and looks into the distance. His bright eyes are intent. His eager body quivers. Suddenly he begins to run from the group, flying over the green grass, his legs carrying him faster and faster.

You have been spotted, and when you and your special friend finally meet, you cling together in joyous reunion, never to be parted again. The happy kisses rain upon your face; your hands again caress the beloved head, and you look once more into the trusting eyes of your pet, so long gone from your life but never absent from your heart.

Then you cross Rainbow Bridge together . . .

~ Author Unknown

Heaven feels very much like Earth to us and we are at ease there. In her book *The Fun of Dying*, author Roberta Grimes describes it as, *"This Heaven is more like Earth than you imagined, but still it is so very different—it is at once both familiar and fabulous. Everything is made of loving energy, most things seem to be somewhat conscious, and because nothing ever decays and night never falls, there is a permanent, timeless beauty to it all."* It seems there is lush green grass, beautiful oceans, lakes and waterfalls, incredible mountains, and the most brilliant array of flowers. Animals lovingly share our existence there, music and all of our favorite things we had on Earth are enjoyed in Heaven.

We will experience a *life review* at some point. The life review is not to be feared. We will be guided through the experiences we have had on Earth and determine what our *Soul Self* has learned. We will experience ourselves through the eyes of others. When we were generous, kind, and loving on Earth to another, we get to feel how we affected the other person through their feelings. If we hurt another person, we will feel the pain and sorrow that the other person felt.

Although we experience a full range of emotions during this review, we are not being judged as *good* or *bad*. It is for us to see and feel the results of our actions, realize where we have grown and where we still have room for improvement. Then it is time for us to forgive ourselves, (no one else judges us) for each mistake, and to celebrate every victory. It seems that it is difficult for us to forgive ourselves in Heaven, because we have not had much practice of that while living on Earth.

We are never alone in our Heavenly journey since we have loved ones around us, angels and guides, who help us through our life review. People whom we did not get along with in life are also nearby, but there is only unconditional love for them, realizing that you all had *roles* to play while you were on Earth, essential for your *Soul Self* to grow and learn.

After our physical deaths, there will be time to rest, explore, and get comfortable with our new surroundings. Most stories of Heaven explain that it is *better than could even be imagined,* and we can have all of our favorite things and people around us. There are colors and sights and sounds that we cannot experience with the senses we have on Earth.

Speaking of our senses, we leave them behind when we leave Earth. Our human body allows us to see, feel, hear, smell and taste. I do believe Heaven will be grand, but it will be different and our experiences of things will be different. You may be able to experience a wonderful amount of love, but you won't be able to experience the feeling of being wrapped in someone's loving arms as you are being hugged.

I had two experiences that assure me that this is correct. After my father died, I had some uncontrollable, painful bouts of grief. Those of you who have lost someone know the pain I am talking about. One evening, just before going to bed, I was in the shower and suddenly the pain of missing my dad flooded through my system. I burst into tears and buckled over, almost falling to the ground because the pain hurt so much. In that moment, I saw my dad standing before me, tall, healthy and strong. The last time I saw Dad he was in a hospital with a broken spine, his body swollen from the drugs he was given and tubes going inside him. However, here in the shower he had a good tan, wore a pale yellow polo shirt and a pair of blue jeans. I was clear that this image was in my mind but it was not a memory, I could see Dad and even see what shoes he had on and his pair of gold wire framed glasses. He reached out to hug me and even though I was soaking wet, standing in the shower, I reached out to hug him. The following message came to me: "Sweetie Pie, where you are is temporary, where I am is forever. You cannot feel a hug in Heaven, so get all the hugs you can on Earth."

A friend of mine died in a car crash on Christmas Eve a few years ago. I dreamt of him not long ago. He, too, was strong and healthy and looking good, much younger than the last time I had seen him. Standing by his side was a little girl, dressed in white. He introduced her as an angel. She had a small silver tray and on it was a cookie, shortbread dipped in milk chocolate, with a single hazelnut on top. It looked like the most delicious thing I have ever seen! I took the cookie, placed it in my mouth and began to chew. There was one problem. I couldn't taste the chocolate. I only experienced a memory of chocolate. When I told my friend of this, he simply said, "There is no chocolate in heaven, just the memory of it. Earth is the only place that you can smell and taste."

Remember my story the next time you have the opportunity to receive a hug, smell a rose, hear a beautiful song, taste a piece of chocolate, or see a sunset. Although Heaven will provide incredible new experiences for us and will be wonderful, it is only here on Earth that we have the five senses. Savor them, will you? I will try to remember to do the same.

Our *Soul Self* must continue the education process in Heaven, too. There is learning to be done and more growth occurs there as well.

We communicate with others, both in Heaven and on Earth, telepathically. We can put words and images in people's minds on Earth, however, *The Voice* speaks to humans much too loudly for them to pick up our messages. Only those that have learned to quiet *The Voice* and let their mind be still, with no distractions, have the opportunity to hear us.

The Illusion of Time

Heaven is exciting and there is much to do and learn, so visiting the Earth plane doesn't happen all that regularly. Certainly, we are only a thought away from those we love on Earth and will be there for them whenever they need us. However, because there is no such thing as time in Heaven, it will seem like only moments have passed, before we are reconnected with those we love.

You may have heard before that *time is an illusion*. It took me years to understand how that could be. I often wondered how psychics could see into the future or into our past. I could sort of understand seeing the past, because it had already happened. The future hadn't happened yet, so how could anyone know the future?

This is the best explanation I have heard. Imagine you are out for a walk and you come across a big boulder. You decide to sit on it and take a break from the walk. Beneath you is just a big rock, a motionless piece of the Earth. From your *perspective*, it is just an object to sit on while you rest before you continue your journey.

Now, remember what I said earlier? The boulder is made up of molecules. Inside the molecules are atoms. Inside the atoms are protons, neutrons and electrons. Inside those subatomic particles you find quarks containing vibrating strings of light energy.

Imagine for a moment that you can see those vibrating strings of energy moving around inside the rock. You watch one start at the top and move deep inside it. Another one starts at the bottom and moves its way up. Then another moves from the left and the right. From outside of the boulder you witness everything that is going on inside it. You can clearly see where something begins and where it ends.

What if you were one of those strings of energy? You might remember that you came from the left and have no idea you are heading to the right. Living on Earth is much like living in the boulder. While we are busy living our lives, we cannot see outside our own perspective.

Heaven is somewhere outside of our current perspective. Our family and friends in Heaven don't experience time because they are not bouncing around in the rock called Planet Earth with us. Psychics and mediums use a specific method that allows them to connect with this other plane, outside of our perspective, allowing them to see the past, present and future and connect with the deceased. I am going to teach you that method in the next chapter.

The Illusion of Space

Where in the world is Heaven? The answer to the question is in the question itself. Heaven exists within this world, within you, within your home, within the trees and the skies and the oceans. Heaven is on

Earth. Like invisible radio and television waves and wireless Internet signals, Heaven is made up of invisible waves of energy.

Remember those quarks we just spoke of that contain the strings of vibrating energy? Two or more strings of vibrating energy can occupy the same exact space. Where you are sitting right now is probably occupying the same space as some radio, television and wireless Internet waves. Where you are sitting right now is also occupying the same space as Heaven.

The Illusion of Distance

In Heaven we communicate telepathically and can literally communicate with anyone at anytime, no matter how far the distance might seem to you and me on Planet Earth. An example of this would be when I first started doing my *Electronic Voice Phenomena* recordings. I have a friend in Australia named Duncan and I had the courage to tell him what I was doing. He asked if I could do a recording to try to connect with his first wife, who died during their marriage. My first reaction was to say, "No," because he was in Australia and I was in Massachusetts, a short 10,000 miles away! However, I was up for the challenge, because my instinct was that if there truly was no time or space, she could leave his side in Sydney and join me in my living room in Massachusetts.

With 10,000 miles and a 14-hour time difference, Duncan and I had a phone conversation, and I held my digital recorder in my hand. I turned on the shower for *white noise* in the background. Duncan lovingly asked his wife to visit me in Massachusetts and try to put a message on my tape recorder. I pressed the *record* button and we did not speak to each other for one minute. I pressed the *stop* button, and told Duncan I would call him back in an hour. Listening to EVPs takes a lot of time. Very rarely does a loud voice appear and most often I have to replay some whispers over and over to see if I can understand the words.

I was nervous when I called Duncan. He is a very professional man and I was calling him to explain what I thought his deceased spouse was trying to tell him. I felt crazy. I told him that I heard a loud, clear, "I love you, Duncan," at the beginning, followed by, "She is a better housekeeper than me." Duncan confirmed that his second wife was a much better housekeeper, that the first wife was a little messy! I told him I heard singing, but it sounded like a woman was singing in French. Duncan responded, "That would be my Mum. She used to sing me lullabyes in French before I went to bed as a child." The last message was something I felt silly sharing with Duncan. Remember the skunk cartoon character named *Pepe Le Pew?* Well, several times on the recorder I kept hearing, "Pepe Le Pew, Pepe Le Pew, Pepe Le Pew." When I told Duncan about that strange message, he was thrilled. He simply said, "Sandra, Pepe Le Pew is what I called my grandfather."

Look up from where you are seated right now. Can you imagine a person that you loved and lost sitting or standing next to you? I will give you some tools to communicate with them soon, but for right now, trust me, *they are there.*

Reincarnation

I am a little ashamed to tell you that I don't always recycle my cans, bottles, and newspapers. Thankfully, I am not in control of the Universe. The Universe, I believe, does *recycle souls,* giving each of us many opportunities to continue our growth.

There is plenty of proof that reincarnation is real. After reading Sogyal Rinpoche's book, *The Tibetan Book of Living and Dying,* I could understand the idea of *soul growth* through reincarnation. The belief in reincarnation also helps us to get through times when a person's life is cut short, for instance when a child dies.

I also believe that we belong to *soul groups,* meaning a group of family and friends that reincarnate together lifetime after lifetime, to give our souls the most effective advancement. Before our lives on Earth, we discuss who will play what role and why. Sometimes we can choose to come back on our own, without the group, as there may be *unfinished business* with a group of souls that still requires our assistance on Earth.

Are there people in your life that you feel so comfortable with, perhaps whom you've known for a long, long time? Just over six months ago I met a man for the first time, or so I think. In the first few days of knowing him we were both clear that this is an extraordinary friendship, that neither of us have ever had a connection to anyone like this. The deep level of love, compassion, and vulnerability was there from the start. It is a pure, unconditional love too, not connected by the typical male-female attraction (although he is quite handsome), but rather what seems like an intense, soul-to-soul bond. I have no doubt I have known him before and there is a purpose to our relationship.

Have you ever wondered about the people in your life? Some of them you would love to reincarnate with over and over again, wouldn't you? Others, you hope you don't have to spend too much time with them here on Earth, and there's no way you'd want to reincarnate with them. However, our relationships (good and bad) give us our souls' optimum growth. Our relationships can serve as mirrors so we can fully see ourselves.

For instance, what are some qualities that you love in a person that you know? You may think someone is smart, loving and downright fun to be with! You know how you can recognize those qualities in that person? Because *you have the same qualities within you.* Now think of someone you don't like and what you don't like about him. Perhaps you feel he is self-centered, mean and cannot be trusted. Remember, people act as mirrors for your *Soul Self* to grow. Somewhere, lurking inside yourself or in your past, you have been self-centered, a bit mean and not trustworthy. It is hard to look at that part of ourselves, but trust me, it's in there. Even if you have always been nice to another person and can be trusted, are there times that you have been mean to yourself and let yourself down, not following through on a promise or something you told yourself to do. We typically treat others much better than we treat ourselves.

After my dad's death, I had some very difficult days dealing with family members. My grief was almost unbearable and the arguments were extremely bad. I hate to argue and could not imagine why a previously loving group of people could now be acting so irrationally (myself included). I have this vision, whether accurate or not, that long before we came into this lifetime, we all agreed who would play each role. Perhaps even my poor dad chose to live his last days in suffering to fulfill his role. You see, it empowers me to believe that we had this agreement for this lifetime. Without the things happening exactly as they did in my life, I would have never learned about grief and would have never written this book.

Evidence that Supports the Theory of Reincarnation

Probably the best-known, if not most respected, collection of scientific data that appears to provide scientific proof of reincarnation, is the life's work of Dr. Ian Stevenson. Instead of relying on hypnosis to verify that an individual has had a previous life, he instead chose to collect thousands of cases of children who spontaneously, without hypnosis, remembered past lives.

To collect his data, Dr. Stevenson documented each child's statements of a previous life. Then he identified the deceased person the child remembered being and verified the facts of the deceased person's life that match the child's memory. He even matched birthmarks and birth defects to wounds and scars on the deceased, verified by medical records. His strict methods systematically ruled out all possible normal explanations for the child's memories. Dr. Stevenson devoted forty years to the scientific documentation of past life memories of children from all over the world. He had over 3000 cases in his files before his death in 2005. Many people, including skeptics and scholars, agree that these cases offer the best evidence yet that substantiates reincarnation. There are many great books on the subject of reincarnation, if you are interested in learning more. A few that I recommend are: *Children's Past Lives: How Past Life Memories Affect Your Child*, by Carol Bowman; *Many Lives Many Masters*, by Brian Weiss; *You Have Been Here Before: A Psychologist Looks at Past Lives*, by Dr. Edith Fiore; and *Children Who Remember*, by Dr. Ian Stevenson. For more information go to WeDontDie.com/reincarnation.html.

Suicide

Suicide is a very tender subject to approach. Unfortunately, in our society, I think it is widely believed that suicide is wrong and therefore anyone who commits or attempts suicide is bad. I personally feel very strongly that, unless I am in another person's shoes and can see life through their eyes, then I am not in a position to judge someone for their actions. I ask the same of you.

I believe that there must be a tremendous amount of pain, depression, or sadness for a person to try to end his or her own life. I cannot imagine the negative words that *The Voice* in their head must be telling them, for life to be so bad that their only option is to commit suicide.

I once heard someone say, "The mind is a very scary place, don't go in it alone." One of the problems that we face, especially in times of grief or depression, is that we are all alone with our thoughts. I am normally a very upbeat, positive person and I can only remember a few times in my life that I ever got really angry or mad, until just before and after my father's death. I will discuss anger as a part of the grieving process a little later on, but I want you to know something: I was terribly depressed and angry and felt that there was something seriously wrong with me. I didn't know anything about grief, so I didn't know that what I was feeling was normal. Have you had that experience, caused by some terrible loss in your life? You may be able to understand what a terrible, dark place it is and how contemplating suicide may happen.

When I was providing meals for race car teams, I once had a man visit me in the kitchen as I was cooking dinner. He told me that he was incredibly sad and in a dark place because his wife had left him for another man. He told me the pain was almost unbearable. I had just finished recording my *How to Survive Grief* CD and had a copy of it in my bag that I had just created on my laptop. I gave it to him and explained that, "Grief is grief, it doesn't matter if it is caused by a death, a loss of a job or your wife leaving you for another man." I told him he may find comfort in the CD and better understand what happens in the brain when grieving.

About six months later, the man walked back into my kitchen, gave me a big hug and said, "Sandra, you saved my life with that CD." I simply said, "Thank you," as *you saved my life* is a common expression I hear when someone is thanking me for something. He stopped me from what I was doing, looked me straight in the eyes and said, "You don't understand. Sandra, you literally saved my life. I was going to commit suicide because I couldn't handle the pain. When I heard you speak on that CD, it was like you were talking just to me. I realized that as awful as it felt, what I was experiencing was *grief*. I took your suggestions of what to do and my life changed. During that time I met a beautiful woman and we are now engaged! I wouldn't be alive if it wasn't for that CD."

Wow. I never knew the impact I could have on one life until that moment. You probably don't know what a positive impact you have on others, do you? Well, I did a little homework and found that one million people worldwide commit suicide yearly due to feelings of grief and depression. I am thankful that I posted *How to Survive Grief* as a free download at SurviveGrief.com. In the first year, several thousand people in 15 countries have heard it.

From the research I have done about people who attempt suicide and have near-death experiences, they are not pleasant. They are painful and scary. One man I spoke with told me that he could not even explain how "dark and unimaginable it was."

Remember, I said that when we die, we have a *life review?* When someone commits suicide, his or her mind still remains after death. They are often very, very hard on themselves, create their own punishment, and their mind can give them terrible images. They can feel the pain and suffering of the people they left behind. They have to work to forgive themselves and it is often very difficult for them to do this, knowing the pain they caused others.

If you are reading this now and contemplating suicide, remember, you cannot escape your own mind, and death is not the answer. Our brains are very fragile, and what you may be experiencing may not be your fault, it could be associated with grief or loss. Please know that most difficulties pass with time and it is possible to live a rewarding life in the future. Your problems still must be faced in the afterlife, with the added burden of knowing that your loved ones are suffering. You are an *Eternal Soul* having a human experience. You are not *The Voice* in your head. Feel free to turn to chapter 10 where I address grief, and know you are not alone and there is help available to you.

The good news is that people who commit suicide do not suffer eternally. They are surrounded by loving souls that work with them to understand their pain and help the *Soul Self* to be healthy again. I witnessed medium Maureen Hancock give a mother a message from her son who had committed suicide. Maureen described the son, telling her that he had a tattoo of a skull and crossbones on his right upper arm and wore a silver cross on a necklace. She told the woman that the son apologized for hurting her, by hanging himself. He wanted the mother to know that he had been taking drugs that had led him to kill himself. He was sorry, but wanted her to know that he was in a great place now, with his favorite uncle and aunt.

Remember the little soul that was waiting in line to come to Planet Earth to learn, love and experience emotions? Well, we were all warned that we would be given *The Voice*, that would make us forget who we really are. The mix of grief, depression, drugs, brain chemistry and *The Voice* telling us negative things about ourselves, may make it virtually impossible for our *Soul Self* to remember who we really are. Again, have compassion for others, as we are not in their minds to know the pain they may be suffering.

I am often asked if I believe in *Hell*. The answer is *no*, I do not believe that after death there is a place we go to suffer for eternity. I believe that Hell exists right here while we are on Earth. Hell is created within our own minds and experienced as suffering. Suffering is when *The Voice* in our head disagrees with the way it thinks things should be. Life can be very, very painful; that is why I feel it is so necessary for you to remember who you really are. The people in your life deserve to know who they really are too.

HOMEWORK ASSIGNMENT

Where in your life are you suffering? Is there a relationship or illness causing you pain? Do you have problems or struggles in your life right now? Do you think something is wrong with your life? Do you compare your life to others and think that your life should in some way be different?

Start to speculate and look to see why your *Soul Self* may have picked that problem to experience in this lifetime. As far as relationships go, why would you have made an agreement with certain other souls to come to Earth and have a problem with them?

You'll have to put *The Voice* in another room while you do this exercise! That voice in your head would rather you become a victim and be powerless to the problems that you have in life. However, engage your *Soul Self*, even if you have to make up or invent reasons that you have certain troublesome people or problems in your life. When you can look at people, or your problems from this perspective, you will begin to have some power. Power is necessary for you to have the results and dreams you say you want, so it is critical to continue looking at your life and your growth from your *Soul Self's* perspective.

Chapter 8

Seeing with Your Eyes Shut

The day science begins to study non-physical phenomena,
it will make more progress in one decade than in all the
previous centuries of its existence.

~ Nikola Tesla, inventor and engineer, b. 1856

com·mu·ni·ca·tion, *noun*

Something imparted, interchanged, or transmitted.

An ability we have as human beings, that tends to set us apart from the animal kingdom, is our ability to communicate. From our perspective, it seems like we are the most advanced species that can communicate our thoughts through language and we speak, write, use sign language and send texts and emails to each other. We believe we also have the unique gift of logic, which can process thoughts and then communicate them effectively, unlike any other species we share our world with.

I will start this by talking about *ants*, those pesky little things that annoy the heck out of us. I know that every spring and summer, I find them traveling around my home, especially in my kitchen, no matter how clean and *crumb free* we try to keep it! As much as ants are a nuisance, you may think of them differently in a few minutes and may hesitate to squash one of them with your sneaker the next time you see one!

I first learned about the communication of ants many years ago when I learned about the bridges they build. Ants are smart; if they want to get somewhere they will. Ants create elaborate tunnel systems underground. But above ground, they build bridges. One kind of bridge they build uses bits of dirt or debris, like a leaf or a stick. If you watch the ants, you will see a group of them work together to move the debris over a hole, so they may have a bridge to cross to the other side.

The second kind of bridge is even more amazing. A group of scientists placed a shallow, round dish of water on a table. In the center of the dish was another smaller dish, whose edges were slightly taller than the original dish. In this dish was sugar, probably the most exciting food an ant could imagine. Using their ant instinct, they detected this feast of sugar. However, when they approached the bowl, they found the water and were, I'm sure frustrated as there was no way to reach it.

What happened next seems to me to be a form of logic and communication. The ants began to build a bridge, constructed of themselves! Ants grabbed the legs of other ants, side by side and constructed a massive bridge made up of their bodies. The ants were able to remain still and stay tightly connected to their fellow ants. This allowed for other ants to cross the bridge and get to the bowl of sugar. Unfortunately, the ants that were part of the bridge ended up in the water, most of them giving up their lives, so that their friends could enjoy the sugar.

I can't help but wonder, how do they communicate to create this plan? Who decides who has to be the bridge and who gets to take the sugar? Do a little research on ant bridges when you have some time. It is truly amazing to watch.

And then there is a slightly larger species, the honeybee. We often see bees in our backyards buzzing around the flowers in our gardens. The bees that we see are called worker bees. Worker bees make up 75–95% of the bee colony. They keep themselves busy by spending their time in our flowerbeds foraging for pollen and nectar to bring back to the colony. It is amazing to me that the bees remember where their hives are, as they can travel over five miles away and remember their way back home. As amazing as this is, even more interesting are the *drones*.

The drone bees are the scouts. They are the ones looking for the new sources of food. When they find an area, let's say your backyard, they return to the hive to communicate with the worker bees the exact location of your flowers. These drone bees do not leave the hive again. They do a dance that tells the worker bees the exact location of your house. The worker bees find your backyard, collect the pollen and nectar and return to the hive. Remember, the drones sometimes have to communicate a distance of five miles or more. Could they have logic, intelligence and a form of communication other than what we know? I say, "Yes."

Rent the movie *March of the Penguins* sometime. Emperor penguins travel over 60 miles (100 kilometers) and meet up with other penguins to mate each year. There are roughly 600,000 total Emperor Penguins around the coastline of Antarctica, each belonging to one of 44 colonies. These penguins travel these long distances and will arrive in their own particular colony within a day or two of each other!

Have you ever been snorkeling and seen the behavior of a school of fish? Maybe you've seen it on TV or in an aquarium. In a split second, the entire school of fish can change direction and swim to another location. Birds do it too, as I have often been amazed at an entire flock of hundreds of birds quickly changing direction and traveling somewhere else. You've got to wonder which fish or bird makes the decision to change direction? Maybe the whole group decides, but how do they communicate this to each other? Clearly they communicate, somehow. I have an excellent video called *Amazing Starlings Murmuration* at WeDontDie.com/AmazingAnimals.html.

We can all agree on the existence of instinct in animals, right? But can we agree on the possibility that logic exists? Here are some examples.

Monkeys can spot a colony of ants or a beehive and realize there is something good inside to eat. Using logic, a monkey can find a branch, remove the leaves and use this tool to stick in the nest to remove the honey or the delicious ants to eat.

Gorillas have been observed using sticks to measure the depth of water and use them as walking sticks to support their posture when crossing deeper water. Orangutans have also been observed using sticks to measure the depth of water. On the island of Kaja, a male orangutan was observed using a pole to acquire fish from a net after observing local humans doing the same while spear fishing.

Have you heard about the octopus that was given an empty peanut butter jar? Well, empty of peanut butter but instead contained water and the octopus' favorite kind of fish. The octopus opened the peanut butter jar and got the fish out. How did he know to do that? Another great story involves another octopus, this time in a large fish tank. On the other side of the room was another tank with a few yummy fish in it. All caught on camera, the octopus left his tank, moved across the room, entered the other tank and ate the fish. Then he returned to his original tank!

Crows are another intelligent species. They have been known to put a nut or a seed, too tough for them to crack, under the tire of a car and wait for the car to break it open. They have been seen bending wires to use as hooks or tools to get something they cannot reach. They have been caught pulling up fishing lines from ice fisherman's holes, eating the bait fish on the end of the hook and gently lowering the hook back down into the hole.

The Elephant Whisperer

South African conservationist Lawrence Anthony was asked to accept a herd of *rogue* elephants on his Thula Thula game reserve in South Africa, but his common sense told him to refuse. However, he was this herd's last chance of survival—notorious escape artists, they would all be killed if Lawrence wouldn't take them. He agreed but, before arrangements for the move could be completed, the animals broke out again and the matriarch and her baby were shot. The remaining elephants were traumatized, dangerous, and very angry. When they arrived at Thula Thula, they started planning their escape. As Lawrence battled to create a bond with the elephants and save them from execution, he came to realize that they had a lot to teach him about life, loyalty, and freedom. He was nicknamed *The Elephant Whisperer* and effectively rehabilitated these mighty animals.

Lawrence Anthony died March 7, 2012. Within two days, after walking 12 hours, the two herds arrived at his home, appeared to be grieving and paid their final respects to the man who saved their lives. They stayed for two days and then began their journey back to the bush.

There are two elephant herds at Thula Thula. According to Anthony's son Dylan, both herds arrived at the Anthony family compound shortly after Anthony's death. "They had not visited the house for a year and a half and it must have taken them about 12 hours to make the journey," Dylan is quoted in various local news accounts. "The first herd arrived on Sunday and the second herd, a day later. They all hung around for about two days before making their way back into the bush." Elephants have long been known to mourn their dead. In India, baby elephants often are raised with a boy who will be their lifelong rider, known as their *mahout*. The pair develops legendary bonds—and it is not uncommon for one to waste away without a will to live after the death of the other.

> *I shall not commit the fashionable stupidity of regarding*
> *everything I cannot explain as a fraud.*
>
> ~ Carl Jung

Just because we cannot explain something does not mean it is not real. We are familiar with *local communication*; we can talk to a friend with our words, create words with our mouths, use sign language, or write a letter and drop it in a mailbox, or email it. *Non-local communication* is something very different. It is a form of communication that does not use any of the things I just mentioned. Let me give you a couple of examples.

Have you had the experience of thinking about a person and just moments later, the phone rings and they are on the line? Or, have you had a dream and then some part of it came true? Have you spoken some words to a friend and they responded, "I was just about to say that very same thing," or, "I was thinking that exact same thought!" Those are *non-local* experiences and I intend for you to have a lot more of them. Why? Because it is in those moments when you have a weird experience like that when you can contemplate the fact that you may not be just your body and start realizing who you really are: *a soul having a human experience.* It is amazing how much *The Voice* wants us to believe that what we have experienced in the past is the absolute truth. The truth, I believe, cannot be found inside us. Do you remember my example of the boulder? From being inside the boulder, we cannot see that we are inside the boulder. Could you imagine a fish trying to explain the water he lives in? To him, it is real and there is nothing else. For human beings, what boulder or fish bowl are we living in, not able to see what is outside our reality? We are moments away from stepping out of our reality into the world of *Remote Viewing*, which will allow us to perceive reality from outside of our own truths, our own limits, and our own perceptions.

Doesn't it seem like mediums and psychics are able to tap into some extraordinary power that gives them access to another realm? What is this power? What do they have that you and I don't have? The answer is, *"We all have this power."* This power is called *non-local communication*, no different than the bees or the ants or the penguins or the elephants.

I had been looking for the common denominator in people that seem to be able to access this other realm, whether they can see the past or the future, or they can connect to our deceased loved ones. There are also some brilliant minds that are able to invent new things or create brilliant pieces of art or music. What are they all doing that lets them have this incredible power?

Our little soul in Heaven was given this answer before coming to Earth. Remember what he was told? Do you remember something about a stop sign? He was told to *stop thinking* to remember who he really was.

This technique is called *being in the present moment*. We talked earlier about *The Voice*, constantly chatting at us and giving us an opinion on absolutely everything. It never shuts up, does it? Stopping this voice will provide you access to this world of non-local communication. It is a really cool world, too, not just for the famous inventors and the psychics.

Before getting on the tram to Planet Earth, each of us was given a guidebook about how to navigate through our lives. Don't feel bad that you didn't memorize yours, I didn't memorize mine either. However, I was able to download a copy off the Internet so we can both review it now. (That's a joke!)

> *On Planet Earth you will receive five senses. You will have the gift of sight, hearing, smell, taste and touch. It will be amazing to you, how delightful these experiences are. In Heaven, every experience you have is through the Divine Mind and on Earth they are much more sensational.*
>
> *You will also be given an incredible range of emotions that will give you bodily reactions through these five senses.*

You will be able to experience the pleasure of touch, you will find the touch of petting an animal delightful or experience the love when holding a newborn baby. However, you will also experience pain. Emotional pain is caused from human interactions. When someone leaves the Earth and returns to Heaven you feel a great sense of loss and the body reacts with a painful emotion called grief. When you do damage to your physical being you will also feel this pain in your body.

As a reminder, the purpose of traveling to Planet Earth is to have an opportunity for your soul to grow and to be educated. You must experience a full range of emotions and have many, many new experiences for that to happen.

To get full value from your visit to Earth, it is necessary that you forget this place and forget who you really are: A Divine, Eternal Being of Light. When you wake up on Planet Earth, you will not remember this place or who you really are. To assure this, we are giving you a voice in your head that will be a constant companion while you are on Planet Earth. It will be with you and grow with you during your entire visit. It will sound like your voice and will sound like thoughts in your head. You will believe that these are true thoughts, coming from your mind. They are not.

The Voice was designed to prevent you from remembering who you truly are, so you can experience the full range of emotions being a human. Those who wish to get extra benefit from being on Planet Earth, will learn to distinguish The Voice from your Soul Self. Through stopping The Voice, you will begin to remember who you really are, an eternal being of light. When you realize this, you will be able to fulfill your wildest dreams and your experience will be that of Heaven on Earth.

Our Addiction to Technology

I was recently at a restaurant in California and noticed 4 men sitting at a nearby booth. I remember thinking that they must be a religious group and thought it nice that these four men took the time to say a prayer together before eating, because I don't see that very much anymore.

However, when I got a closer look, these men were not praying at all, they were all looking down at their cell phones either texting, checking email, or surfing the Internet!

I am the first to admit that I am a technology addict. I hear the beep of a text message when I am driving and the urge is so strong that I often glance down while I am driving to see who is texting me. I know it is wrong and it is illegal, but I promised to share my truths with you and that is one of them. I also find that many, many, many times throughout the day I feel the strong sense to check my email, just in case something so important has happened that I must tend to right away. However, there is never anything that happens that is so critical it needs my immediate attention. Even while writing this book, I made a promise to myself that I would write for an hour at a time and only check email during my breaks. Guess what happens? I broke my promise because my addiction to technology was very strong.

I know I am not alone, am I? How many of us are in the company of other people and end up looking at our phones or other devices and not enjoying the people we are sitting with? I believe as a whole, many of us living in the modern world are losing our ability to communicate, to experience love and other emotions, due to this addiction we have to technology.

Don't get me wrong, I am not asking anyone to give up any of their toys. There is no way I am giving up my cell phone, computer, iPhone, Kindle, or GPS! It is not the time to say we are wrong or bad for being addicted to technology, it's just time to notice. It is only when we can notice *something* that we can have the power to use something as opposed to us being *used by it*.

If we want to connect with the part of ourselves that lies outside of our current truths and our current perception, we have to learn to set aside both *The Voice* and the things that distract our minds. I encourage you to spend time engaging in conversation with other people. Your fellow human beings can be an awful lot of fun, you know! Remember, try not to allow *The Voice* to persuade you to check your email or answer a text message while you are with others.

Remote Viewing

I'd like to now tell you about my miraculous journey into Remote Viewing. I will also give you the tools you need to experience that you are much more than you think you are.

I took a course in remote viewing with a physicist named Russell Targ. About 50 of us were in the course. Honestly, I was very skeptical, but Russell Targ is a man of scientific background who has spent a lifetime studying ESP, extra sensory perception. In fact, as I write this, Russell's latest book just arrived at my house. The book is titled *The Reality of ESP—A Physicist's Proof of Psychic Abilities*. The first book I read by Russell Targ was *Limitless Mind: A Guide to Remote Viewing*, after attending his workshop.

Russell Targ was born in Chicago in 1934. He received a BS in physics from Queens College in 1954 and did graduate work in physics at Columbia University. He is one of the founding fathers of the laser beam and received two National Aeronautics and Space Administration awards for inventions and contributions in lasers and laser communications.

As a boy, Russell would often meet a new person and would have images appear in his mind about that person. He saw images of the houses they lived in and the pets that they had. He would accurately tell people what he saw in his mind. The people assumed he was doing some sort of magic trick, but Russell knew there was something else happening here.

Unlike some of the psychic courses I had taken in the past, in which the instructors and participants seemed to be what I refer to as a little *woo-woo* (wearing gypsy-like clothing and speaking in metaphysical language) I felt I was in good hands for the weekend, learning remote viewing from Russell Targ, as he is a credible resource with a scientific mind. I encourage you to learn more about him at ESPresearch.com because this world is fascinating.

Friday evening was mostly lecture. I learned about Russell and his past studies. However, what I really wanted was to get busy and see if I could *remote view* myself. After a fair amount of lecture, my wish was granted.

We were each given a sketch pad of paper and instructed to close our eyes, clear our minds and *see, using only our minds*, what was in the bag Russell was holding. We were to draw images on the paper and not use our conscious mind to try to figure it out. Believe me, *The Voice* in my head was quick to point out that this was a stupid, waste of time, I shouldn't have spent my money on this and if it was to be real, it would work for everyone else, but not for me.

Thankfully, we were told to let that voice go, not to pay any attention to it. We were to use our intention and ask ourselves what images do we see of what is in the bag. We were to pay attention to things we don't normally see in our mind. What came to my mind while focusing on the bag, were engine parts, silver engine parts. I also saw an X or a cross or a + sign. I drew them all on the paper. When Russell opened the bag he took out a small toy helicopter. Maybe the engine parts told me it was mechanical and maybe the X was the propeller of the helicopter? It was cool. I wasn't convinced it was anything more than a coincidence, but I still enjoyed the evening.

That night, before we left the classroom, Russell gave each of us a brown paper lunch bag. Our homework was to find a unique object that we would put in the bag. The next morning we would choose partners and then remote view the objects in the bags. I was excited about this!

Before class, I found my object. In my suitcase, I had a large, plastic serrated knife. It was about 8 inches long and 1½ inches wide, bright green. I had to buy it just before one of my race weeks, when I had to prepare some sandwiches for the team members and I hadn't yet unpacked my normal set of knives from our equipment truck. This plastic knife was definitely unique!

I went to class that morning, nervous because *The Voice* started telling me that remote viewing would work for everyone but not for me, that I would get a partner that was much smarter than I was and it wouldn't work. However, Russell reminded us that this voice is normal and I was just supposed to let my mind become still, concentrate on any new images that came to it and to avoid judging what I saw.

My partner was named John and I coaxed him into going first. He was just as nervous as I was. I pulled out my bag and set it in front of John to remote view. I purposely fluffed up the bag so it looked like it was full, not flat. I didn't want to give John any clues!

John closed his eyes and began to relax. Then, he told me that it seemed like my object was *flat*. He took his hands and stretched them about 8 inches wide. "It is about this big," he said. I tried to keep a poker face, not giving him any reaction that his images were right. I asked him to draw what he saw. It looked like a ruler in his drawing. He then drew what looked to be the serrated, blade part of the knife. He kept saying, "King's crown, I see something that looks like a King's crown." Of course I knew that the serrated blade looked like a crown but did not agree or disagree. Then he said, "Sandra, you use this in your right hand and it's very, very light." I am right handed and this knife was extremely lightweight, being cheap plastic. Lastly he said, "It is green and there is a cloud shape on it, I see a cloud, maybe on a handle?" I had no idea what this meant, as far I knew there was no cloud on it. Russell Targ said our minds won't be 100% accurate, because our imagination gets involved while we try to remote view.

Fifteen minutes had passed and it was time to reveal the item that was hidden in my bag. John's jaw dropped when he saw the green, flat, serrated, light, 8 inch knife that he knew he had identified correctly. My jaw dropped when John said, "Oh, Sandra, here's the cloud." John pointed to the logo of the company that made the knife. It was a cloud shape with the name of the company inside of it. John and I both sat there, stunned, amazed because this sort of thing shouldn't be possible.

It was my turn to remote view. I was still scared, but if young John was courageous enough to do it, then I could too! So, I took a deep breath, looked at the outside of his bag and closed my eyes. The first thing I saw was silver, so I wrote that down. The next image was of a silver ring, with three gemstones on it, one blue, one red and one green. The next image was of a clothespin, used for hanging up clothes to dry. John asked me what it was about the clothespin that was significant. "Open, close," I told him. Something clearly opened and closed with this object. The next thing I saw was a strawberry. He asked what was significant about the strawberry. I said, "Something about the texture, I am feeling the bumps on a strawberry as my fingers brush up against it, I think this object has bumps." He finally asked me what size it was. I drew on the paper a rectangle, about three inches wide and four inches long.

The bell rang and my 15 minutes of remote viewing were over. John opened his bag and pulled out his cell phone. It was silver and almost exactly the same size as the rectangle I drew! It was a *flip phone* and did indeed *open and close* like the clothespin I saw in my mind. The phone had bumps on the number keys and running my fingers over it was the same feeling as touching the strawberry I felt with my eyes closed. The coolest part for me is that the controls on the phone were gem colored squares on a silver ring! There was a green button for talk, a red button for end and a blue button for menu . . . all the images I saw in my mind. I was thrilled, I was a remote viewer and all I could say was, "Wow!"

This was the first time I experienced anything like that. Me, Sandra Champlain, having an experience of ESP! But you have to know this, *everyone* in the entire class was able to correctly remote view. John and I were not the special ones. Everybody could do it. Some people got more details correct but there was not a single person who could not see some detail of what was in the bags. You know what that means? You will be a remote viewer very soon.

From this experiment there were more lectures and more experiments, each one equally as fascinating. We were given envelopes and had to remote view the pictures that were hidden inside of them. For me, the envelope I had to remote view contained images from the past. In my mind, I saw a round well and a fountain. I saw an old building in a town square and the shape of the windows reminded me of combs. There was a lot of activity, as children seemed to be running around and vendors were selling their wares in a marketplace. To me, it seemed like an old European town.

When the picture was revealed, it was a picture of a courtyard in some old European town. The round well was there but there was no fountain. The building looked similar. The bricks were also the same shape as I saw and the windows did look like combs. But where were all the people and the activity? I asked Russell this question and his answer gave me goosebumps. "Sandra, you remote viewed this place as it was in the past. This is a European town square and there used to be a fountain in the center of the well. The activity you saw would have been going on over 100 years ago."

Russell explained that we could remote view the past, present and future. This was the first time that I learned that we are in *the boulder* and we can use remote viewing to see outside of our current perspective and connect to the past, present and future.

He told of some great stories of people who can see the past and the future. Remote viewing is not new and some people are not even aware that they are doing it.

In 1898, fourteen years before the RMS Titanic ship was built, a man named Morgan Robertson wrote a book called *Futility, or the*

Wreck of the Titan. The similarities between Robertson's work and the *Titanic* disaster are astonishing. Robertson described his fictional ship, the *Titan* as "the largest craft afloat and the greatest of the works of men," "equal to that of a first class hotel," and, of course, "unsinkable."

Both the ship he *created* and the real ocean liner, were British-owned steel vessels, both around 800 feet long and sank after hitting an iceberg in the North Atlantic, in April, "around midnight."

While the novel does bear some curious coincidences with the *Titanic* disaster, there are quite a few things that Robertson got wrong. For one, the *Titanic* did not crash into an iceberg "400 miles from Newfoundland" at 25 knots. It crashed into an iceberg 400 miles from Newfoundland at 22.5 knots! I am teasing because he is very accurate. Also, both the *Titan* and the *Titanic* had too few lifeboats to accommodate every passenger on board. Fascinating, isn't it?

We did many different types of experiments in Russell Targ's weekend course, including remote viewing of people's health conditions. I've heard of psychics that could tell what was wrong with a person but had no idea I would be able to do this. "The problem," Russell said, "is that most of us have never been to medical school to be able to properly identify the inner parts of our bodies."

We got right into the exercise and each participant took a partner and was given a blue index card. We wrote down a name of a person close to us on the card and, without showing our partner, had to remote view that person's health condition. I wrote down my uncle's name and *The Voice* in my head kept insisting that I wouldn't be able to do this, so naturally I let my partner to go first.

My partner was quiet for a moment to clear her mind and said, "It is a man, a relative, he has dark hair. He's a big man. He's got problems with his sinuses, I am guessing because he's crying a lot. She was pointing to her back, just under her ribs and said, "He is having problems with an organ." She also saw that he had hip problems and felt like he had an operation. I believe my partner clearly described my uncle. He fit the description, had to have a kidney replaced and had a hip operation in the past. I didn't know about any sinus problems, however, my grandmother (his mom) had just died weeks before. I now believe the crying was from grief.

When it was my turn I got an image of a woman with long blond hair with bangs and blue eyes. I somehow knew that she was a mother of four children. I kept feeling like she was unhappy, felt like she couldn't tell the people closest to her about her feelings and that she had throat problems. These images and feelings seemed very much like my imagination, but I didn't know this woman so I told my partner everything I felt and saw. Guess what? I was right. Her friend fit the description, had four kids, was unhappy because she always tried to be nice and not tell people how she really felt and suffered from acid reflux.

That night I had gone to bed and decided to try my own kind of experiment. It seemed to me that the only way to conduct a remote viewing experiment was to have a partner. I knew there had to be a way to do this solo, without a partner.

While in my room I noticed a *Woman's World* magazine. Women's World was my grandmother's favorite magazine and I bought it for her every week. After Grammy died, I still continued to buy them, just to stay close to her memory. I decided to see if I could remote view the pictures that were in the magazine. I hadn't opened it before, so I didn't know what pictures were inside.

I thought to myself, "Show me the images from page 27." My mind was flooded with all kinds of new images. I saw grapes, a wine glass, the statue of Liberty, a beach ball, a little bird, some ice cubes, red lipstick, a lollipop. I listed about 20 different things in total.

I was so excited when I turned to page 27 and guess what happened? *Nothing.* Not a single image of what I just saw was correct. "What in the world did I see?" I said to myself. "Must be my imagination that created them." To be honest with you, I was disappointed. *The Voice* was quick to tell me what a lunatic I was and told me everything

I had experienced that weekend was just coincidence. Is *The Voice* in your head as negative as mine? Oh, it's horrible sometimes!

Before turning out the light and going to bed, I decided to thumb through the pages of the magazine. That's when I noticed the Statue of Liberty on page 7, a little bird on 14, the glass of wine on page 8, a beach ball on page 38, the ice cubes in a drink on page 29, the lollipop on page 34 and the lipstick on page 17. Almost all of those images that I saw in my mind were somewhere in that magazine! I can still feel that excitement as I am talking to you now. I went to bed that night with an indescribable feeling that there really is so much more to me than I had realized. There is also so much more to *you*. By the way, I did that experiment again 2 days ago. As always, *The Voice* told me that I couldn't do it and it wouldn't work. To my surprise, twenty-nine out of thirty-seven images were in that magazine!

There's more to life than meets the eye.
There is more to you than you know.

The next day in class I was so excited to share my magazine experiment with the group. They all seemed interested and so did our leader, Russell Targ. Since taking that class, I occasionally pick up a magazine and hold the intention of seeing what is on the page before I open to a random page. Yes, I do see images in my mind's eye that are on the pages. This exercise never fails to give me goosebumps.

We moved on to learning about remote viewing the past, present and future. We had already viewed the past and present, but how can we view the future? Russell explained some of the experiments he used with trading on the silver market and remote viewing what the price of silver would do from day to day and how to invest in the market. Eight out of eight times his team made correct predictions on the price of silver. Eight out of eight times they made money on their investments.

One important thing to mention here: remote viewing can be used to predict the future, when you do it from a place of inquiry and scientific experimentation. However, when greed comes in to the experiment and you wish to use this ability to know how to correctly win a bet in Las Vegas, remote viewing will not work. Russell Targ proved this to himself and so did I, when I tried to remote view which slot machine I should play at a casino to win big bucks (only to leave with empty pockets).

Russell told us that time and space are just illusions. There is nothing real about it. There are only moments of *now*, which are made up of all the experiences that have ever happened to everyone, everywhere. It was very hard for me to understand this at the time, so if you aren't getting it, it's okay. I get it now, because I can imagine the atoms bouncing around in the boulder, like I spoke of in chapter 6. You will understand it more fully in time.

The final exercise we did in class was to remote view the future. Russell had two bags, each containing some kind of unique object. He told us that in 15 minutes he would flip a coin that would determine which bag was to be opened. However, we were to remote view the contents of the correct bag before the coin was tossed! I remember *The Voice* telling me this was impossible, but I continued to pay attention to the instructions.

Out came my notebook and I closed my eyes, holding the intention of seeing the object that would come out of the bag in 15 minutes time. The first thing I saw was a round ball, about the size of a tennis ball. It was dark brown, like a belt made of leather. "No, not a ball, more like a hockey puck," I thought. A couple of random images came to mind . . . teeth, a lemon, then a woman's stretchy bracelet. Thinking back to my friend John, I wondered what it was about the bracelet that was a clue. "Something you hold with two hands and pull or stretch," I told myself. A teacup then came to mind, silver. Then I saw a hook. My mind was trying to figure this out, but then I remembered Russell telling us that our minds can only see images of parts of the object and not to try to figure it out.

Soon, the time was up. It was now time to open the bag. Before the flip of the coin, many of us raised our hands and shared what we saw. There were many similar characteristics that we saw: silver, small, brown round leather item, a hook and a cup.

The coined was flipped. It landed on *heads*. The first of the two bags was opened. Russell reached into his bag and pulled out a small object, brown, round, leather-like about the size of a tennis ball but shaped like a hockey puck. He lifted the cover and a hook was exposed. Pulling on the hook (which became the handle), the shape of a silver teacup started to arise. Russell pulled the cup with both hands and twisted it into place. It was the same stretch as I felt of the woman's stretchy bracelet. The hidden object was a one-of-a-kind, antique, portable, collapsible, silver tea cup! Wait until you try this! You will have a, "Wow!" experience yourself. There is nothing like that feeling.

I left the weekend really wanting to know more about remote viewing and how to best practice it. I went to a bookstore and found a deck of flash cards with pictures on them to see if I could remote view the pictures on the cards before turning them over. The deck that I bought is used to teach people Spanish words. Each card had an image along with the word for that image in Spanish. I recommend buying such a deck to practice on your own. My favorite experience was seeing an image of a *rubber ducky* in my mind before I shuffled the cards. I was disappointed to pull the card out of the deck and see that it was a colorful drawing of a ladies' hat filled with flowers on the brim. However, when I looked closely at the drawing, one yellow object was not a flower, but a rubber duck!

I have taught remote viewing to men, women, and children. I have done it on the telephone when the other person was 2,000 miles away from me and she and I would remote view what was on each other's coffee tables. I taught my 13-year-old niece to remote view, by hiding items in a shoe box and taking turns remote viewing the contents. I was recently traveling with my friend Travis in Vancouver. I knew that

I was going to teach him remote viewing, so I had some objects hidden in the drawers of my hotel room. Skeptical at first, he accurately described elements of the items hidden in the drawer. He got so good that during the last experiment we did, he simply said, "It is a hairbrush." I was trying to play it cool and simply told him to go open the drawer and look. Yes, it was my hairbrush in the drawer.

I remote viewed the subtitle of this book as well. For years, I knew that this book would be titled *We Don't Die*. However, I could not figure out a subtitle. I wanted something that you would be interested in reading, without sounding too metaphysical or spiritual. No matter how hard I tried, I didn't like any of the subtitles I came up with. Travis knew about my frustration and he told me he would try to think of a catchy subtitle as well.

About a week later I was traveling on a flight to California and the subtitle, *A Skeptic's Discovery of Life after Death*, came into my mind. I loved it! It said exactly who I was and what I had done. In my excitement I sent Travis an email with those seven words. Then, I got a message, "Call me right away," from Travis and it sounded important. (You must know that even though Travis and I had been great friends, I know some of the topics I spoke about probably seemed a little weird to him). I called Travis and I could tell by his voice that something had happened. He then told me, "Sandra, before I went to bed last night, I thought of those same 7 words for your subtitle. How is that possible?"

As unbelievable as it seemed, for me it was an experience of remote viewing. He and I simply both tapped into the same future reality, one where this book has already been written and we were both just remembering the subtitle. Maybe he created the subtitle and I read his mind or he tapped into my future mind. Either way it is remarkable, isn't it?

How to Remote View

I do recommend you read one of Russell Targ's many books. Both *The Reality of ESP* and *Limitless Mind* give much more information than

I tell you here about remote viewing. You can get the full story and description of remote viewing and learn from Russell's 40 years of experience, including his work with the Stanford Research Institute. Russell was the cofounder of a 23-year, twenty-million-dollar ESP program supported by the CIA, NASA, the Defense Intelligence Agency, the US Army, Air Force Intelligence, and other government agencies.

It is now your time to learn to remote view. I recommend trying it with a friend or someone else you trust. It is important for one person to act as the *interviewer* and the other as the *receiver*. Each person should have a notebook for the exercise. I find it helps when both people write down the words and images that the receiver talks about as the receiver will have his or her eyes closed throughout much of the session.

The interviewer starts by hiding an object in a bag, box or drawer. If you are doing this on the phone with a friend, put the object on a table with no other items on that table. The object you use should be at least a few inches big but smaller than a breadbox. The remote viewing mind loves unique items, so pick an item with different characteristics that your mind will find interesting.

A dimly lit room is preferred, to help relax the mind. If you are the one doing the remote viewing, write your name and the date on the top of the paper with the words, "I am a remote viewer."

The interviewer then says, "I have an object that needs a description."

The receiver should write down any initial images that come into their mind. Often, we get so excited about remote viewing and anticipate what we might see, or worry that we will get it wrong, that our mind is already full of images. Take a few minutes and write down every image that you see. Try to relax and clear your mind. Take a deep breath. Draw a line beneath all the original images and label the images you just wrote as *Initial Images*. They may or may not be related to the object that needs description, but your mind will focus on them if you don't have them written down.

If you are the receiver, you should then close your eyes and relax.

Have the intention to see elements of the hidden object. Pay attention to any shapes or forms that begin to come to your mind. Your interviewer should say, "Describe the surprising shapes and images that appear in your awareness." Feel free to draw pictures or write down images of things that come into your mind. Very often your initial images will be the most important and set the tone for the entire experiment. Remember, remote viewing will show you parts of an object, not the overall object.

Don't try to figure out what the object is. Your analytical mind will take over and your *Soul Self* that is remote viewing will be shut down, so you won't be able to continue until you relax again. When you write down all the images that have appeared in your mind, take a short break. Chat with your interviewer for a moment or two about something else and take some deep breaths. Close your eyes again and pay attention to any new images come into your mind about the hidden object.

The interviewer can help you stay focused by asking you questions like:

> What are you experiencing now?
>
> How do you feel about the target?
>
> Are there any new or surprising elements?
>
> What are you experiencing that makes you say that? (Remember how I saw the strawberry and the clothespin? What I was experiencing was the texture of the bumps on the strawberry and the opening and closing action of the clothespin.)

The interviewer can also have you imagine that you are holding the object in your hand and ask you:

> Does it have a color?
>
> Is it shiny?
>
> Does it have sharp edges?
>
> What could you do with it?
>
> Does it have moveable parts?

Does it have an odor?

Is it heavy or light?

Is it wood, plastic, metal, or glass?

If need be, you can repeat this process, until you get all the bits of information from your remote viewing mind. The process should take about 10–15 minutes, no longer. The problem I find is that *The Voice* in my head tries to control the experiment before too long. It starts to try to figure out what the object is and tells me that I will be wrong. By the way, you have to be willing to be *wrong* to effectively do remote viewing. When you can take the pressure off and decide that this process should be fun and it's okay to be wrong, you can end up being more accurate. It is also important to trust the person you are doing the remote viewing with. If one of you makes fun of the other, it will be very difficult to want to try to do this again. No one likes to be laughed at.

When you are finished making notes, take a moment and review them with your partner. After reviewing, you can reveal the object and take a few minutes to debrief what you saw and what you didn't. You will be amazed by some of the fine detail your mind can pick up from the object, things that may not be noticeable unless you hold the item close to your eyes.

Here's another rule: write down everything that you see when you remote view. Often, the interviewer will reveal an object and you might say, "Oh, I saw that in my mind, I just didn't write it down!" Here's the deal: you must write it down for it to count. While I was remote viewing with Travis, I got an image of his blue bottle of cologne in my mind. I assumed that because I saw him with this bottle earlier, my imagination gave me the image and therefore I was not remote viewing it. So I did not write it down. What did he have hidden in the drawer? The blue, cologne bottle.

In *Limitless Mind* Russell Targ compares our ability to do remote viewing to our ability to play music. Certainly, there are child prodigies like Mozart who can remote view very naturally. However, we can all practice and become phenomenal piano players or remote viewers if we practice.

I promise you this, when you remote view you will have an experience of being who you *really* are. You will be seeing outside of your five senses and outside of the boulder you are living in and what you experience may just leave you saying, "Wow, how did I do that?"

Remember, you are that young soul who came to Planet Earth to experience emotions and use the 5 senses. You are now learning to quiet your mind and get in touch with your Soul Self, who can create and fulfill just about any dream you can come up with.

HOMEWORK ASSIGNMENT

It is time to remote view! Remote viewing might require you to become courageous, as you may not be ready to share with people that you are reading this book and you are now experimenting with Extra Sensory Perception.

1. Remote view with another person, whether that person is with you physically or is at another location. With our cell phone technology, you can do this experiment with someone at a distance and have them send you a picture of the object that you just remote viewed.

2. Remote view with a magazine or a deck of flash cards. Hold the intention to see the images inside of a magazine. Write down every image. When you go through the magazine, you have to look at the pictures very carefully, as sometimes the pictures are small within another picture.

3. Visit Russell Targ's website ESPresearch.com and learn more about Targ and his experiments. Currently, there is a free application to use on many phones or devices called *ESP Trainer*. It is very fun!

4. Visit WeDontDie.com/remoteviewing.html and you will find some places online to test and practice your remote viewing skills.

Remember, please be gentle with yourself and realize that the more you practice the better you will get.

Last, I want to remind you that you must be courageous and step through any fear that you may have to ultimately achieve the results that you want in life. I know the feelings of fear and anxiety can be very uncomfortable, but think about it this way: when you are doing the thing you are afraid of, you are not afraid in that moment, are you? Please push yourself through your fears and you will have an extraordinary life.

I would love to hear about your experiments! Please feel free to share them at WeDontDie.com/remoteviewing.html.

Chapter 9

Reconnecting with Those You Have Loved and Lost

A friend's hand is always there . . .
you just have to reach out for it.

~ Unknown

re·con·nect, *verb*

To be linked together again.

The Loveometer

When someone we love dies, it leaves a huge hole in our hearts. The pain we experience is called *grief* and it feels like part of us is missing. The pain at times seems unbearable.

I do believe that we are souls put here to have a human experience and the biggest task we each have is to experience love. That means give love, show love, be loving and receive love. Is there a way to tell if we are on track being human and we are experiencing love? Yes, I call it the *Loveometer.*

Imagine an instrument that looks like a thermometer. One end says *Zero Love* and the other side says *Maximum Love*. The amount of pain you feel from grief is in direct correlation to the amount of love you have in your heart, as pain would not be present when you lose someone, if not for love. If you were to hold this Loveometer in your hand, while feeling your grief, what love temperature would it read? I have a sneaky suspicion you have hit *Maximum Love* sometimes, haven't you? You might feel the Loveometer pushing beyond maximum, feeling like it will burst.

Grief certainly does hurt and feels like something horrible has happened to you. You could choose to look at grief another way: that your *Soul Self* is right on track. Part of the reason you are on Earth is to love with all of your heart. Feeling intense grief means you have done just that. You should be proud of your capacity to love fully. Not everyone has experienced true love.

Relationships and Soul Growth

In the beginning of this book, our young soul was given a guidebook to study before coming here:

> *Earth is the only place in all of the universe where you can feel a wide range of these emotions. You are given a pencil and must circle the top three emotions that you want to experience the most on Earth. Being the wise soul that you are, you circle: Love (of course, that's a given), Generosity (because it feels good to help others), and Independence (who wouldn't want that?). Of course, you don't read the fine print that tells you that you are NOT given these emotions, but instead you will be given situations where you are able to experience these emotions.*

Ninety-nine percent of the time situations that allow you to have maximum soul growth contain an element that you cannot control. That element is other people, and we call our interaction with these other people *relationships.*

I will define relationships as *any interaction you have with any person.* Often, when we hear the word relationship, we think of a romantic relationship. That is not what I am speaking of here. When you hear me use the word *relationship,* I mean *any* interaction you have with the people that surround you in life. For example, you have a relationship with your spouse, your friends, your boss, your coworkers, your kids, your parents, etc. You even have relationships with your dry cleaner, your postal workers and the people that work at your bank. Take a second and look at all the relationships you have. Quite a few, huh?

For our soul to grow, we must have these relationships to work out what we came here to do. It is a widely shared belief that we create *soul contracts* with others, before coming to Earth. Some of these contracts give us great opportunity to practice being loving and generous. While others give us the perfect foundation to practice compassion and forgiveness. You may have a few of those in your life. Do you have people that you are angry at or have had a disagreement with? Do you have people you are not talking with right now? Take a look and identify what the opportunity for your soul to grow is in one of these relationships. There is *always* a soul growth that takes place, always.

Once, I got very hurt by a woman who told me that I'd look much better if I lost weight. Just the way she said it really hurt. I didn't see it at the time, but my soul certainly did grow out of that experience.

I learned to be *compassionate.* I got to see the situation from her point of view. This allowed me to have a relationship with her and love her for the woman she is. I learned that when someone says something that upsets me, it is because I believe what they are saying is true. I didn't get upset when my little five-year-old niece said, "Auntie Sandy, why are you fat and Momma is skinny?" Certainly, big kids and little kids speak the truth. It is what we do with that information that counts.

I got to experience both *love* and *generosity* in my relationship with my grandmother, who I called "Grammy." I moved to Massachusetts to be close to her and when I was not traveling, cooking for the race crews, I spent time with her almost every day. Grammy was easy to be with, never demanded anything and was *grateful* for everything. Her life couldn't have been easy and surely was filled with heartache. She lived just one week short of her 91st birthday and experienced going through the Depression and the deaths of a younger brother, her husband, many friends and eventually, the death of several of her brothers and sisters. Grammy had died before I learned about grief, so I wasn't able to talk with her about it. What I can now see is how strong a woman she was. Grammy was an angel to me and her soul clearly had learned its life lessons and it was time for her to move on. She was *loving, generous, grateful, wise, funny, never complained and never said a bad thing about anyone.* She wasn't afraid of death either. Grammy would always say, "When God calls me forth, I cannot come fifth!" In fact, those words came out of her mouth just moments before she passed away.

The relationship I have with my mom has taught me love, compassion, and *forgiveness.* My parents divorced when I was a teenager and I believed Dad was right and Mom was wrong. In my teens and my college years, I didn't have a good relationship with my mom. I always believed that my mom was the cause of my parents' divorce. It wasn't until years later, 1991 to be exact, that my relationship with my mother changed. Mom and I sat in a restaurant for hours, drinking lots of wine and discussing our past memories. I was able to share with her the pain I felt growing up and how difficult my life had been, especially around the time of their divorce. Mom shared with me her entire past. She shared the experience of coming to the United States from Germany during the World War. She talked about her childhood, her siblings and some of the beliefs she had about life and about herself.

She spoke of her mother's death when she was 20 years old and how she raised her younger brother. She told me about the relationship she had with my dad, both the good things and the problems.

I got to see my mom's life through her beliefs and experiences. I got to forgive my mom for everything I thought she did wrong and forgive myself for having the resentment I had held toward her. We were able to *clear the slate* and start our relationship again. For the past 21 years, Mom has been my closest love and has supported me more than any other human being ever has.

What it took was each of us being *willing* to see life from the other person's perspective. We were then able to forgive each other and clear the slate and create a whole, new relationship, based on love, trust, respect and a lot of fun. Mom and I laugh a lot!

My soul has grown from the emotion of love. Love from family, friends and pets, both giving and receiving. I have also grown in *romantic love* and *self-love*, too. I first got my first taste of romantic love at the age of 16 and loved my boyfriend dearly. We shared dreams of getting married, having a family and living happily every after. But that didn't happen. Before my 17th birthday, my boyfriend had found someone else: my best friend. The summer went by and this young gentleman came crawling back to me, apologizing because it was me he truly loved. We dated our senior year in high school and just before our senior prom he told me that he was in love with my new best friend. I can still remember the severe pain I felt when he said those words.

You and I unconsciously make decisions about who we are in those tough times in life. Looking back, I clearly made the decision that there would always be someone better than me, that a romantic relationship would not happen for me and definitely, I could never trust a friend. For almost the next twenty years I lived my life feeling unlovable, very alone and didn't trust anyone.

I never gave up hope. Time and time again, I got back on that horse and kept dating. But the same thing kept happening to me, a man would break up with me for another woman. Little did I know then that I unconsciously held the belief that I was unlovable and if I was displaying that I was *unlovable* to the men in my life, no wonder they broke up with me!

My soul finally became aware that I am lovable and the way I learned that was from self-love. In author Dov Baron's book, *Don't Read This: Your Ego Won't Like It*, he provides a wonderful exercise that helped me develop this self-love. Every day for two weeks, when I woke up in the morning, I would take out a sheet of paper and a pen. On the first half of the paper, I would write why people love me—all the good qualities that people have told me about myself. On the second half of the paper I wrote down all my successes. Looking at these 14 pieces of paper after two weeks, there was no way that I could hold together the belief that I am unlovable. What developed in me after the exercise was self-love, now being able to see myself as the loving, generous, playful soul I am, one that wants to help other people's dreams come true. After doing Dov Baron's exercise, I have had the confidence to write many of the words you now read. Although I had started writing *We Don't Die* several years ago, the majority of the book was finished after developing that self-love.

The grief of losing my dad also gave me the courage to start dating. I realized I had a huge fear of rejection and did not want to experience the pain of a breakup again. The pain of grief was so severe that I thought I could have died after the death of my father, but I did not. I realized that if I could live through the pain of losing my dad, I could certainly live through the pain of a romance ending. I have met some new, incredible men because I was willing to be more vulnerable and started dating.

The relationship I had with my dad taught me a bunch, too. People often ask, "What is the thing that you are most proud of?" My answer, since May 11, 2010, is "Being by my dad's side during the last months of his life."

My dad was an incredible father. He was a pilot in the US Air Force and went on to become a captain for American Airlines. He had cancer 30 years ago and miraculously went into remission. He spent his years inspiring cancer and AIDS patients and anyone in need, to live a good life. He was a generous friend to many and gave so many people hope. Dad became an avid bike rider after his first time with cancer and rode a bicycle across the United States five times, raising money for charity. He loved his airplanes, loved being a flight instructor and loved flying in formation with his buddies at *Spruce Creek Fly-In*, a private community for golfers and pilots. He had a hangar close to his house and loved being in the air. Even in his seventies, Dad still enjoyed bicycling 20 miles a day, until his back started giving him problems.

His back pain led to finding out he had a cancerous tumor that had broken part of his spine. Although it was radiated, Dad suffered with an extreme amount of pain. He had a pain pump attached to him that gave him medication regularly and when the pain got too bad, he could press a button for more. It was tough seeing Dad like this. The man who had so much life and spirit was now regularly in the hospital, spent a short time in Hospice regulating his pain medication, went into two nursing homes and back to the hospital. Although he suffered physically, he was his old positive self mentally. I know things got very tough for him, especially towards the end, but he played the game of making the day brighter for every person who walked into his hospital room. He would ask the nurses or aides about themselves and their lives, he would ask them what they loved to do. He knew that when a person talked about what they loved, that would make them happy. He also would share an inspiring or funny story with them just to put a smile on their faces.

What my soul learned from my time with Dad was how to be *strong*. In the past, I never liked hospitals, couldn't handle the sight of needles or bodily fluids. None of those things mattered when I was with my dad. I became a *fighter* and gave everything I had to make sure that Dad was cared for the best way possible. I tried to be the best companion I could be and did everything I could to bring a smile to his face. Dad and I watched comedy movies and good documentaries. We talked about some of the things that our minds were capable of. He loved my stories of remote viewing and mediumship. We played a *gratitude game* every day and would take turns back and forth saying all the things we were grateful for. I personally believe that feeling gratitude, feeling love, and having a good laugh are essential to the healing process, so I made them a priority everyday. I brought him ice cream, his favorite muffins, and had a stash of goodies tucked away for him in the hospital's refrigerator. I felt like a cruise director, making sure my passenger had the best trip possible. I am extremely proud of myself for that and didn't know that I could be that strong of a person. My soul had a major growth spurt, spending that time with Dad. Without Dad, this book would not be in your hands right now.

You may have experienced grief in your own life and know that it brings a lot of pain and suffering, especially in our relationships. Over 45% of sibling relationships end when a parent dies, 70-80% of couples get divorced when their child dies, and over 90% of couples divorce if one of them is diagnosed with a life threatening illness. Grief comes after a death of a life or relationship, but what many people do not know is that grief comes before the end. I experienced this within my own family.

I now have two years of research behind me as why humans do some of the things we do during grief, but when Dad was dying, I had no idea. What I did know was that there were many disagreements between my siblings and me, which led to incredible fights and as a result, our relationships came apart. I made them wrong as much as they made me wrong. I had no idea that during the time of *anticipatory grief*, the memory and perceptions in our brains become faulty and that what *we believe is reality* may not be the truth. In my eyes, my siblings, once some of the closest and most fun human beings in my life, became different. There is no doubt that I became different in their eyes as well.

If you have ever experienced a death or the breakup of a relationship, you know it is awful. You are not just grieving the loss of the person that died, but you may also grieve the loss of people that are still alive and that can be even worse.

My soul got some very advanced growth lessons from my siblings and I am grateful for that. I was driven to find out why we all became so different and what happens during grief that made our family come apart. I found amazing evidence of how our brains work during grief and how brains work under the stress of an illness. I cannot even imagine what was happening in my dad's brain. He surely was experiencing grief and fear, all the while taking huge amounts of pain medication that has been proven to destroy memory and brain function.

My siblings and I fought about "What Dad wants . . ." and it was amazing that he told me one thing and they told me he wanted another. My mind was quick to believe they must have been lying and I'm sure they believed that I was lying. I then began my studies with Dr. Daniel Amen, the world renowned brain expert and author of the bestseller, *Change Your Brain, Change Your Life: The Breakthrough Program for Conquering Anxiety, Depression, Obsessiveness, Anger and Impulsiveness.* Looking at brain scans of people who are under the influence of drugs, it was clear to me that my dad's brain function was very, very poor. I believe now that Dad told us kids different stories. It is not his fault; in that moment his brain did the best it could. Depression and grief result in similar faulty brain functions and those of us experiencing grief do not have the full brain capacity of people not experiencing it. Our memory, perception, communication and understanding are faulty, resulting in incredible misunderstandings, fights and often, relationship breakups.

This book would not have been created if not for my family. What seemed like the worst thing imaginable at the time has now allowed this information to come forth from two years of investigating grief. Over one million people end their own lives because of grief and depression and many relationships end as well. Heidi, Steve, Karen, Uncle Joe, Auntie Fran, Donna, Grammy, Mom and Dad, I owe you much gratitude. Without the *soul contracts* we made before we got to Earth, there would be many more suicides and relationships ending. I know for certain that the words within this book have already saved lives and many relationships from ending.

Forgiveness

Now seems to be the perfect time to bring up *forgiveness*. I used to believe that when we spoke about forgiveness, we were saying that what the person did was acceptable or okay. Oh, I was mad when someone said, "Just forgive them," because I didn't believe people should be forgiven. Especially for violent, cruel, or illegal acts.

What forgiveness means is to stop being resentful towards someone. I heard someone say once that resentment is like *taking rat poison, then waiting for the other person to die*. Resentment is painful and can eat us up inside. Forgiveness is simply giving up the right to be resentful. Whether the person did something right or wrong, you are no longer going to have the rat poison killing you from the inside out. I urge you now to forgive and let go of any resentment you may have toward a person or yourself.

A special ingredient you can add to forgiving someone is compassion. Remember, the best place to stand in an argument is on the other person's side.

In the case of my family, I saw how my actions could have created the perception they had of me and how their actions created the view I had of them. Add to that, our grieving brains were so inefficient at processing information. It is no wonder there were arguments. I feel it is so important to be compassionate with each other and practice forgiveness.

HOMEWORK ASSIGMENT

Make a list of the relationships that you have or had in your life, dead or alive. Start with the ones closest to you (even the people you may disagree with or be mad at) and list them all on paper. Even if people are no longer in your life but made a big impact on you, write their names down too. Next to each name, write an emotion you experienced because of them and the gift your *Soul Self* got because of them. You'll be writing down words like love, jealousy, faith, trust, anger, forgiveness, generosity, tenacity and things like that. Any emotion or learning that you did is perfect. Write them all down. Let me know about them if you'd like, you can email me at Sandra@SandraChamplain.com.

As we move into the *Reconnection* phase of this chapter, you may consider calling or writing the people to tell them, "Thank you. Thank you for allowing me to grow as a person." Let them know how they made a difference for you. Be sincerely grateful, see their actions from their side and generously thank them for the difference that they have made in your life. If that person is deceased, we'll now be talking about getting in touch with them and having this conversation. A little extra note in this assignment: before you get into communication with this person, take a few minutes and think about what makes them so special to you. We often live lives forgetting how special we are and how special the people around us are, as *The Voice* often tells us the negative stuff. So take a deep breath, quiet your mind and listen to the good your *Soul Self* has to say about yourself and others.

Reconnection

Many people believe that they must go to a psychic or a medium, hold a séance, or a do an *Electronic Voice Phenomena* recording to reach someone who has passed from this life to the next.

Certainly, you can do those things and they will give you the proof you need that your loved ones are still with you. There is nothing wrong with wanting evidence.

You just did a little remote viewing not long ago. (Well, I hope you did the exercise and didn't let fear stop you). You remember how easy it is to clear your mind and see into the past, present or maybe the future? All you have to do is clear your mind again to connect to the realm where you can talk to your folks in the hereafter. They really are *here, just after.*

I mentioned that there are invisible radio and television waves coexisting in the same space that you are occupying right now. Our deceased loved ones are right here, too. Someday your body will not be on the Earth but you will be back, as well. You will exist in a magical world and be invisible to your friends and family, but you will be here, visible or not.

As you contemplate if you are ready to connect with a deceased person, whether it be your dad or mom, your spouse or your friend, I want you to know something: that person is right there, right now in front of you. They may be sitting in the seat to your left or on the couch to your right. They may be standing in front of you or they may be lying in the bed beside you. They have only been a thought away since the day they passed and can be with you at a thought's notice, until it is your time to go.

I want you to pretend for a minute that the person is there in front of you or sitting on a chair beside you. What would you say to them? As hard as it may be to believe that they are there, know this: that mediums do this exact thing. They relax their mind, just like when we did when remote viewing and wait for images to appear of people they do not know, as opposed to objects they do not recognize.

Most of the mediums have had lots of practice communicating with the hereafter. Each time you practice, you will have better results. The resources in this book will give you the sources you need to consult a medium, a spirit artist, or someone who can help you record an EVP. You may also go to WeDontDie.com/EVP.html to get detailed instruction of how to do a recording.

A gentleman that I connected with online, Phil Graham, made an accidental discovery in 2002. Before this, he did not believe in psychics or life after death and most definitely did not believe in afterlife contact.

Since then, Phil has shared his simple discovery, called *Coffee Time*, with thousands around the world. His information is free and you will find his technique very comforting and reassuring that your loved ones are still near.

Phil says, "If someone dear to you has passed away and you miss them, let me assure you there is life after death and those in it are contactable, not just by a gifted few, but by ordinary non-psychic people. You just need to relax, listen and recognize the signs." Sounds like the same advice about remote viewing, doesn't it? Again, all connection happens when we can relax and calm *The Voice* inside our head. To see a great video about Phil and the instructions for *Coffee Time*, please visit WeDontDie.com/CoffeeTime.html.

As a special gift that I have for you, for giving me your time in reading this book, I have recorded a CD simply called *Reconnections*. You will be able to quiet your mind and reconnect with the soul of the loved one you lost while listening to it. To listen to your copy of *Reconnection* please go to WeDontDie.com/Reconnections.html.

Sometimes, the people we need to talk to are alive and for whatever reason (they may be angry at you or you may be too afraid to call them), you will still be able to connect with their souls. As you learned from remote viewing, it is easy to connect with a space far away from where you may now sit.

HOMEWORK ASSIGNMENT

Reconnect, reconnect, reconnect. It is time for you to say everything you need to say to them. Imagine they are right there in front of you, in many cases they will be. If the person is alive, trust that they will be receiving the message. It is your time to speak and say everything that you need to say. It is also time to forgive, so that you no longer have to carry around the pain. Trust me, this will allow you room to create and experience many great, new things in your life.

Have you ever heard the expression, "What you resist, persists?" When you avoid doing this assignment, it will keep popping into your head reminding you to do it. Might as well get it done now. It is easier than you think, if you allow yourself to listen to the *Reconnections* audio.

Remember this one very important thing I like to say:

What seems like our imagination is often not,
it is simply a connection with the Eternal.

A Last Word about Relationships

As human beings, we can often feel alone or lonely. Although you may not be able to see the love you have around you, it is there. There is a whole team of invisible people in front of you, behind you and by your sides who want you to have the greatest life possible.

It is mandatory for soul growth that you spend lots of time talking with other people. Don't spend too much time being alone or being distracted by modern technology like emailing or texting. Your personal relationships provide you with the atmosphere for your soul to come out and play, learn, grow and experience *love*. That is the reason you came to Earth to begin with, remember? When you spend too much time alone, *The Voice* will take over and make you forget who you *really* are.

You are an eternal soul having a human experience,
who can create and fulfill any dream you can imagine.

Chapter 10

Surviving Grief

When one door closes another door opens;
but we often look so long and so regretfully upon the closed
door, that we do not see the ones which open for us.

~ Alexander Graham Bell, inventor and educator, b. 1847

grief, *noun*

Deep prolonged mental anguish, intense sorrow, emotional suffering caused by a loss, a disaster, or a misfortune, especially by the death of a loved one.

"What is Grief and Why do we experience it?" I gave you the definition of grief above, but if you have ever experienced it, I am quite sure you would disagree with that definition. What we feel when we are grieving is much, much worse than words can possibly describe. My definition would be more like this:

grief, *noun*

An assortment of terrible feelings that last a long, long time, including: shock, disbelief, anger, rage, fear, sadness, sickness, and uncontrollable crying to the point of being buckled over in pain with no relief in sight. Having a feeling of emptiness that certainly life will never be the same again. Not being able to concentrate, having other areas of life suffer including massive miscommunications in relationships with spouses, siblings, friends, and coworkers. Life feels like it is falling apart.

To me, grief is the most painful emotion we will ever experience as human beings. We all experience grief a bit differently and for different periods of time and there is no formula for how long you can expect it to last.

You may wonder, "Why does grief have to hurt so bad if death is normal?" If you are grieving right now I guarantee that you are not alone. For the last 300,000 years our Earth has been spinning with human beings living on it. Every day on Earth, there are nearly 340,000 human births and over 142,000 deaths. Over a year, there are over 124 million births and 52 million deaths. Every second, four of us are born, while every 1.8 seconds, one of us dies.

Often, when a woman learns that she is pregnant, she receives multiple copies of a certain book, *What to Expect When You're Expecting*. When the special day comes and the baby is born, we rejoice and celebrate. Out of *nowhere*, a cute, little life gets created and we feel incredible love for that little being. Then, one day, we return to that *nowhere* in death. As normal as death is, very few cultures celebrate it and certainly, there is no one book given when someone dies. My goal is for the book you are holding, *We Don't Die*, to be given as an appropriate gift when someone experiences the loss of a loved one.

We do not celebrate death, we grieve. We begin to feel the most painful emotion that exists. We may not like it, but grief is something we all must experience in our lives. Grieving is not taught in schools and remains a mystery until we are faced with it.

Unfortunately, it may be difficult to learn about grief while you are grieving, because your brain is literally rewiring itself in *survival mode* to deal with a new reality after your significant loss. If you have been grieving as you read this book, you may have found trouble concentrating on the words. It is not your fault and there is nothing wrong with you; poor memory and concentration are parts of grief.

An incredible amount of energy is used, by the brain for grieving. There are areas of your brain that are literally readjusting right now to deal with the loss. These are the same areas you use for memory, learning, concentration, perception and communication. Not only do people find it hard to learn while grieving, but often you will find listening and retaining information is not so easy. This means that your work and relationships may suffer.

During grief, you may find people saying to you, "I told you that already, weren't you listening?" Or, someone will be talking to you and you'll want to respond, but you just can't come up with the words you want to say. You try to recall some bit of information, something you know well, the word will be right on the tip of your tongue, but it does not come to mind or come out of your mouth.

Your perception and your view of the world and the people in it can be way off, too. Your view of reality may not be the truth, but it is your truth, because you are the only one living in your brain. Let me give you an example. Your boss may ask you, "What time will you hand me that report you've been working on?" What you perceive is, "He thinks I'm not doing my job, he is always on my back for something. I can't stand him, I am going to look for another job." What really happened? Your boss just asked you a simple question and you made up the rest.

How about this example? You and your siblings have always been reasonably close. You have heard stories about how families come apart when there is a death and you vow with your brothers and sisters, "That will *never* happen to us." Your mother then passes away. Each sibling, along with your father, begins the grieving process.

Your family meets to discuss what to do next and how to handle funeral arrangements. Beside your perception being way off, childhood memories could come flooding back and the miscommunications begin. Your sister begins to ask about Mom's wedding ring, something Mom had promised to her. She is grieving and wants the ring because it was special to Mom.

Often, we want to be reunited with a person so bad, that we feel like, "If I could just have one of her things, I would feel better." Unfortunately, it does not work that way. Your sister wants the ring to be close to your mother's memory. How might the other siblings perceive this? One might say, "She's greedy, I knew it, she is going to go after everything."

You may have a brother who is a psychologist. He brings up the fact that you all need to remain calm and address things one at a time, perhaps make a list of how to navigate through the funeral and burial process. What might be the perception of another sibling? "He was Mom's favorite, he could do no wrong in her eyes, he got the good grades, went off to college and now helps people." Another sibling might say, "Pay no attention to him, remember, people go into the careers they most need. He couldn't figure out his own life so he became a psychologist." The family begins fighting.

There are now five adult children who just lost their mother, all with varied perceptions, not having a clue what happens to the brain during grief. The result? Over 45% of sibling relationships end after a parent has died and a staggering 70–80% of marriages end in divorce after their child dies. Ultimately, the reason for most of these situations is simply not having proper brain function during the grieving process.

There is also a phenomenon called *anticipatory grief*, in which the grieving process begins before a death. If a person is told they have a life threatening illness, they may experience anticipatory grief. This was the case within my own family. As my dad's cancer got worse, so did the anticipatory grief. Once a loving family, this grief within the minds of all of his adult children led to anger and catastrophic arguments.

Ninety percent of marriages end in divorce over anticipatory grief. For example, imagine a woman is diagnosed with breast cancer. Both the husband and wife are flooded with a range of emotions: *shock, anger, fear, denial, sadness, disbelief* and *numbness* to name a few.

The woman may invest her time in finding the best doctors, the best nutrition, research the topic to the fullest, add some alternative approaches to the regimen the doctor has given her to beat the cancer. She also now sees life as an opportunity and chooses to do all the things in life that she had been putting off. She plans a trip to Italy, she gets in touch with her old friends from high school, she volunteers at a local homeless shelter and she begins writing the novel she had created years back in her mind.

However, her spouse is handling his anticipatory grief another way. He is now frightened to lose his wife. She is his best friend, his confidant, his soul mate. This once powerful, independent man now wants to stay home and takes a leave of absence from work, so he may nurture his bride during her time of need. After all, he knows he may not have too much time left with her. He is frightened to lose her, doesn't leave her side and wants to do everything for her.

You might imagine that this would drive the wife crazy as this woman is ready to do all the things she has dreamed of doing. Meanwhile, the husband is frustrated because he cannot understand his wife's behavior. Both have a very different view, or perception, of the situation.

What happens to this couple? That all depends. First, they could grow apart and ultimately get divorced, regardless of the health of the wife. Or, one or the other could lose their health, die and the other live with regrets the rest of his or her life. The best case scenario? You could hand them each a copy of this book and tell them to "Read chapter 10 first!" This will allow them the opportunity to learn about anticipatory grief and how to deal with it, when it arrives.

Let me make sure you understand this: grief comes into your life before and after a death. Remember, the loss of a job or finances, or the breakup of a relationship can all cause grief. If you don't feel quite right in your own life right now, look to see if you have experienced a loss or a significant change.

I believe that with knowledge comes power. We do realize that our bodies cannot survive death and no matter how much we believe in life after death, we will all experience grief. We know it is going to hurt terribly. We experience more loss the older we get, as our friends and family grow older, too.

Grief must run its course, but we can educate ourselves in preparation for it. It is not a pleasant subject; I am sure you have noticed that there is not a New York Times best-seller called, *What to Expect When You're Dying*.

When you grieve, you may feel angry or spend your time thinking about regrets. I would ask you to redirect your energy to learning how to heal and how to continue your life.

Why do we grieve? The answer is simple: because we love. If we didn't have love and connections to others we would not grieve. Think about people you do not know very well that have died. You may feel bad for their family and friends, but you don't know the person, so you don't feel too bad and you do not grieve.

However, imagine someone close to you dies. A person or pet that you love and cherish has passed away. The pain of your grief can be crippling. Most of us who have felt grief agree that we would do anything to prevent losing someone we love. We can stand pain from an injury, we know that eventually we would heal and the pain would leave us. Healing from grief has no guarantees, it could take six months, it could take years. We all grieve and heal in different time. I believe the pain caused by grief certainly does lessen over time, but that feeling of missing another will never quite go away. There is no way to avoid experiencing grief, but there are ways to lessen the pain and the time spent grieving.

We will now turn to the brain to look for some answers about grief. We know that animals, as well as humans, experience grief. Grief is essential for the survival of a species. Imagine a bear cub, raised by its mother, relying solely on his mother for food and protection. One day the mother disappears and now the bear must survive on his own. The bear experiences grief. His mind goes into shock. The bond he had with his mother is now broken. For this bear's survival, his brain must rewire itself and become accustomed to the fact that there is no mother now to feed and protect him. Grief alerts him to the fact that he is now responsible for his own survival. Without grief, the bear would either starve to death or become the prey of another animal.

Humans act the same way as animals. Our bodies and our minds get used to the sounds, touch, sight and smell of another person. This is done through chemicals present in our bodies. When we are in the presence of such a person, a particular mix of neurotransmitters and hormones are produced. This forms a physiological identity of the other person in our body and a bond is created in our brains. We literally become addicted to this person through this bond. We call this bond love. This same bond often occurs with the pets we may share our homes with. Although they are not human, the bond can be just as strong and sometimes stronger, depending on the amount of time we spend with them.

The human brain operates much like your automobile, on fluids called neurotransmitters. Just as your automobile uses brake fluid, antifreeze, transmission fluid and oil, your brain runs on these neurotransmitters. Some give us energy, like those related to adrenalin, some control body movements, such as dopamine and some control our mood.

The neurotransmitter associated with grief and depression is called serotonin. Serotonin is a slow-acting neurotransmitter that is associated with sleep, appetite, energy, alertness, memory, concentration and mood, just to name a few.

When a person we are close to dies, we no longer can experience that person alive and, due to the stress on our system, more serotonin is used up than the body can replace. Our minds are conditioned to have that person alive, so when the person dies, the system goes haywire and into turmoil. Depending on the degree of the bond, the body may go into shock, very much like an addict who stops getting his fix. If you can imagine a person who is dependent on a chemical or alcohol and doesn't receive it, they would go into *withdrawal*. Although they may appear normal from the outside, their sense of reality may be false. The same holds true for the person grieving a significant loss.

During the grieving process, the brain continuously uses serotonin much faster than it can create it. Our memory quickly begins to fail, our perception changes and we see people and situations a different way. Fear, anger, disbelief, denial and sadness set in, all part of the grieving process. However, one day the weeping and the grieving will end as serotonin gets restored. At that point, the body becomes emotionally and physiologically stable and we feel calm. Our bodies are no longer addicted. The grieving phase is then over.

Symptoms of Low Serotonin

1. Your sleep cycle is off. You find yourself not being able to sleep or you sleep at strange hours. Serotonin, you see, controls our sleep cycle.

2. Concentration and attention will drop. Grieving students might experience a drop in grades. You might put odd things in the refrigerator; perhaps you'll find your missing cell phone in it! You find yourself inside the grocery store, having no memory of why you went shopping in the first place. You feel forgetful and your brain may seem cloudy at home or at work.

3. You lose physical energy. You can sleep for over ten hours and you still feel tired when you wake up. You feel that you don't have the energy to make it through the day no matter how much caffeine you consume.

4. You feel emotionally unsteady. You may cry at any moment for any reason. Driving down the highway you hear a song on the radio, the scent of the dish detergent makes you think of your deceased mother, you read a greeting card and a picture or saying causes you sadness. By the way, crying is an important part of the grieving process for toxins to be released. Research has shown the tears of a grieving person have a different chemical makeup than other tears you may cry.

5. Sexual interest, appetite and general interest will rapidly drop. You will stop answering the phone, stop visiting with friends and stay home with the curtains closed. Normally a social butterfly, while grieving, you may find yourself wanting to be left alone.

Each human brain is unique. How long it takes to adjust varies from one individual to another. It will depend on the particular brain and on the magnitude and significance of the change. A person that loses a child will often have a much harder time coping with grief than a person who has just lost their job. The most painful grief is often felt by a person that loses their lifetime mate. We often hear of a spouse dying soon after their longtime partner dies. Their pain from grief may be so severe that they *die from a broken heart.*

The length of time you experience grief and its intensity depend on how well you can accommodate it. I say accommodate, because there is no point in fighting, reasoning, or attempting to eliminate or heal the grieving process. Grief is a basic survival task and not an illness. Although the adjustment process can feel awful—it is a natural and very much needed process. To fight the adjustment process or to try to eliminate grief is as senseless as trying to fight the fact that we need food, drink, or sleep. We will not only fail but also risk doing serious damage to ourselves. As uncomfortable and painful as the grieving process may feel, it is essential to our brains and must be experienced fully.

I encourage you to consult your physician, a person that you trust and that knows you. There is level of deep grief that can be diagnosed and a prescription can help until the brain begins to function more properly. However, to take a medication in times of normal grief, the sadness may be masked and a person may feel better, however when they stop taking that medication, the sadness will return. Have you ever heard the expression, "What you resist, persists?" When a person avoids feeling grief, the grief will return until it is fully felt. That is true with any emotion, the only way to truly release an emotion is to fully feel it.

Again, I do encourage you to start with your physician and diagnose whether what you are feeling is severe grief requiring medication or normal grief. Both are extremely painful.

Other things we may use to numb the pain such as alcohol, caffeine, sugar, or nicotine also do harm in the long term. Attempting to avoid feeling emotions by consuming one of these can have the effect of blocking or slowing down the grief process. Blocking grief comes at a great cost because it means we do not adjust to our new reality and therefore cannot be present in our lives and function properly.

The implications of not grieving can be serious. When grieving does not occur, a person's mind may not accurately perceive the reality they live in. By trying to turn off grief, people often develop real depression, suffer physical symptoms and their relationships and work performance greatly suffer.

Warning Signs of Grief—When You Should Consult Your Physician

When your serotonin level drops to dangerous levels, your *mind speed* seems increased. You feel like your mind is racing at what seems like 200 miles per hour. Severely depressed and grief stricken people often tell their doctors, "I can't get my mind to stop."

You feel your brain turning against you. It will reach in your memory bank and pull out every bad thought from the past it can find, including the arguments you had with the now deceased person and how you failed them. You will be tortured by your own thoughts, feeling sad and guilty.

As your mind speed picks up, the *garbage truck* may arrive. While the brain is already torturing you with the past, your mind can create thoughts that seem like torture to you. Your mind may tell you things like:

You are a burden to your family and friends

You have failed and disappointed those closest to you

No one really cares about you

Your children would be better raised by someone else

Your family would be better off without you

You are going crazy and there is no hope

It would be better for everyone if you weren't around

You would be better off dead

You should probably kill yourself

To the non-grieving mind, you can see that these messages really are garbage. However, to the severely grieving, your mind will try to make you very uncomfortable. You may be flooded with thoughts of violence (against yourself and others), you may believe you are being condemned by God, or you will think you deserve this condition for some reason. Your garbage might also tell you that if you seek professional help (from a physician, psychologist, psychiatrist, or counselor), you will be committed to an institution forever. *Please realize that these are signs of a very low level of serotonin and you must see your physician.*

> *If you have ANY questions whether your grieving*
> *is normal or not, see your doctor.*
> *I cannot repeat this enough, "If in doubt, see your doctor."*

For normal grief, with normal low serotonin levels, the only way to end the grief is to live through it and let the brain spend the necessary time rewiring itself for your survival. Unfortunately, we can feel numb, uncertain, be in disbelief, depressed, angry, vulnerable, confused, and afraid during this time.

The process of grief is physical. Building new brain connections and neural networks is exhausting. It uses up much of our energy and we don't often have much mental energy left for anything else. Unfortunately, we cannot choose when we want to grieve and must continue to use the same brain while it is going through this adjustment period. We must continue to work, make decisions, take care of our family, maintain relationships and fulfill responsibilities. This is where life gets difficult.

Because our brain considers adjustment to change crucial to survival, it will make it a top priority and will allocate as much energy and resources as possible to the adjustment process. This is because, from our brain's point of view, we are in danger as long as our mental image of reality does not match our actual reality. Everything else that we have to do just has to take a backseat. Our brain does not care that we have to go to work, raise children, pay bills, drive cars, run businesses, care for others, cook and do the shopping.

Most of us are busy people with responsibilities and commitments, but our grieving brain is not leaving us with enough energy to function as we normally do. This can leave many people feeling terribly inadequate and dysfunctional. In a world where we must work and live with others, the grieving process puts an incredible strain on our relationships.

Over 100 years ago, grieving was not what it is today. Children often grew up on farms, saw animals die and watched the deaths of their elders. The old or sick family members were cared for by family during their final days. Even after death, it was the family's responsibility to wash and dress the body and have the wake at the house. Families worked together and stayed together during the grieving process. Even though there were tears of sadness, death was a normal part of life. People's brains 100 years ago were not thrown into such a survival mode because experiencing a death was a part of normal life. Grieving then was not nearly as torturous as it is today.

Today, we don't see much of death. We live our lives unconsciously thinking that death happens to other people. Our elders and sick die in hospitals and nursing homes. It is rare that we see a farm, let alone live on a farm and see the birth and death of animals. Death is kept quiet and away from society, for the most part. We have not been given any tools that our elders had for dealing with death and grief.

Then, without warning, death pays a visit to your life. You may get a phone call that someone close to you has died and your brain goes full force into survival mode, to readjust to this significant change. You may find out that someone you love has an illness and is going to die. Again, through anticipatory grief, you'll experience the same shock and emotions associated with grief even though that person has not yet died.

Grief is a very hard journey on anyone. We need our friends and family to be there for us, to listen to us, to provide a shoulder to cry on and to depend on them for support. However, this can be a very hard thing for a family to do, because they are all going through grief at the same time. Each brain is being used for its own survival, so chances are others will not have the mental ability to be compassionate about your needs. What we need are friends, but often a friend is fearful, does not know what to say and ends up disappearing from your life, instead of being there to console you. I intend for this to stop. When people fully understand grief, we may move through it together, as opposed to coming apart. If you don't like someone's actions towards you while you are grieving, simply know that they do not understand the grieving process. Feel free to share *We Don't Die* or send them to *SurviveGrief.com* to help them understand.

Earlier I spoke of the relationships that suffer or can even end during grief. The words you are now reading have already saved some families and relationships from the pain of coming apart. *You see, if you get divorced from a spouse or end a relationship with a family member, you will grieve the loss of that person as well as the person that died.*

A term that is frequently used when describing another during grief is *true colors*. The meaning is that people spend their entire lives pretending to be kind, decent, and generous. We have heard it often when a person seems to become selfish, angry, greedy, or void of emotion, that the person's *true colors* have come out.

I would ask you to consider that people's true colors are the mannerisms and attitudes that the person has shown consistently in their life, not in the time of grief. Deep down, people are still the same as they have been in the past. However, when they experience grief, their body goes into shock and a new, temporary, set of emotions takes over as the brain tries to survive.

We need people when we grieve. If the grieving process is properly understood, more people will have compassion with each other . . . no matter if it is happening now or if something happened 20 years ago. It's never too late to apologize and make amends.

Please remember the symptoms of grief are the brain's physical and emotional response to the loss that has occurred. No matter how smart you are and how much you may have read about the subject, your body will still have to go through grief.

The following are more detailed mental symptoms of grief:

Impairment of the short-term memory: for example, you may not remember conversations and activities as they really occurred, or you may say you are telling the truth and the other person is lying.

Diminished concentration and attention span

Distorted perception: for example, you may get angry and cut a person out of your life because you heard an unpleasant "tone" in the way they spoke to you or you may assign an incorrect meaning to something a person did, for instance, "Judy balanced the checkbook and she knows that's my responsibility, now I don't trust her anymore."

Feeling absent-minded, forgetful, and distracted
Focusing on the negative aspects of life, with a sense that everything is
     going wrong
Loss of interest in what you previously enjoyed
Difficulty in dealing with responsibilities
Fear of going "crazy"
Difficulty making decisions
Feeling stupid
Inability to think about the future and make plans
Worrying about not achieving or not living up to your usual standards
Worrying that you will never feel good again and will always feel the
     way you do now
Worrying about absolutely everything

As a reminder, please be gentle and compassionate with yourself
and others while grieving. Unless you are in someone else's shoes, you
don't know how difficult a time they are having. Do your best to listen,
do not make them wrong for their behavior and choices, and love
them. Thankfully, with mutual respect and patience, relationships can
withstand this tough time and sometimes grow stronger due to grief.

Supporting Others through Grief

Perhaps the greatest mistake someone attempting to comfort a grieving person can make is to insist on how they must be feeling. Instead,
friends and relatives of the bereaved should be patient with whatever
emotions the individual may be feeling, without deciding whether
these emotions are appropriate.

Most grievers need to talk, often repeating the same story every
time you talk to them. I request that you be a listener, ask if there
is anything you can do for them, let them know you will always be
there for them. Eventually grieving will end and you won't hear the
story again.

Remember, someday you will grieve, and we all need support.

What Not to Say to Someone Grieving

Even if you are thinking this, please do not say, "They had a good long life," or, "It was their time," or, "God needed another angel in heaven." What can you say? "I am here for you and I care about you." "I am not in your shoes to know what you are feeling, but I will do whatever you need me to do." Sometimes that means simply listening.

People will appreciate those words, yet they may not take you up on your support. Grief is often a solitary experience and the only way to go through it is alone. Others will never be able to understand exactly how you may be feeling, so be patient with whatever may come, and that will help the keep the relationships strong.

If it is believed that grief is interfering with a person's life, then counseling may be in order. I have some grief coaching resources online at WeDontDie.com/GriefSupport.html.

I chose to include the technical aspect of what is happening in the brain during grief so you can be gentle on yourself and your loved ones who may be experiencing grief. Remember, grieving people are in survival mode. They have no choice whether they wish to experience grief or not. I will now discuss the stages of grief. You will be able to refer to them when you feel stuck in an emotion. Often, when we can recognize what stage we are in and realize it is normal, we can step out of it. I am reminded of a hamster running in a spinning wheel. He gets exhausted running and running. At some point he realizes he is in a wheel and not going anywhere! Similar to grief, when you realize that you are running and running and not going anywhere, you can gently step off the wheel.

The Five Stages of Grief

The five most well-known stages of grief were introduced by a Swiss-born psychiatrist, Dr. Elisabeth Kübler-Ross, who spent over

40 years working with thousands of dying children and adults and their families.

Please note that it is a common misconception that stages happen in a certain order. At any time during your grieving, one of these emotions can appear. We may experience some of them repeatedly.

The five stages are denial, anger, depression, bargaining, and acceptance.

1. *Denial*—Denial is a conscious or unconscious refusal to accept facts, information, or reality relating to the situation concerned. Denial is a defense mechanism and perfectly natural. Denial means that you do not accept the death or loss as the truth.

2. *Anger*—Anger can manifest in different ways. Grieving people can be angry with themselves or with others, often those closest to them. Many intense feelings of blame get directed toward other people—like relatives, friends, or doctors, who did not seem to help the person enough before their death.

It is so common to feel anger at oneself for failing to prevent the death or blaming oneself for not doing more. Feelings of anger towards the person who has died are often particularly distressing and confusing. The griever may feel abandoned by them.

Knowing that experiencing anger is normal may help keep you detached and non-judgmental when experiencing the anger of someone who is very upset. Again, anger is a natural and common response to loss. It is rare to experience no anger during grief and, for some people, feelings of rage can be very intense. The protest 'Why me?' reflects a general sense of helplessness at the unfairness of life, as does anger at others for carrying on their lives as if nothing happened.

3. *Bargaining*—Traditionally, the bargaining stage for people facing death can involve attempting to bargain with God or the Universe. Some people may bargain to feel the pain of cancer, so their loved one does not have to feel it. People facing less serious trauma can bargain

or seek to negotiate a compromise. For example, "Can we still be friends?" when facing the breakup of a relationship.

4. *Depression*—Shows an acceptance with emotional attachment. It is quite natural to feel sadness, regret, fear and uncertainty. Depression shows that the person has begun to accept the reality.

5. *Acceptance*—This stage varies according to the person's situation, although broadly it is an indication that there is some emotional detachment from the situation. People dying can enter acceptance a long time before the people they leave behind and this can often cause turmoil.

Since Dr. Elisabeth Kübler-Ross' passing in 2004, there has been much more work in the area of grief and there are even stages within stages, which I will cover next and, like the original five, can be experienced at any time during the grieving process.

Shock—The death of someone close to you comes as a tremendous shock. When someone dies unexpectedly, this shock is intensified. When someone takes their own life, or dies in a violent way, the shock can be particularly acute. Shock is common during the days and weeks immediately following a death. Some experience it more severely and for a longer time than others.

Numbness—Your mind will only allow you to feel your loss slowly. What has happened may seem unreal or dreamlike. The thought, "This can't really be happening to me," may occur. The numbness of early grieving may itself be a source of distress and misunderstanding if one wonders, for example, why one cannot cry at the funeral. As a note, numbness only delays emotional reactions and may be a help in getting through the practical arrangements. The *protection* provided by shock gradually wears off and emotional pain soon begins.

Disbelief—It is natural to have difficulty believing what has happened. When a death was untimely and sudden, it is even harder to grasp that the loss is permanent and real. On one level it is possible to know that a loved one has died. On another, deeper level it may seem impossible to accept. A large part of you will resist the knowledge that the person who has died is not going to be around any longer.

Confusion, panic and fear are common during this struggle between knowing that the person has died and disbelief.

Searching—Numbness and shock tend to give way to an overwhelming sense of loss. Many grieving people find themselves instinctively *searching* for their loved one, even though they know that they are dead. This may involve calling their name, talking to their photographs, dreaming they are back, or looking out for them amongst people in the street. This denial of a painful reality is a natural part of grief.

Anguish and Longing—The understanding that a loved one is really dead brings with it tremendous misery and sadness. As the loss begins to make itself felt, longing for the person who has died is common. Powerful and desperate yearnings to see and touch them, to talk and be with them, may be felt. You may even cling desperately to one of their belongings just to feel close to them. The intensity of emotions is often frightening and may leave you feeling devastated. Emotional pain is often accompanied by physical pain. It is common to go over and over what has happened, replaying things in your head or talking them through. The need to talk about a loved one following a death is part of the natural struggle to counteract their loss.

Physical and Emotional Stress—Losing someone close to you is a major source of stress. This stress may show itself in both physical and mental ways. Restlessness, sleeplessness and fatigue are common. You may also have bad dreams, memory loss and difficulty concentrating. You may experience dizziness, palpitations, shakes, difficulty breathing, choking in the throat and pains in the chest. Sadness may feel like a pain within. Muscular tension may lead to headaches and neck and back pain. Loss of appetite and nausea are also very common. Sexual interest may also be impacted. The physical effects will eventually pass with time.

Guilt—Guilt or self-blame is also common during grief. Guilt may be felt about the death itself. It is extremely painful to accept that we were not able to prevent the death of a loved one or protect them.

Feelings of responsibility are common and people often judge themselves harshly under these circumstances. Our relationships before the death are another common source of guilt. Sudden death interrupts close relationships without warning.

Since our lives are not usually conducted as if every day might be our last, we assume there will always be the future to sort out tensions and arguments or to say the things that have been left unsaid. Regrets often take the form of "if only." "If only I had done this," or "If only I hadn't said that."

Occasionally a death may bring with it a sense of relief for those left behind, particularly if there had been unhappiness and suffering for the deceased or loved ones beforehand. This feeling may also cause a person to feel guilty. Lastly, guilt may be felt for surviving, for remaining alive when the other person is dead.

Despair—Feelings of despair are common during grieving, once it is realized that despite all the anguish and longing, the loved one will not be coming back. Relationships often suffer because despair is draining and you may feel no interest in others.

A person may be left feeling both powerless and hopeless. Life may no longer seem to make sense or have meaning. Feelings of "not giving a damn" about anything or anyone are common and suicidal feelings are not uncommon. Please don't take these feelings lightly! I encourage you to see a doctor or therapist if they occur.

Fear—Fear is common in grief. Violent and confusing emotions, panic and nightmares may make grief a frightening experience. You may fear a similar event happening again. You may fear for yourself and those you love. You may fear *losing control* or *breaking down*.

Grief and Depression—The feelings of the newly bereaved have a lot in common with those of people suffering from depression. Like depression, grief can bring profound sadness and despair. Life may not seem real anymore. It may be hard to see a way forward.

People who have had such a loss are likely to be more prone to sadness and depression for a number of years. For some, these feelings may be particularly severe and prolonged. When grief gives way to a longer lasting depression, further help may be needed.

Caring for Yourself

The loss of someone close is unbelievably stressful. It can help you to cope if you take care of yourself in certain small but important ways. Here are some that might help:

Remember that grief is a normal emotion—Know that you can and will, heal over time. Know that you are not alone and you will get through this. It hurts tremendously, but what you're feeling is normal.

Participate in rituals—Memorials, funerals, and other traditions will help you get through the first few days and honor the person who died.

Spend time with others—Informal gatherings of family and friends can bring a sense of support and help people to not feel so isolated in the first days and weeks of their grief.

Talk about your feelings—Some people find it helpful to tell the story of their loss or talk about their feelings. Sometimes a person doesn't feel like talking and that is okay, too. No one should feel pressured to talk. You will eventually stop talking about it, but keep on talking until that day comes.

Journaling or writing—Even if you don't feel like talking, find ways to express your emotions and thoughts. Start writing in a journal about the memories you have of the person you lost and how you are feeling since the loss occurred. Write a song, poem, or tribute about your loved one, even if you never show it to anyone.

Exercise—Exercise can help your mood. It may be hard to get motivated, so modify your usual routine if you need to. Try not to think too much! Put on your sneakers and go outside for a walk. Sunshine will do you good, as well.

Eat right—You may feel like skipping meals or you may not feel hungry, but your body still needs nutritious foods. Dr. Daniel Amen's bestselling book, *Change Your Brain, Change Your Life*, gives readers an excellent prescription of foods, vitamins and activities to heal your brain.

Join a support group—If you think you may be interested in attending a support group, look on the Internet for grief support groups. The thing to remember is that you do not have to be alone with your feelings or your pain. WeDontDie.com/GriefSupport.html.

Let your emotions be expressed and released—Don't stop yourself from having a good cry if you feel one coming on. Do not worry if listening to particular songs or doing other activities is painful because it brings back memories of the person you lost; this is common. One day, when you least expect it, the pain will be gone.

Create a memorial or tribute—Plant a tree or garden, or memorialize the person in some fitting way, such as running in a charity run. There are now websites you can create in the memory of a loved one. I created JohnChamplain.com in memory of my wonderful father. This not only got my mind on something positive, but his friends who could not attend the funeral had a place to post a picture, share a memory, or send a condolence message.

Getting Help for Intense Grief

If your grief is not letting up for a while after the death of your loved one, you may want to reach out for help. If grief has turned into deep depression, it is very important to tell someone.

How do you know if your grief has been going on too long? Here are some signs:

You have been painfully grieving for 4 months or more and you aren't feeling any better.

You feel profoundly depressed.

Your grief is so intense that you feel you can't go on with your normal activities.

Your grief is impacting your ability to concentrate, sleep, or eat.

You feel you cannot go on living after the loss, or you think about suicide, dying, or hurting yourself.

It is natural for loss to cause people to think about death to some degree. However, if a loss has caused you to think about suicide or hurting yourself in some way, or if you feel that you cannot go on living, it is important to consult a physician right away.

Counseling with a professional therapist can help, because it allows you to talk about your loss and express strong feelings. Many counselors specialize in working with teens or children who are struggling with loss and depression. If you would like to talk to a therapist but are not sure where to begin, ask an adult or school counselor. Your doctor may also be able to recommend someone.

How to Lessen the Pain

Faith—Do you now have stronger beliefs about life and death? It may be extremely helpful for you to get involved with your religion and speak to a member of clergy or attend regular services.

Be active—When you get involved in a project or volunteer to make a difference for another, it may take your mind off your loss for a little while. Again, this activity will let a little serotonin start being replenished in your brain.

Children and animals—The laughter of a child or visiting a pet store and petting the puppies can make things feel so much better while grieving.

Play some music, read a good book, call a friend, go to a movie—These may be the last things you feel like doing, but any one of these activities will give your mind a break and will cause some healing to occur.

Unfortunately, even during these activities, you are in the adjustment period and waves of grief will still hit you. I was cooking at a racetrack in Canada and remember making a big batch of scrambled eggs with many people around. Without warning, I burst into tears uncontrollably thinking about the loss of my wonderful grandmother. Our brains need to go through the adjustment period, no matter what distractions we give them.

These waves of grief are often very intense, most of the time without a signal that they're coming. For lack of a better expression, we must *ride the waves*. When we fully experience the pain, the sadness, the tears and all the emotions, it allows them to dissipate. Anger, rage, fear, dread, guilt and denial are other emotions that will surface. It is very important to feel these feelings and to notice what it is you are feeling. As much as it hurts, it is a normal way your body must process grief.

I told you to experience these emotions, not act on them. When anger arises, do not yell at your spouse or your coworker. If you feel guilt, do not sit there stewing for two hours, thinking about what you should have done differently. Rather say, "I am feeling guilt." Feel what guilt feels like in your body and where you feel it and eventually those sensations will disappear.

Remember, "What you resist, persists." Avoid feeling emotions and they will return to find you.

The Present Moment Technique

One great practice anytime you are overcome with emotions associated with grief is being in the *present moment*. You have had some experience with this already with remote viewing. Going to the same place can provide freedom from pain.

Find something to pay attention to. You may see a plant sitting in the room or a sneaker on the floor by your front door. Notice everything you can about the object—the size, the color, the texture, each intricate detail. Fully investigate the object and even touch it, noting how it feels on your fingertips. You know what you just did? By being in the present moment and only paying attention to one thing, you re-circuited some brain patterns in your mind.

Anytime you get flooded with those unbearable feelings of grief, get your mind into the present moment. First, recognize what your body is doing. For instance, your body may be feeling incredibly sad and crying hysterically. Stop everything and notice what your body is doing. "I'm producing a lot of tears, I can hardly breathe, my heart is racing, my stomach feels sick, I feel like I have pressure on my chest."

From there, find something to bring you even more into the moment. If you are sitting in your car, you may focus on the steering wheel. In your office, you may concentrate on the movement of the second hand of the clock. You could use your other senses, concentrating on the sound, smell, touch, or taste of something. If you pick sound, you could notice the sound of the cars in the background, the notes in a piece of music, or the varied sounds of the birds chirping. There is no wrong way to do this exercise. You simply have to get into the present moment. Be advised, *The Voice* will want to think thoughts and disrupt your peace of mind. Simply try to bring your mind back to the present moment when this happens. Even taking a few deep breaths of air and concentrating on every inhale and exhale will make a big difference.

We, as humans, develop habits of grieving like any other habit, good or bad. You may have a good habit of brushing your teeth and you may have a bad habit of feeling guilty. You may have a good habit of recycling your bottles but have a bad habit of being angry at a person.

The more you think any thought, the easier it is for it to become a habit and the more you will do it. There are neural patterns being created in your brain every time you repeat something. So, if you want to lessen the pain of grief, you must realize that anytime you think a reoccurring negative thought, you are increasing your grieving time. Catch yourself in the act of thinking a negative thought, then get into the present moment, trying to not think about anything. Let the emotion just be and it will disappear. Then replace the thought with a positive one. Even a little thing like looking around your environment and finding something you are grateful for (like sunshine or the sound of birds chirping) will make a big difference for you.

HOMEWORK ASSIGNMENT

What losses have you experienced in your life? Did you then experience any emotions that we discussed that are a part of grief? Have you felt them fully or tried to avoid them? If you have been avoiding feeling grief, consider *opening up the wound* and allow yourself to feel the emotions. Cry if you need to. The pain will not last as long as you think it might. By doing so you will create the space for something new and good to come into your life.

Remember to practice self-love: forgive yourself and others, as the brain of a grieving person is unsteady. Also share what you know and help others understand grief. You may be saving someone's life, literally.

As we let our light shine, we unconsciously
give other people permission to do the same.
As we are liberated from our own fear,
our presence actually liberates others.

~ Marianne Williamson

Chapter 11

The Genius of the Human Body

What spirit is so empty and blind that it cannot recognize the fact that the foot is more noble than the shoe, and skin more beautiful than the garment with which it is clothed?

~ Michelangelo, Italian sculptor, painter, architect, & poet, b. 1475

ve·hi·cle, *noun*

Any means in or by which someone travels or something is carried or conveyed; a means of conveyance or transport.

Do you like cars? If money were no object and you could have any car in the entire world, what would it be? Okay, maybe you already have one of those, aren't you lucky? But if you could have another, what would you get? Something sporty? Something luxurious? Something classy? Heavy duty or reliable? The good news is that when you came to Earth so long ago, you got a priceless vehicle for traveling. I like to call it your *Energy Vehicle*, also known as the amazing human body.

Your Energy Vehicle

The body is not a permanent dwelling,
but a sort of inn which is to be left behind
when one perceives that one is a burden to the host.

~ Seneca, Roman philosopher, mid-1st century AD

We have discussed the mysteries of both *Outer Space* (planets, stars and the Universe) and *Inner Space* (the quantum mechanics of our tiniest particles). Your human body is the next mystery to discuss. Your body is an incredibly complex and intricate system, one that still baffles doctors and researchers on a regular basis, despite thousands of years of medical knowledge. Here are just some incredible facts about the energy vehicle you call your body:

You spent about half an hour as a single cell. All life has to begin somewhere, and even the largest humans spent a short part of their lives as a single-celled organism when sperm and egg cells first combined. Shortly afterward, the cells began rapidly dividing and forming the components of a tiny embryo.

Every day your body produces 300 billion new cells. Your body not only needs energy to keep your organs up and running but also to constantly repair and build new cells to form the building blocks of your body.

Three hundred million cells die in your body every minute. While that sounds like a lot, it's really just a small fraction of the cells that are in a human body. Estimates have placed the total number of cells in the body at 10–50 trillion so you can afford to lose a few hundred million without a hitch.

Your brain has about 100 billion nerve cells. These cells can hold five times as much information as the *Encyclopedia Britannica*, or any other encyclopedia, for that matter. Scientists have yet to settle on a definitive amount, but the storage capacity of the brain in electronic terms is thought to be between 3 to 1,000 terabytes. The National Archives of Britain, containing over 900 years of history, would use 70 terabytes, making your brain's memory power pretty darn impressive.

There are 45 miles (72 km) of nerves in your skin.

Nerve impulses to and from your brain travel as fast as 170 miles (274 km) per hour.

Your heart will beat three billion times in your lifetime and pump 48 million gallons of blood.

Your brain operates on the same amount of power as a 10-watt light bulb.

Your brain is much more active at night than during the day.

Your body is estimated to have 60,000 miles of blood vessels. To put that in perspective, the distance around the Earth is about 25,000 miles, making the distance your blood vessels could travel if laid end to end more than two times around the Earth.

Scientists have counted over 500 different liver functions. You may not think much about your liver except after a long night of drinking, but the liver is one of the body's hardest working, largest, and busiest organs. Some of the functions your liver performs are: production of bile, decomposition of red blood cells, plasma protein synthesis, and detoxification.

Over 90% of diseases are caused or complicated by stress. That high stress job you have could be doing more than just wearing you down each day. It could also be increasing your chances of having a variety of serious medical conditions like depression, high blood pressure, and heart disease.

The tooth is the only part of your human body that can't repair itself. If you've ever chipped a tooth you know just how sadly true this one is. The outer layer of the tooth is enamel, which is not a living tissue. Since it's not alive, it can't repair itself, leaving your dentist to do the work instead.

The bones in your body are stronger than some steels. Of course your bones can still break, but pound for pound bone is stronger than steel.

The length from your wrist to your elbow is the same as the length of your foot.

On average, you breathe 23,000 times a day.

We humans do not see with our eyes—we see with our brains. The eyes are basically the cameras of the brain.

On average, you speak almost 5,000 words a day—although almost 80% of speaking is self-talk (talking to yourself).

brain, *noun*

The portion of the vertebrate central nervous system that is enclosed within the cranium, continuous with the spinal cord, and composed of gray matter and white matter. It is the primary center for the regulation and control of bodily activities, receiving and interpreting sensory impulses, and transmitting information to the muscles and body organs. It is also the seat of consciousness, thought, memory, and emotion.

Isn't the human brain fantastic? You and I each have one of these remarkable things, but have no idea of all the ways it functions to keep us alive and allows us to live the lives we do.

While there are many complexities of the brain, I am only going to talk about a couple main topics here, as they relate to who we *really* are, what we want and how to use this brain to get some results.

Your brain is made up of two sides, the left and the right, that each has its own specific duties. You have a dominant side of your brain, just like some of us are left-handed and some are right-handed. There are a few of us that use our brains equally, just like there are some ambidextrous people who can write with both their left and right hands.

The right side of your brain controls muscles on the left side of your body and the left side of your brain controls muscles on the right side of your body. Also, sensory information from the left side of your body crosses over to the right side of your brain and information from the right side of your body crosses over to the left side of your brain. Therefore, damage to one side of the brain will affect the opposite side of the body.

Each hemisphere of the brain is dominant for certain behaviors. For example, it appears that the right brain is dominant for spatial abilities, face recognition, visual imagery, music and art. The right brain is the creative part. *Right brainers* tend to go into jobs that require creativity and visual imagery. Musicians, artists, actors, athletes, psychics and mediums are some of the careers of right brainers.

The left brain may be more dominant for calculations, math and logical abilities. The left brain typically likes numbers and can strategize and figure things out. Computer programmers, scientists, bankers and lawyers would most always be left brain dominant people.

Remember our experiment with remote viewing? When you calmed your mind and relaxed, what you were doing was relaxing your left brain. *The Voice*, which is constantly narrating your life, is in your left brain. The part of you that was able to remote view and connect with the past, present, future, as well as your deceased friends in the hereafter, is your right brain. Just as *The Voice* lives in your left brain, your *Soul Self* inhabits your right brain.

I encourage you to watch a video by scientist Jill Bolte Taylor, a left brain analytical person, who had suffered a massive stroke. A blood vessel exploded in the left hemisphere of her brain and as the blood filled her left brain, she witnessed her speech, logic and reasoning abilities shutting down. She tried to pick up a business card and call a colleague for help but when she looked at the card she just saw black dots and couldn't differentiate what she was looking at. She couldn't figure out how to move her arm to dial the phone. In time, the left brain kicked in enough so she was able to get help for herself.

However, most of the time she was alert and awake in her right brain and the experience seems remarkable. As her left brain was shutting down, Jill felt *one with the universe*, that she was connected to everything that is and ever was. What she witnessed was only beauty, peace and love. It was a place that she is certain all of us can get to, if we can just practice putting our left brain on hold for a while. To see this incredible video please go to WeDontDie.com/JillBolteTaylor.html.

Just like in remote viewing, when you can learn to quiet your left brain, you can have access to the magic of the universe, which actually isn't magic at all, it is reality. *The Voice* in your head and your left brain are responsible for you believing that you are separate from others and they will continually try to convince you that what you experience in life is reality, when it is really a grand illusion.

The Intelligence of the Human Body

*There is more wisdom in your body
than in your deepest philosophy."*
~ Friedrich Nietzsche

You are living in one amazing energy vehicle, I can tell you! Your body is not just any old vehicle. You currently own one of the highest performance vehicles in the world, even if you think you need a little repair! I work with race car teams and I know that the body you live in is a Porsche, a Lamborghini, a Ferrari, an Aston Martin, a Bentley, or a Maserati. With all its intricate details and performance abilities, your vehicle outperforms the world's most expensive cars. In fact, your body is priceless; it is literally impossible to get the parts needed to keep your body on the road forever.

We are often not aware of this high performance machine we live in and so we don't treat it like one. We don't always give it the right kind of fuel it needs, exercise it often enough, keep it in good repair, or keep it off the road when it needs a rest. We'll get into that shortly.

Did you feel excitement when you did the exercise in remote viewing? I hope so. Amazing that our minds can see images in a magazine we haven't opened yet or elements of an object on your friend's coffee table a thousand miles away, isn't it? Well, I hope you are sitting down for this: *Your body has the same incredible ability that your mind does.*

Applied Kinesiology and Muscle Testing

Applied Kinesiology is a fairly new branch of science, which was developed by doctors, chiropractors and acupuncturists in the United States and is amazingly efficient at balancing the body so that it can return to excellent health, energy and emotional strength. It stands apart from any other type of health technology largely due to its use of *muscle testing*.

The basis of Applied Kinesiology is that the body is like a piece of electrical equipment that is controlled by an incredibly complex computer, our brain. Our brains are continually in communication with each of the 639 muscles in our bodies.

If a muscle is electrically in balance, it is possible to measure a constant electrical signal from the brain to that muscle and back again. However, when the body is overstressed (due to a chemical, emotional, structural, or electrical cause), the electrical signals in one or more muscles go weak.

This is the basis of muscle testing, the main tool used in applied kinesiology. For example, if a person has a particular muscle in their *arm out of balance*, then they will not be able to hold their arm in a certain position when the kinesiologist applies pressure to it. If you and I were doing this experiment together, we would stand face to face. I would lift my right arm parallel to the ground and keep it strong. You would take a couple of fingers and try to push down on my right wrist. If I were to say, "My name is Sandra Champlain," and pushed down on my wrist, my arm muscle would stay strong and you would not be able to push it down. If I were to say, "My name is Mickey Mouse," my arm muscle would become weak and you could push it down very easily.

Psychiatrist Dr. David R. Hawkins, author of *Power vs. Force: The Hidden Determinants of Human Behavior*, did some experiments to test the validity of this theory. In one experiment, Dr. Hawkins put a thousand people in a room, each with a sealed envelope. Half the room was given organic Vitamin C and the other half a packet of NutraSweet (an artificial sugar substitute made with aspartame). None of the participants were aware of the content of their envelope. Each person was tested using muscle testing. The result was that half of the room went weak while the other half stayed strong. The 500 people who went weak were holding the envelope with NutraSweet and the 500 who stayed strong had the organic Vitamin C. Dr. Hawkins' experiments have proven our bodies' natural ability to be the ultimate truth detector.

Dowsing

Everything has an energy vibration, whether it's the sound of our voice, invisible radio waves, the book or device currently at your fingertips. Even your fingertips carry a vibration within them, as your tiny molecules contain atoms, the atoms contain protons, neutrons and electrons, which contain quarks, that are made of strings of invisible, vibrating energy.

Dowsing is an art that any of us can learn, to use our body to pick up the subtle energy fields of virtually anything you can imagine. You may have a picture in your mind of an old-timer walking around with a wooden stick or branch with a V on one end or a pair of *divining rods*, looking for an underground water supply to dig a well.

Several years ago, I took a course on dowsing, after doing my share of investigation on the Internet. I traveled to a small town near Augusta, Georgia and met Joey and Jill Korn. They offered a weekend retreat in their home. I have to be truthful, I did not read the course explanation, but I liked the looks of Joey and Jill, they seemed normal enough, the price was right and I wanted to look for underground water. However, the workshop was much more than I could have anticipated.

Several students gathered at their beautiful, home on the lake. It was a great location and the other students were wonderful. Joey and Jill brought in food and wine and we all joined in cooking and washing dishes during the weekend. Everybody was especially excited to find out that I was a chef and I had some fun cooking *Beer Can Chicken* with Joey.

The first day we learned a lot about dowsing, tracing back to the people that dowsed years and years ago. We learned about the divining rods or the branches that people often used. All along I assumed that somehow these tools were necessary and magical. It was then that I was told that we are the magical ones; like in kinesiology, our bodies can pick up the subtle energy vibrations around us and we then can unconsciously signal the rods or the piece of wood to move.

We each received a set of dowsing rods from Joey. (You can see a picture of them at Dowsers.com) They are thin copper tubes about four inches long with what seemed to be radio antennas on the end. We each did what we could to steady the rods and hold them in front of us, pointing forward. We were instructed to say, out loud, "Rods, this is the neutral position." (We were training the rods!) Then, we had to make the rods move so that each tip pointed out, parallel to our bodies. One tip pointed left, one pointed right, both were a full ninety degrees from where they started out. "Rods, this is the position when I am standing over an underground stream of water," we each told our rods.

With dowsing rods in hand, we headed outside. Joey dowsed and found an underground stream and each of us took our turn stepping onto this patch of grass. We held the rods in the parallel position and told the rods, "This is what an underground stream feels like." We all looked foolish and began aimlessly walking around trying to keep our hands and rods neutral and just waiting for something to take place. We were told to have the *intention* that our bodies could sense the streams. We were to try to keep our minds quiet and try not to think (sound familiar?). Can I tell you how silly we all looked? Ten grown adults walking around with copper tubes in our hands. I tried to be serious and not laugh, but then it *happened*. As I walked, my rods opened all by themselves! It was a weird feeling, yet so cool! I stepped back, away from the supposed *underground stream* and the rods closed back up again. I stepped forward and, again, they opened. I was now a dowser! We walked around his backyard for several minutes until each of us found some underground streams and felt comfortable using our dowsing rods.

We went back into the house for more lecture and practice. We learned that *everything vibrates with energy*. We dowsed the television, refrigerator, clock radios and the microwave oven. The rods opened and closed, then opened again, the closer we got to the electrical item, due to the positive and negative currents in fields of energy.

We then started dowsing people! There is a band of energy that emanates out of each one of us. Have you heard of *chakras*? I remember once hearing about auras and the chakra system that supposedly we each have, allowing us to produce waves of energy. Now, here in Georgia, I was picking up that subtle energy with these rods. We found that we could manipulate our energy fields. If we thought a sad thought, our energy was detected close to our bodies. If we thought a happy thought or recalled a favorite memory, our energy field would grow much, much larger, often fifteen feet away from ourselves! This was a fun and very, very cool experiment.

The streams of energy that come from us start at the top of our heads and run to the base of our spine. No chakra energy is sent out from our legs or arms, just from our core bodies. Many say the history of chakras can be traced back to the *Upanishads* (ancient Hindu scriptures that established the core teachings of Vedanta) which are believed to have been passed down orally for approximately a thousand years before being written down for the first time between 1200–900 BC. It is believed that we each have seven of these chakras, which you may imagine as fans, twirling inside us and blowing energy out of us. These invisible chakras are said to produce our *life force* as human beings.

Our dowsing master, Joey Korn, referred to our bodies as *energy vehicles*. Our invisible, energy vehicle surrounds every moment of our lives. It is highly concentrated about six feet in front of us and about four feet behind us. It grows larger when we feel good and retreats when we feel bad.

Have you heard of the *Law of Attraction* and the *Art of Manifestation*? There has been much controversy about the book, *The Secret*. Some people read it or watched the movie and hoped that they could think certain thoughts or envision life a certain way and then it would magically come true. I enjoyed *The Secret* but think some people are missing a certain element to have their dreams fulfilled, that element is *action*. I, the chef, will share the precise ingredients and the recipe for success so that you may have the results you'd like in life. It is easier than you may think, but it does require some work.

When we dowsed the human energy vehicle (also known as each other), we charted a certain pattern of lines that extended from us. This map or system of energy lines coming from our bodies is the identical pattern of the *Tree of Life* that is in the Kabbalah. Kabbalistic knowledge was believed to be an integral part of Judaism's oral law given by God to Moses on Mount Sinai around the 13th century BC, though some say that Kabbalah began with Adam. It is believed that the Tree of Life is the universal energy out of which all things are created.

Joey taught us *applied kinesiology* (which I described earlier) and we were able to do the muscle tests to detect areas of the room that held a negative energy. Have you ever gone into a room or been around a person and felt *bad vibes*? That is the kind of energy we were looking for. We could also pick up these areas of invisible negative energy fields with our dowsing rods.

Joey explained that energy is energy and will always exist. We have positive, negative and neutral energy. Neutral and negative energy can be shifted to positive energy. "How?" you ask. Saying a prayer the proper way can turn energy positive!

The Power of Prayer

I grew up Roman Catholic and was taught to pray. As you know, I questioned my faith and questioned what is real and what is man-made. Prayer seemed like a good idea at some point in my life, (like when I really wanted something), but it wasn't something I regularly did.

While at the dowsing retreat, Joey spoke to us about the power of prayer. Over lunch we talked about the importance of *blessing* food or saying a prayer before we eat. Just before we ate our meals Joey asked us to *dowse* our plates of food to detect if there was any energy radiating from them. Raw fruits and vegetables seemed to have some energy coming from them while cooked food had none.

Just then, Joey said a prayer and blessed the plates of food, holding the palms of his hands over them (by the way, it's not necessary to do this hand motion, but it seemed to be appropriate). He said something like "God, if it be Your will, please bless this food, please put good life force into it so that we may be strong, healthy and feel good by eating it. We thank you. Amen."

He spoke briefly and to the point. I learned that the actual words or the hand gestures we do have nothing to do with the actual blessing or healing. Healing all comes from our *intention* behind our words. To effectively pray or bless something or someone, you must *feel* with all your being, that you want that change to happen. Guess what? When we dowsed our plates of foods after Joey's prayer, the rods showed positive energy. Oh, forgot to tell you, we trained the rods to cross each other like an X whenever we found positive energy.

The fun didn't stop there. After lunch we started making people stand in places of negative energy, making sure they were weak by doing the arm test. We then had them take their watch, ring, or glasses off. We blessed their rings, watches and glasses. When the people put those items back on, they became strong! The skeptic in me feels the need to tell you that we did *double-blind* tests. People were not aware if they were standing in a negative energy field and time and time again, we proved that blessing or praying for an object or a person worked and they became strong.

When I got back to my house I decided to do a science project with dowsing and blessing. I had gone on a trip to Costa Rica and brought back a set of eight bottles of hot sauce that I was going to give to my chef friend, Pieter, who loves hot sauce. They were all in the same size bottles, just with different labels. For fun, I lifted a random bottle, did not look at it and blessed it with all my might! I put healing energy into that bottle of hot sauce. Without looking, I put a little piece of tape on the bottom of the bottle, so I could eventually know what bottle I blessed. I lowered the bottled and mixed it up with the seven other bottles, still with my eyes closed. I then placed the bottles on the floor and separated them by eight inches or so. I pulled out my handy dowsing rods and had the intention of finding the bottle that I blessed. There was no movement over any of the bottles except for one. An X was formed with the dowsing rods over one bottle. I lifted the bottle and it had the piece of tape on it. There is no question in my mind that prayer works!

I have often heard of people consciously creating a *safe bubble of energy* or *light* around them, visualizing a glowing pink or white bubble that protects them. I believe what is happening then, is that a prayer is being accepted by the universe and an invisible field of good energy then surrounds that person or thing. Yes, silently I bless every airplane I get on, visualizing a bubble of loving energy around it to keep all of us passengers safe and infuse us all with love and good things! I'm sure *The Voice* in your head might be commenting about me right now!

My friend, Jessie told me about the book, *Science and Health with Key to the Scriptures*, written back in the late 1800s by a woman named Mary Baker Eddy. She explained that reading the book leads us to know that we are perfect, spiritual creatures and that miraculous healings are possible when we think from this view of our perfection. Jessie has witnessed miracles in her own life and encourages the *testimonial* section of the book be read first. I shared this information with a friend of mine who shared it with a friend of his who was painfully suffering from Stage IV (four) colon cancer. Over the course of a month, his wife read *Science and Health* to him. The latest tests now show that this man has no trace of cancer in his body! Did reading the book cure him? There is no way to know for sure. However, we know the power of the mind and the power of prayer. I personally do believe that anything is possible and this book is a free download.

To be on the receiving end of being blessed or having been prayed for can be life saving. There have been thousands of scientific tests done about the power of prayer and the healing that occurs in groups of people who are *prayed for* as opposed to those who are not. Research shows that those who get prayed for, heal more than people who are not prayed for. You, at any time, could put your hands on a person, say a prayer for them with the intention of their healing and send positive energy to them. For more information on the powers of the mind (medical intuition, remote viewing and distant healing) I encourage you to read both *Limitless Mind* by Russell Targ and *Your Eternal Self* by R. Craig Hogan, PhD. In those pages you will learn about some of the incredible research done and much more evidence of the power of your mind.

Messages in Water

I stumbled across Dr. Masaru Emoto's *Hidden Messages in Water* when I was watching the movie *What the Bleep Do We Know* several years ago.

Dr. Emoto is a Japanese author and scientist, best known for his claims that human consciousness effects the molecular structure of water. I became intrigued with him, did as much reading as I could and watched every video I could find.

Dr. Emoto's first experiment that I watched showed him looking under a microscope at water droplets. He set out to compare Tokyo's water with water from of a beautiful waterfall.

He froze small droplets of water from each water supply and watched them under a microscope as they began to melt. The water droplets from the waterfall produced images of perfect snowflakes, as they began to thaw. The droplets from the city water in Tokyo resulted in very ugly, strange patterns as they melted. Clearly there was a difference.

Dr. Emoto searched for neutral water that would not show a negative or positive pattern. He began to use distilled water for his experiments and noticed that no image formed as these droplets melted. This was the neutral starting point for the amazing new experiment to come.

He put distilled water in bottles and wrote words on each bottle. Words like *love, happiness,* and *faith.* On some bottles he wrote the words *hate, war,* and *anger.* He then took the water and placed droplets from each bottle onto trays and froze them. When the droplets began defrosting, the droplets from the positive words formed beautiful snowflakes-like images, perfectly symmetrical and gorgeous. The droplets from the negative words showed very uneven patterns, almost disturbing. I knew that our words had power, but did not realize that written words could make this amount of difference.

The experiment went on to have bottles of distilled water around pieces of music. Each time the water spent time with beautiful sounds, the frozen water droplets formed gorgeous crystals. On the flip side, when the water was subjected to rough sounding music, the shape of the droplets became disturbing. So, be careful what you listen to!

My favorite experiment of Dr. Emoto's was the one in which he invited people in Japan to participate. He asked families to cook a pot of rice, then take the cooked rice and divide it into two glass jars. One jar would be placed in one room, the second jar in another room. Daily, the family members would talk to the rice. In the first room they would praise the rice, love the rice and speak nice words to the rice. In the other room, they scolded the rice, hated the rice and were angry at the rice. Over the course of the month, the *loved* rice turned a golden brown color and produced a sweet, nutty smell when the jar was opened. In the other room the *hated* rice turned black and smelled foul and rotten. Have you ever heard of someone who talks to their plants say that they grow much better? I believe this is the same phenomena.

Interesting, isn't it? The power that our words, thoughts, music and intentions have? If we can have this kind of effect on droplets of water, just think what impact we can have on our bodies and on the things around us. 60% of our bodies are water, right?

The months before my dad's death held some very difficult moments. One thing he mentioned often was that he did not want to be *alone with his thoughts* and that he appreciated the time my siblings or I could be with him. As positive as he was, he was human and I can only imagine he suffered from fear (of death or the future) as much as from the physical pain. I showed Dad the documentary about Dr. Emoto's experiments with water droplets and rice and he was amazed! I brought Dad a photo of two jars of rice, one black and one white, from Dr. Emoto's experiment. While he was alone, he would see the images of rice on his wall to remind him of the power of thinking loving and positive thoughts and to discourage him from thinking negatively.

The power of our words, thoughts, blessings and prayers are astonishing. I believe that each of us has the healing powers of the spiritual beings we follow. Up to this point we have not been aware of it, but it is now the time to wake up. There is much that our minds and bodies can energetically detect and impact.

Here is a gift from master dowser Joey Korn. It is a way for you to bless the energies in your life:

> *In my dowsing research over the past thirteen years, I have found that the most powerful way to keep the energies around you, in your home or office, balanced and beneficial is to keep your own energies balanced and beneficial, as well as those who share the space with you. This includes the Earth energies associated with what dowsers call geopathic stress. I've devised a very simple blessing formula to help you to integrate the blessing process easily into your life. You can also use it to bless others, your home, and objects you wear.*
>
> *If you will include these five components in your blessings, and do so often, you or whomever you bless will stay energetically balanced, as will most of the energies around you. Staying balanced will help you heal and help you react more appropriately to issues and circumstances in your life. Negative thoughts and emotions are what I call "anti-blessings." They have the exact opposite effect as blessings. Turn your anti-blessings into blessings. And turn your prayers from pleading into beckoning, asking God to bless you with energy to help you to accomplish whatever want to in your life.*

The Five Components of this Simple Blessing Process are:

1. Address the Divine in some way.
2. Ask to be blessed or charged with energy.
3. Make a statement of what you want to accomplish.
4. Express gratitude.
5. Close the blessing in some way.

Each component is important. The first three are to make it work; the next two are for you. It is important to feel and express gratitude and to turn our blessings over to a Higher Power.

So here's a simple blessing:

"Dear God (or however you address the Divine),
Please bless (or charge) me (or someone else or an object you
    wear) with energy,
To bring healing and balance to my/his/her/our complete being,
Physically, emotionally, mentally, and spiritually,
Thank you,
Amen."

Joey Korn and his wife, Jill are amazing, fun and loving people. Their website is: Dowsers.com

How to Maintain Our High-Performance Energy Vehicles

Take care of your body. It's the only place you have to live.

~ Jim Rohn

Like the high performance Lamborghini, there are things we must do to keep our energy vehicles looking good and performing their best. Of course we must keep them clean, but we must also give them the best fuel, oils and lubricants. We must have routine service performed on them, we must keep them in good running order by driving them, we must not over stress them and we must park them from time to time.

If the body be feeble, the mind will not be strong.

~Thomas Jefferson

Our bodies are amazing and, as much as we all know that we should take care of them, we often don't. I won't go on too long about this, as we all know what we should do to keep ourselves healthy. I want to give you a new reason to maintain good health. The healthier you are, the more effectively you can use this invisible life force that you are part of. The healthier you are, the better you are at remote viewing, the better your chakras are spinning and generating energy, the more your thoughts and prayers have an impact on people and things around you and ultimately, the faster you can have some of your dreams come true. I honestly mean that. In chapter 14 you will be given some action steps to have some of the things you desperately want come true. The healthier you are, the more energy your vehicle creates, combined with the other practices we will soon discuss, the faster your dreams will come true.

Don't take this the wrong way, I do not mean that if you have forty pounds to lose and are a smoker, that you cannot have a dream come true until you lose the weight and stop smoking. The moment you change some habits and behaviors, your energy shifts toward the positive, allowing results to start happening. All we humans can do is the best we can. Some days you might need a little compassion and forgiveness towards yourself and simply recommit to doing your best.

Please be gentle on your body, for it is a magnificent creation. Do not blame it if you don't like your weight or shape or the length of your nose. It is that negative voice in your head that needs to be silenced. Practicing remote viewing, meditation and being in the present moment will help turn off *The Voice*. Anytime you can get 100% into the present moment will help, even if only for a short while. Practice, practice, practice and just do the best you can.

> *"Games lubricate the body and the mind."*
>
> ~ Benjamin Franklin

I am not sure if the *games* Ben Franklin was talking about were physical games like tennis and basketball or if he meant games for the mind, such as crossword puzzles or tic-tac-toe. There is more than enough evidence that physical exercise strengthens the body while mental exercises strengthen the mind. A friend of mine does a daily *WOG* (part walking, part jogging) while wearing headphones and listening to an audio book. Seems like a great way to exercise the body and mind at the same time, doesn't it?

Tune Up Your Brain

I have had several opportunities to learn from the worlds' leading brain doctor, Dr. Daniel Amen, author of many books including *Change Your Brain, Change Your Body* and *Change Your Brain, Change Your Life.* He gives excellent advice on caring for the most powerful, three pound super-computer that controls your energy vehicle, your brain. The information below is some of the advice Dr.Amen wrote in an article called *Seven Ways to Optimize Your Brain and Your Life.* The full article can be found at WeDontDie.com/DrAmen.html and the amazing Dr. Amen's website is AmenClinics.com.

Protect Your Brain

Protecting the brain from injury, pollution, sleep deprivation and stress is the first step to optimizing its function. The brain is very soft, while the skull is really hard. Inside the skull there are many sharp bony ridges. Several brain areas are especially vulnerable to trauma, especially the parts involved with memory, learning and mood stability. In order to be your best, it is essential to protect your brain from injury. Wear your seatbelt when you're in a car and wear a helmet when you ride a bicycle, motorcycle, or go snowboarding. Make sure children wear helmets.

Dr. Amen's brain imaging research has shown that many chemicals are toxic to brain function. Alcohol, drugs, nicotine, too much caffeine and many medications decrease blood flow to the brain. When blood flow is decreased the brain cannot work efficiently. It is hard to be your best when brain activity is diminished. Stay away from substances known to be toxic or those that decrease brain activity.

In a similar way, sleep deprivation also decreases brain activity and limits access to learning, memory and concentration. A recent brain imaging study showed that people who consistently slept less than seven hours had overall less brain activity. Sleep problems are very common in people who struggle with their thoughts and emotions. Getting enough sleep every night is essential to brain function.

Scientists have only recently discovered how stress negatively impacts brain function. Stress hormones have been shown in animals to be directly toxic to memory centers. Brain cells can die with prolonged stress. Managing stress effectively is essential to good brain function.

Feed Your Brain

The fuel you feed your brain has a profound effect on how it functions. Lean protein, complex carbohydrates and foods rich in omega-3 fatty acids (large cold water fish, such as tuna and salmon, walnuts, Brazil nuts, olive oil and canola oil) are essential to brain function. Unfortunately, the great American diet is filled with simple sugars and simple carbohydrates, causing many people to feel emotional, sluggish, spacey and distracted. Start the day with a healthy breakfast that includes protein, such as eggs, lean meat, or dairy products.

Many people struggle with energy and mental clarity after lunch. Dr. Amen has found that eliminating all simple carbohydrates at lunch (sugar, white bread, or other products made from white flour such as bagels and white pasta, potatoes and rice) can make a dramatic difference in energy and focus in the afternoon. An additional benefit of skipping sugar and simple carbohydrates at lunch is that most people do not feel hunger until dinnertime. He also believes taking a 100%

vitamin and mineral supplement is important. Many people do not eat like they should on a regular basis.

Kill the ANTs (Automatic Negative Thoughts)

The thoughts that go through your mind, moment by moment, have a significant impact on how your brain works. Research by Mark George, MD and his colleagues at the National Institutes of Health demonstrated that happy, hopeful thoughts had an overall calming effect on the brain, while negative thoughts inflamed brain areas often involved with depression and anxiety. Your thoughts really matter. Dr. Amen calls them ANTs, I call it, *The Voice*. James Allen, author of the short book, *As A Man Thinketh*, speaks beautifully of this fact.

Dr. Amen firmly believes that once you learn about your thoughts, you can choose to think good thoughts and feel good or you can choose to think bad thoughts and feel lousy. You can train your thoughts to be positive and hopeful or you can just allow them to be negative and upsetting. How you feel is up to you! You can learn how to change your thoughts and optimize your brain. One way to learn how to change your thoughts is to notice when they are negative and talk back to them. If you can correct negative thoughts, you take away their power over you. When you think a negative thought without challenging it, your mind believes it and your brain reacts to it.

Work Your Brain

Your brain is like a muscle. The more you use it, the more you can use it. Every time you learn something new your brain makes a new connection. Learning enhances blood flow and activity in the brain. If you go for long periods without learning something new you start to lose some of the connections in the brain and begin to struggle more with memory and learning. Albert Einstein said that if a person studies a subject for just fifteen minutes a day, in a year he would be an expert and in five years he could be a national expert. Learning is good for your brain.

HOMEWORK ASSIGNMENT

Begin to see yourself as a soul with a body,
rather than a body with a soul.

~ Wayne Dyer

Give gratitude for the tremendous, self-contained, high performance vehicle that you live in. One that generates its own electricity and only requires a little food, a little water and a little movement to sustain it for many, many years.

Enjoy the pleasures that only the body can give you through the senses, such as: the warmth of being cuddled up on a soft bed with the person or furry pet of your choice; the sound of your favorite music or birds singing on a Spring day; the smell of hot cinnamon rolls in the oven or the scent of your favorite person's cologne; the sight of a double rainbow after a rainstorm or the flickering of a candle's fire; the taste of your favorite flavor of ice cream or the tartness of a lemon.

Chapter 12

Riding the Emotional Roller Coaster

*At the end of your life, it's friendships, emotions, and thoughts
that you take with you, rather than what's in your bank
account. So, even though people don't have a lot here, they are
a lot richer in many ways and we can learn from that.*

~ Sebastian Vettel, race car driver,
Formula One World Champion, b. 1987

roller coaster, *noun*

**A small gravity railroad, especially in an amusement
park, having a train with open cars that moves along a
high, sharply winding trestle built with steep inclines
that produce sudden, speedy plunges for thrill-seeking
passengers.**

*You notice that off in the distance a big, long line is forming.
Almost like the line that forms for a really popular ride at an
amusement park. There is a big, flashing sign overhead that
says, "This Way to Planet Earth." You slowly approach, having
no idea what this Planet Earth is all about.*

You make your way to the end of the line and see a man,
standing alone, patiently waiting. Casually, you ask, "Excuse
me, sir, what is this line for?" This guy can barely get the
words out, he is so excited. "Oh my goodness, don't you know?
Didn't anybody tell you? Everybody is doing it! It's Earth,
Planet Earth! There is excitement to be had, adventures to go
on, emotions to feel."

Our little soul coming to Planet Earth was so excited, wasn't he? Just think, we were that soul once and our wish came true. We get to be living here on Planet Earth right now! Emotions can feel really good, can't they? I can think of the time I got to fly upside down in an airplane for the first time, I had the biggest smile on my face as I experienced the fun! I remember all those Christmas Eves when I could barely fall asleep because of the excitement of Santa Claus bringing me toys while I slept. I think of the times I've laughed so hard that I started crying and the muscles in my face started hurting because I smiled so much. I remember the love I felt sitting in a movie theater and holding my grandmother's hand and I remember the good feeling of my muscles being massaged after working very hard at the racetrack. Yes, these feel-good emotions make it easy to love being on Planet Earth.

But then there are the others, the times of fear, sadness, rejection, jealousy, grief, regret and anger and the times of pain and suffering. These are the times we forget that it was us that wanted to come to Planet Earth in the first place.

Our emotions do feel like a roller coaster ride, don't they? So many ups and downs, one minute you feel great and the next you feel horrible. Emotions seem to have a life of their own. One minute they don't exist, then they show up and you feel them, then they disappear as abruptly as they arrived. There are good emotions we want to hang on to and negative emotions we want to get rid of.

The fastest way to get rid of an emotion is to experience it fully, really feel it. Remember the expression, "What you resist, persists?" Emotions are that way. If you are feeling sadness and try to change it into something else, you cannot. Sadness will sneak back in when you least expect it. The next time you want to get rid of an emotion try this: feel it fully. If you feel sad then cry. Cry your eyes out if necessary. Feel where in the body you are experiencing the emotion. Then, only after you have experienced it fully, will it move out of your system.

As good and as bad as they can feel, I want you to know that emotions do two important things. First, experiencing emotion causes *soul growth* and that's a good thing. We can have faith that great things are on the horizon because we have felt a myriad of emotions on Earth. I'm sure the negative emotions even give us extra credit points when we get to Heaven. The second thing experiencing emotions does is provide results in our lives. Let me explain.

Remember my experience of dowsing human energy patterns? The stronger the feeling of joy, the larger the energy that radiates from our body (our energy vehicle). I believe that these strings of invisible energy travel outside of us sooner or later and find their way back to us, like a boomerang. Energy leaves us as strings of vibrating light and comes back to us as strings of vibrating light, this time in forms of *matter*.

For example, imagine a guy wants a new cell phone. Although the old one works, it is slow, it has tape holding it together, it doesn't have all the features that the new ones have and this poor guy feels embarrassed carrying it around. Money is tight for him and he cannot justify buying a new phone when the old one works. Embarrassment and being jealous of what other people have won't attract a new cell phone to this guy. Negative emotions won't cause any good energy to be radiated from his system.

What he must do is try to think about reasons he wants that cell phone. He must create and feel *desire*. He begins to think "A new cell phone will make it easier for me to stay in touch with people I love, I can imagine their smiling faces while talking to me on the phone, I can access the Internet and stay more connected to my business and help my employees make more money to support their families and live better lives." It is important that he start feeling grateful for cell phone technology and the phone he's already had and feel gratitude for the new one as if he has already received it and is now using it for the good things.

Can you now imagine the kind of energy that he is putting out into the world? Those vibrating strings have a sneaky and miraculous way of coming back to those who send them out. It may not be the very next day, but he might get a special offer in the mail for a discounted cell phone or a relative might get a deal and want to put him on his plan to save them both money.

I cannot give you scientific proof for this theory and probably won't be able to until my day comes to cross the bridge into Heaven. I do know that I have produced some incredible results for myself and so have others, by using this formula. I'll give you more details about that in next chapters.

Everything we can do in heaven, we can do on Earth.
It just takes longer because of the illusion of time.

It seems the results are instantaneous and show up quickly in Heaven, as there is no such thing as time in the Hereafter. What we wish for gets created in a blink of an eye. We want a mansion, a rainbow, or a hot fudge sundae? We just think it and it is there for us to enjoy.

While this may sound like something from the movies, imagine for a moment that it is very possible to have those things we really want appear in front of us, here on Earth. Our dreams definitely can come true and we can cause things to appear.

How are you doing as you read this? Are you listening or has *The Voice* in your head started telling you that Sandra is getting a little *out there, a little weird and into some of this woo-woo stuff*? *The Voice* does not want you to remember who you really are, remember that! This will all fall into place and will actually feel good for you to do some of the result producing actions, so just sit tight!

Don't let *The Voice* make you forget who you really are! As a reminder, you are an eternal soul here having a human experience. You can remote view, you can *see* pictures inside a magazine before opening it. You can connect with loved ones that have passed away. You live in a miraculous world that allows you to travel in a high performance energy vehicle. The planet you live on is only one of 50 billion in our galaxy, which is only one galaxy out of 100 billion galaxies in the universe. We are made up of molecules and if you put a camera inside a molecule, there would be nothing to see, its contents invisible. We truly are miraculous beings.

The difference between snapping your fingers in Heaven and having a new cell phone show up and snapping your fingers on Earth and it taking a little time for that cell phone to show up has to do with four factors:

Time
Emotions
The Voice
Other people's agendas

Here on Earth, we have the illusion of time. What seems like a second in Heaven may take 6 months here on Earth. Our emotions are the fuel behind whatever it is we wish to create. Be forewarned: it is *impossible* to emit a full charge of happy, grateful, desire-filled energy 24 hours a day. We also have *The Voice* in our head, trying to convince us that we are not special, not worthy and it does not let us remember who we really are. Last, we have other people's energy vehicles (their wishes, dreams, and desires) getting caught in traffic with our own.

A Cherokee Legend

An old Cherokee is teaching his grandson about life. "A fight is going on inside me," he said to the boy.

"It is a terrible fight and it is between two wolves. One is evil— he is anger, envy, sorrow, regret, greed, arrogance, self-pity, guilt, resentment, inferiority, lies, false pride, superiority, and ego." He continued, "The other is good—he is joy, peace, love, hope, serenity, humility, kindness, benevolence, empathy, generosity, truth, compassion, and faith. The same fight is going on inside you—and inside every other person, too."

The grandson thought about it for a minute and then asked his grandfather, "Which wolf will win?"

The old Cherokee simply replied, "The one you feed."

High Octane, Result-Producing Emotions

We need the best fuel for the best results. The following emotions will supercharge your dreams into becoming reality: desire, hope, faith, excitement, enthusiasm, love and gratitude. It is critical to first establish what you really, really want in life then muster up every bit of desire so you want it very badly. I want you living in this miraculous world knowing your dream is not only possible, but it's coming your way! I want you on the edge of your seat and excited about it. I want you loving your life, the people in it and the dreams that are coming true. Most importantly, the grand daddy of all the result producing emotions is: gratitude. You must feel grateful for that which you already have and that which you wish to receive, as if it has already come true. I have an audio to help you with this called The Breakthrough Visualization. You can listen or download it at WeDontDie. com/BreakthroughAudio.html.

Cheap Fuel, Poor-Performance Emotions

There are some emotions that you want to try to avoid. This list of emotions causes your energy vehicle to stall, to be much, much smaller than it should be and causes it to send out mixed signals about what you want, preventing you from producing the results you really want in your life. The emotions to avoid are: jealousy, hatred, revenge, greed, anger, anxiety and fear. I know it is not possible to avoid fear but there is one way to the other side of fear and that is straight through it. Having *courage* and doing the thing you are most afraid of, can produce great results, fast.

Programming Your GPS and Getting on the Road

You need to know where you are going before you travel to a destination, right? The same thing goes for fulfilling your dreams. You need to have a clear vision and desire of what you want and how it will feel when you get there. There are many *experts* who talk about achieving goals this way, although one thing they often forget to mention is that you have to be sitting in the driver's seat, turn the car on and begin to drive! I learned about being a human GPS from extraordinary author Mike Dooley, creator of the daily *Notes From The Universe*, available at TUT.com.

It is great to visualize, to use emotions, to be grateful, but you and I must take conscious action toward making our dreams become reality as well. In our cell phone example above, you cannot sit at home and wait for a cell phone to appear. You must start investigating which one you want, have conversations with people about cell phone options and keep your eyes open for good deals. There is soul growth at stake here, so it is critical you do your part and take action toward making your dreams come true. Your emotions will be the fuel to help you get to your dreams, but it is vital that you start driving toward them as well.

However, when we travel by car, it is not always smooth sailing. We often have things that come up. We run into construction, or our vehicle malfunctions. Sometimes we have a passenger on board that needs something and takes us off our course. Below are the common roadblocks we experience, making it difficult to stay in a positive, result-producing emotional state.

Roadblock #1: Fear

I am sure that everyone can agree, fear stops us from having the things we want in life. We have fear of everything, don't we? Some of the most common are the fear of taking action, fear of having conversations, fear of rejection, fear of the unknown, fear of what other people will think, fear of getting hurt and fear of failure.

Fear is a natural part of our lives. Fear can be a good thing, because it can literally save your life! It is appropriate to fear jumping off a cliff because you may hurt yourself or worse yet, kill yourself. Our basic sense of fear is responsible for our survival. That is a good thing.

However, we have all experienced some painful events in our lives, haven't we? *The Voice* remembers those events and creates fear in our minds so that we don't experience the pain again. For example, the first time you loved someone romantically, perhaps you were open and vulnerable and shared everything with them, with all of your heart. Then, maybe that person broke your heart. Deep inside you know that being open and vulnerable is necessary for any relationship to work, however you now experience a real fear and *The Voice* tells you that you should *never* be open and vulnerable again, because it can hurt too much if a relationship ends.

Can you see that this fear has been created by *The Voice*? We end up creating our own self-fulfilling prophecy. We ultimately create the pain that we are trying so desperately to avoid. If you are not open and vulnerable in a relationship, neither person experiences the deep level of connection that we know is part of a loving relationship. Sooner or later, the other person may leave and you may end up being heartbroken again. This unnecessary fear, created by *The Voice*, causes your worst nightmares to come true.

Anytime fear comes up in your life, take a look to see what you are afraid of. I bet that at some point in your past you experienced a pain or a failure and *The Voice* doesn't want you to make the same mistake twice. *The Voice* is not your friend (or foe for that matter). It is simply something we all have that keeps us from remembering who we really are and the power we have.

What do you want in your life? I mean really, really want? Could it be a new career or traveling to a far off land or maybe you want an intimate, wonderful relationship with a soul mate. Why don't you have that thing now? I am sure you can give me reasons like: "My current job is just fine," "I don't have the time to travel," or "I just haven't met the right person yet." While it's possible some of those things are true, I bet you that there is an underlying fear beneath one of those desires that is preventing you from having that dream come true. Could it be that you are scared to change jobs because you don't know if you would be successful in the new job? Could you be afraid of traveling because you have never ventured outside of this country, don't speak the language at your dream destination and are afraid of the unknown? Perhaps as much as you say you want a soul mate relationship, it is scary to be out there dating new people and you are afraid of getting your heart broken again.

The secret to achieving your wildest dreams is
to search for what makes you afraid and then go do it.

Taking this step is truly the answer to living a miraculous, result filled, dream life. Think of a time you were afraid to do something and did it anyway. You were courageous, weren't you? What results do you have in your life right now that you wouldn't have? I, myself, experience fear very often, constantly wondering what will happen and worrying about how things in my day will play out.

He who is brave is free.
~ Seneca, Roman philosopher, mid-1st century AD

Do you think creating this book was fear free? Hardly. I have been talking about writing a book for over five years. One day my Mom said, "Sandra, I am sick of hearing you talk about writing a book. Stop talking about it and just do it."

Those words of hers made me realize how scared I truly was. So, I decided to do a little research on book writing. I found *Rick Frishman* and his *Author 101 University* weekend training course. I signed up for it, booked my airline ticket to Las Vegas and hotel room. The fear kicked in on the way to the course. I was afraid of meeting other people, not being good enough and certainly believed that I was not good enough to be an author.

While at the course, I got the basics I needed to begin writing, but then I had to write a book proposal and let a prospective publisher know who I was, what my book was about and why I was writing it. I moved through this fear and did create the book proposal but my fear was at an all time high (my knees were weak, my heart was pounding and my hands were shaking) as I handed it to David Hancock, founder of Morgan James Publishing. I waited several weeks fearfully for a response, knowing that Morgan James only publishes just over one hundred of the five thousand book proposals that they receive each year. *The Voice* kept telling me not to get my hopes up. "Other people publish books, Sandra," it said, "you don't." My taking this action, regardless of the fear I felt, did produce a result. I got a call from the amazing Kristen Moeller who read my proposal and said, "Sandra, we want to publish you." Sometimes fear stops me, but this time it did not because I so desperately wanted to share with you the information you have been reading in *We Don't Die*.

One way to work through your fear and become courageous is to recognize the physical characteristics of fear. Often, you will feel your heart racing and your body shaking, even your knees feel shaky. Your hands may feel cold and sweaty, your mouth can get dry and throat tight, finding it difficult to get your words out. For me, I feel nauseous and like my heart is beating so fast that it may explode. Fear feels awful. When you can recognize the bodily sensations and realize that *The Voice* is trying to persuade you to be afraid based on some memory of your past, very often you can become courageous in that moment and take an action. A little side note here: fear and excitement feel the exact same way. We have the same bodily sensations when we are going on a ride at an amusement park or just before we are about to kiss that special someone for the first time. If you can convince yourself that you are really experiencing excitement, not fear, it may help.

There is no way to prevent the experience of fear. But here is something to realize: fear is only present *before* you do the thing you are afraid of. When you are in the midst of the action, doing the thing you were afraid of, fear is not present. Imagine being afraid to have a conversation with a person. We can spend weeks imagining the conversation and being afraid of what might or might not happen. It takes a long time before we work up the courage to pick up the phone and make the call. However, the moment you start talking and are in the action of actively speaking and listening to the other person, the fear is gone. What I am saying is, "Fear is useless." Unless it is used for your survival, experiencing fear is a waste of time. Go do something courageous today, will you? Your soul will grow *big time* and you will have an awesome result in your life.

I forgot to mention, the three main fears humans all share are death, failure and being alone. Your life and the lives of those people most important to you will never be the same because you now know that *We Don't Die*. You realize now that you can never die and failure is an illusion. Your *Soul Self* can never fail, because everything you experience is growth for your soul. Also, you are never, ever alone. Your invisible loved ones surround you now and you have many people who love you.

Roadblock #2: Suffering

Suffering prevents us from being able to experience positive emotions. Suffering occurs any time we think something should be one way and it turns another way. We suffer if we don't get a job we interviewed for or if a person we fall in love with doesn't show their love in return. We suffer most when we experience physical pain. When our bodies hurt and pain is present, it is nearly impossible to access the positive emotions that bring about positive results. There are, however, a few tools we can use. Three useful tools that my dad used when he was suffering from pain were laughter, gratitude and visual imagery.

Watching comedy movies, telling jokes, or sharing memories of fun times help create laughter. There are many books about laughter being the best medicine. I do believe that laughter does have healing benefits and I know that it causes endorphins to be released in the body, which helps pain subside.

Visual imagery also helps with pain. You can release pain through visual exercises you do in your mind, including quieting the mind. An excellent resource is *Jon Kabat-Zinn*, who is the founding director of the Stress Reduction Clinic and the Center for Mindfulness in Medicine, Health Care and Society at the University of Massachusetts Medical School. In his books, lectures and CDs, he teaches *Mindfulness*, a medically proven technique that can reduce pain, tension and anxiety in your body. More information can be found at MindfulnessCDs.com.

We suffer when we believe we are *victims*. We often don't like our job, our house, our friends, our family, or our bodies. We think we are too tall, too short, too thin, or should not have a certain ailment. We suffer when we don't have enough money and we don't have enough time. We suffer when things don't go the way we want them to go and we suffer when people are being different from how we want them to be.

The best cure for a *victim mentality* is to realize who you really are. It is time to stop listening to *The Voice* and allow your *Soul Self* to speak. You are a magnificent, eternal soul who is on Earth to learn lessons. The only way you can learn lessons and grow is to be in a world with pain, problems, frustrations and other people who each have their own agenda. When you are suffering, take a minute and believe that it was *you* who created this situation so that you could learn and grow from it. *The Voice* will try to convince you that this is not the truth. If you listen to *The Voice*, you will suffer and things will not ever change. You, my friend, are not a victim so please ask *The Voice* to stop complaining and trying to convince you that you are one.

The only way to have lasting results in your life is to become responsible for your life. Everything you have and you don't have in your life, right now, is because you created your life the way it is. You created it and you can change it. That may seem like good news or that may seem like bad news. Either way, knowing this is the first step to REAL POWER.

Roadblock #3: Other People

Don't you find other people often get in your way of being happy? Come on, be honest. Other people can often make us feel bad or ruin our days. How can we ever expect to be vibrating with a high level of miracle producing energy with other people around?

I am laughing as I write this because it really occurs to me that some people can give me an incredible amount of pleasure and others can cause me a huge amount of suffering. You know some of those people? Well, we'll get through this together.

In fact, let me remind you that the other people in our lives are necessary. Oh, that hurts to admit. How much do I love making other people wrong so I don't have to be responsible for my life? I do it all the time. It is fine to make people wrong, but I want you to know that doing so won't give you any real power in your life. Your soul won't grow and you'll probably have a few enemies.

What is the answer? If we take responsibility for everything that happens in our lives, we will see that we were responsible for having these people show up in our lives. Maybe they made a soul contract with you before you came to Planet Earth. You asked to learn patience and compassion? That person that really annoys you volunteered to be in your life, wasn't that generous of them? Now they are in your life on Earth, complain to you often, nothing is ever good enough for them and they constantly tell you that you are the problem and you should change.

It is easy to want to be right and put that person in their place, isn't it? Oh, how often we want to argue, don't we? Ah, but arguing and being judgmental causes negative emotions that don't allow us to have the results we want in life. What do we do? It is actually quite simple: even when you know you are right about something, don't be right. Better to look at the situation from the other person's perspective, try to understand where they are coming from and drop it.

I believe all people do the best they can with the things that they have learned in their lives and all people generally come from a good place. Instead of getting annoyed with a person, why not try listening to them with love in your heart. Look at them as the young soul they are that came into this life for their own sets of reasons for their soul to grow. Know that every conversation you have with them, they may give you a gift. They may tell you something interesting that will help you in life or they may be there to teach you compassion or forgiveness.

If you can dream it, then you can achieve it.
You will get all you want in life
if you help enough other people get what they want.

~ Zig Ziglar

If you can find the gift that this person is to you, your emotions will shift to the positive. To shift them even higher, try this: get the person to talk about what they love about their life. Anything at all. Ask them what they love about their kids or what they love to do in their free time. Ask those kinds of questions, even have them talk about a favorite memory. You know what will happen? They will turn into a happy, wonderful person in front of your very eyes! You will also be much happier and apt to share something you love about your life, raising those positive emotional vibrations tremendously and sending an incredible amount of strings of energy out to the universe. They say, "Be careful what you wish for, because you just may get it." Anytime you make a difference for another person, you dramatically increase the joy that you feel in life and the results you have as well.

Gratitude

Gratitude is the secret weapon for feeling good and having results show up in your life. This is good news because gratitude feels good and we like to feel good.

There are two ways to live: You can live as if nothing is a miracle; you can live as if everything is a miracle.

~ Albert Einstein

The Voice won't be interested in you feeling gratitude. Gratitude is *The Voice's* enemy; it would much rather you feel fear or doubt.

Gratitude helps with pain relief. When Dad was in the hospital, he and I would each take turns telling each other what we were grateful for. We each had to share at least twenty things and would take turns going back and forth. We would be grateful for our deep sea fishing trips, or the laughter of my sweet, young niece and nephew. We found when we relived these experiences, we would start to feel good again. The endorphins released from feeling grateful alleviated some of Dad's pain and made me feel happy too.

Gratitude can turn a bad mood into a good mood. Try this sometime: put on your favorite music, sit down with a piece of paper and write out fifty things you are grateful for. Allow yourself to feel grateful and think of why you are grateful for these things. Hmmm, sounds like some great homework for you at the end of this chapter!

You'll learn very shortly a *recipe* that will help you get the results you want in your life. Gratitude is one of the main ingredients.

In closing this chapter, being in a state of negative emotion doesn't feel good and doesn't help you produce the things you want in your life. It is essential to get *The Voice* in your head to stop telling you negative things and having you experience fear.

Stay out of your head for a while. Go outside, call a friend, do something you enjoy, put on some happy music and dance (even if you don't feel like it), or get into the present moment and experience the miraculous world we live in. These are just a few practices to experience result-producing, positive emotions.

HOMEWORK ASSIGNMENT

1. Stop complaining. Begin to look at every person, every event and everything in your life as something that you created. Look for why it is necessary for it to be in your life for soul growth.

2. Do something you love today. Play your favorite song, read a book that you enjoy. It doesn't have to be big and it doesn't have to take long, but it must make you feel good.

3. Set a timer for five minutes and write out the things you are most grateful for. You don't need to rush and it's not important how many items you write down. What is important is how you feel when you write them, it is important that you feel gratitude for them.

4. Make a difference for another person. It can be a person you know or a stranger. Give them a sincere compliment or let them know that you appreciate them. Let them know the difference they make in your life. They will feel good and you will feel good. Then, watch for good results to start happening in your life and in theirs.

Chapter 13

It Is All in Your Mind

Watch your thoughts, for they become words.
Watch your words, for they become actions.
Watch your actions, for they become habits.
Watch your habits, for they become character.
Watch your character, for it becomes your destiny.

~ Mahatma Ghandi, b. 1869

The life that you believe is real, the emotions you have and the five senses you delight in experiencing, all occur in one place, inside your mind. Life is an illusion for the soul, but for us it seems incredibly real. We believe things to be real because we experience them with our five senses. Life is like a puzzle we cannot solve. Do you remember those Chinese finger traps we had when we were kids? They were tubes made just large enough to put your left and right index fingers in either end. Once your fingers were in, you were trapped. It was a simple prank, but no matter how hard you pulled, you could not get your fingers out. The more you pulled, the tighter the trap was around your fingers and the more frustrated you got.

Life is like a Chinese finger trap. Remember what our young soul was told?

Warning: once you arrive on Planet Earth, you will forget all about this place. You will forget that it was you who chose these emotions to experience and these parents. You will forget that you were given a guidebook. That is why it is critical that you memorize it now. We need you to forget, so you may experience the fullest range of emotions possible for your soul to grow.

To help you believe that you are a person of Earth, not the eternal soul that you really are, we are giving you a companion for your journey. This companion will be within you at all times. It will remember your past experiences and remind you of that past. You will never feel alone as we have created a voice that will talk to you inside your mind all the days of your life on Earth.

During your stay, there will be some guides that will appear on your journey, to help you along the way. It is essential to listen to each person you meet, because they might be one of your guides. In case of an emergency, there will be only one way to get help. You will be able to access this guidebook through your thoughts. To achieve this, you must stop the voice inside your mind and quiet your senses. We have put reminders around the Earth in the form of STOP signs. These signs will be a reminder to you, that you must stop your thinking and quiet your mind. Then, have the intention of getting an answer to your question and the answer will come in that stillness.

The way to get out of the Chinese finger trap is similar to how to access the guidebook. One must stop to get out of the trap. By simply bringing the fingertips together and not pulling, the finger trap comes off your fingers. By simply stopping your thoughts, you can get out of the trap of thinking you are only human.

Stopping the thinking is also known as *being in the present moment.* The present moment is the gateway for remote viewing to take place, for psychics to tap into your future and for mediums to connect with your deceased loved ones. The present moment can take you out of pain and into moments of great inspiration.

There is such an incredible sense of peace and freedom that arises when *The Voice* stops talking and your mind is quiet and there is nothing there. However, where there is nothing there, *everything* is there. Everything being you, your *Soul Self*, tapped into all of the cosmos.

Did you know that some of the greatest minds in the world would tap into this peaceful place and then the ideas for some of their greatest inventions would appear in their minds? We are talking about Leonardo DiVinci, Thomas Edison, Henry Ford, Alexander Graham Bell, Albert Einstein, Walter Russell and more. Look at some of the accomplishments of these extraordinary people: Clint Eastwood, George Lucas, Tina Turner, Sting, Michael Jordan and Steve Jobs. Do you know what they all have in common? Whether they called it "quieting their mind," "visual imagery," "meditation," or just "being still," profound ideas came to their minds when that inner chatter from *The Voice* in their heads was not taking place.

They say that there is a bank of *Universal Knowledge* that we can all access when we quiet our minds. Some call this place the *Akashic Records*. I call it the *guidebook* that our souls connect to when we quiet *The Voice.* Whatever it is called, it surely is magnificent. Not only does it allow us to get great ideas, access the past, present and future, it allows us to communicate with those we cannot see and it allows us to turn our thoughts into reality

> *Every genius thinks INWARDLY toward his Mind instead of outwardly toward his senses. The genius can hear sounds coming out of the silence with his inner ears. He can vision non-existent forms with his inner eyes and he can feel the*

rhythms of God's thinking and His knowing—which are
a blank slate to the man who believes that HE is his body.
When a human rises to the exalted state of genius, he becomes
a co-Creator with God."

~ Walter Russell, b. 1871

Walter Russell

In 1963, Walter Cronkite referred to Dr. Walter Russell as "The Leonardo da Vinci of our time," on the national television evening news, when he announced Russell's death.

Walter Russell was an amazing man. At a very young age he told his parents of a mystical experience he had while in the woods. Some would call it *cosmic consciousness*, but young Russell believed he communed with God. His parents thought him to be a troubled child and the words he spoke and the words he wrote seemed to be nonsense to them. They thought maybe he should be institutionalized.

When brought to a proper teacher, the writings of this young man were determined to be as extraordinary as the writings of the brilliant poet, Walt Whitman. Walter Russell was a genius. Walter did not claim that he was anything other than an ordinary man, even until his death.

In the book, *The Man Who Tapped the Secrets of the Universe*, Russell says,

I believe sincerely that every man has consummate genius within him. Some appear to have it more than others only because they are aware of it more than others are, and the awareness or unawareness of it is what makes each one of them into masters or holds them down to mediocrity. I believe that mediocrity is self-inflicted and that genius is self-bestowed. Every successful man I have ever known, and I have known a great many, carries with him the key that unlocks that awareness and lets in the universal power that has made him into a master.

In one lifetime, Walter Russell was a sculptor, a painter, an author, a musician, an inventor, an architect, a scientist, a composer, a physicist, a mathematician, a philosopher and a philanthropist. The United States government had Russell create sculptures and paintings of the presidents and they were done with amazing accuracy. Russell was also an equestrian and a champion figure skater. Whatever Walter Russell touched, he was a genius.

Russell taught thousands of people how to reach this Universal Intelligence by holding a question in their minds and going to that quiet place we all have within. With enough practice, patience and intention, all answers to everything are available to each of us.

My dowsing friend, Joey Korn, introduced me to the amazing works of Walter Russell. Joey is an expert on Walter Russell and can point you in the right direction if you want to learn more. Joey carries all of Walter Russell's books at Dowsers.com.

Have you ever gone to bed at night and had a problem in your mind that you needed an answer to? Then, the next morning you knew the answer. I believe we access Universal Intelligence when we sleep. Have you had some insight or vision of something new while taking a bath or a shower? Our minds are normally relaxed just before falling asleep at night, when we wake up in the morning, while relaxing in the shower or bathtub and even sometimes when we drive a car, we may get a great idea.

If you realized how powerful your thoughts are, you would never think a negative thought.

~ Peace Pilgrim

Destroying Negative Beliefs

We now know that we are eternal souls having a human experience here on Earth. We know that we are able to connect with a *universal intelligence* that makes wondrous things happen. We know that we must have full desire to achieve our dreams. We know that fear and negative emotions must be avoided at all costs and that gratitude, love, excitement and positive emotions must be experienced. However, there is still one barrier that will prevent us from achieving our dreams: the negative beliefs we have about ourselves.

What are the negative beliefs that you have? Just wait about three seconds and *The Voice* in your head will begin to tell you things like, "You're unlovable," "You're overweight," "You have no confidence," "You're a failure," "You'll never amount to anything," "You are stupid," "You are a disappointment," etc. What is your voice telling you now? Take a second and write them down. We will need to know what they are so we can begin to eliminate them, which is essential to you having incredible results.

The mind is its own place, and in itself,
can make heaven of Hell, and a hell of Heaven.

~ John Milton

If I haven't told you this enough, you deserve having all the things you want in life. You waited in that line in Heaven and have spent a long time on Earth. I bet there are things you still want, as there are things I want. You deserve to have those things. You are a special person and there is no one like you. You work hard, you care for people, you have love in your heart. You deserve some magic in your life and much more happiness. There is a level of joy that you deserve to experience that you have not felt yet. You deserve to feel the magic of life and share it with the people you love. That's why you came here and I ask that you take the necessary steps that will make those things real for you.

As I explained in my story of growing up, *The Voice* has been telling me some extremely disempowering statements about myself. I read an excellent book by Dov Baron titled *Don't Read This: Your Ego Won't*

Like It. He compared the ego (*The Voice*) to a grumpy, old man. This old man is so set in his ways and he does not like change. I could relate to what he was saying immediately!

Dov Baron explains that in our first years of life, our minds are wide open to the information that comes in. We believe the information to be truth. Our ego (*The Voice*) then develops within us and that information gets filed away in our subconscious minds and in every cell in our body as *the truth*.

For instance, one of my first painful experiences in life was getting lost at that amusement park. The fear is still a memory in my mind and body, although it happened when I was a little child. The *truth* that my ego told me was, *"I am unlovable, there is something different about me and I don't matter."* Is any of this true? Absolutely not. What simply happened is a four year old child with bad vision got more excited about seeing some brightly colored balloons than paying attention to where Mom and Dad went.

I have known for a long time that my ego constructed those beliefs, however, when something goes wrong in my life, it is automatic that *The Voice* tell me those statements are true.

For instance, is it any accident that I have remained single and am now well into my forties? How *lovable* do you think I may have appeared to romantic partners if *The Voice* was telling me, "I am unlovable."

In your life, have you had the same things seem to happen over and over and over? When I attended the Landmark Forum weekend seminar, it became clear that when the same things keep happening to a person, *the problem is that person*.

As I said earlier, *The Voice* inside my head constantly tells me things like "I am not enough, I don't matter, there is something different about me and I am unlovable" and has given me a fabulous set of skills that I am grateful to have. I am nice, generous, independent, intelligent and very loving. I give to others what I feel that I did not receive myself.

There is nothing wrong with any of those skills, as they have made me the successful woman I am today. However, my dream is that someday I am married to a man that is my best friend and together, we make a profound difference in the world, sharing this message, *We Don't Die*. If I hold onto my negative belief that "I am unlovable," can you see that I will never have that dream fulfilled? It is a necessity for each of us to identify and not to listen to the negative words *The Voice* may be telling us.

There were some excellent exercises in *Don't Read This: Your Ego Won't Like It*, to gain mastery over *The Voice*. This particular exercise will pave the way for some extraordinary results and I invite you to try it. First, take a look at the struggles you have had repeatedly in your life. It may help to look at yourself from an outsider point of view and ask, "What kind of beliefs does this person have about themselves?"

For instance, one of the beliefs that *The Voice* has convinced me of is:

I am unlovable. I will remain single and alone
for the rest of my life.

You want to do this for every one of the beliefs that you have about yourself, if you want to have power. Next I want you to feel how true that belief is for you.

I want you to know something. From the time we are born until about seven years old, our brains believe the information we receive as *the truth*. As we get older, all it takes is one or two times for something similar to happen and *The Voice* will have us believe that thing is the absolute truth. So, at five years old if someone laughed at your drawing of a horse, you may never draw or paint ever again in your life! This happened to a woman that I know. After doing the work to destroy her belief she found she has an incredible, natural creative ability and produces wonderful artwork.

I have quietly lived my whole life deep down believing that there was something wrong with me and that I am unlovable. All because a sixteen-year-old boy's hormones attracted him to some other girl. Ridiculous, right? But I have lived the following thirty years single and never in a long-term relationship. Coincidence? I don't think so.

The next part of the exercise is to make a list of all the evidence that you have that the belief is the truth. For me, guess what happened? I started laughing. I laughed and I laughed and I laughed. What makes me, Sandra Champlain, different from any one of the seven billion people on Planet Earth? Oh sure, they are special and deserve love, but I don't. *The Voice* is quick to point out, "If you lost a few pounds you'd be more attractive." I could not find any proof of that either. I was able to smile thinking about all the handsome men from my past that found me attractive no matter what size I was. There is also proof that overweight people do get married, so that belief got destroyed too.

> *A man's own self is his friend. A man's own self is his foe.*
>
> ~ *Bhagavad Gita*

Not only did I laugh, but I also gained power. Something shifted inside me, big time. Another great exercise Dov suggests is to spend two weeks or more doing this: upon waking in the morning, take ten minutes and write out the *things other people love about you* and the *successes you have had in your life*. I can honestly say this exercise has me feeling great every day I do it.

It takes time to destroy negative beliefs, because they have been with us for so long, often since we were kids. Negative beliefs are simply habits and we know habits can be changed. Whenever you take a few minutes to do the above exercises, you will get your power back.

> *Every minute spent worrying about "the way things were" is a moment stolen from creating "the way things can be."*
>
> ~ Robin Sharma

Change Your Thoughts, Change Your Results

The biggest thing we have working against us in achieving our own dreams is our mind. It is interesting that we unconsciously believe that things are the truth, even when they are not true. *The Voice* has been our constant companion since day one, which we listen to as the truth and it prevents us from remembering who we really are: eternal souls having a human experience.

> *Whatever you hold in your mind will tend to occur in your life. If you continue to believe as you have always believed, you will continue to act as you have always acted. If you continue to act as you have always acted, you will continue to get what you have always gotten. If you want different results in your life or your work, all you have to do is change your mind.*
>
> ~ Unknown

Dr. Jacques Dallaire, author of *Performance Thinking*, has worked with high-level athletes, race car drivers, occupational specialists and business professionals for over forty years, giving them the tools to stop negative thoughts and increase their mental sharpness and focus. I absolutely love how he describes our beliefs, comparing us to elephants and fish:

> *Circus example. When a baby elephant is born into the circus, the elephant trainer tethers the elephant to a chain that is attached to a stake driven into the ground within the elephant enclosure. The purpose of this restraint is to teach the elephant to remain in its enclosure, and when it is small, the chain actually prevents it from wandering outside of the relatively restrictive space defined by the length of its chain. The baby elephant pulls on the chain, but it cannot escape its confines because it is limited by that restraint. It effectively learns that pulling on the*

chain is futile and that its confinement to a small enclosure is a permanent condition of its life. Over a relatively brief period of time, it stops pulling on the chain altogether. It comes to accept an internal representation of itself as a captive creature that is incapable of breaking free, and it continues to reflect this belief in its behavior. As it grows to become a full-size elephant, the elephant does not pull on the chain, because it has learned that it is futile, even though it could pull the stake out of the ground with ease as a full-grown elephant!

Aquarium example. When a city aquarium was looking to create a new marine exhibit that featured large, somewhat aggressive game fish, it ran into a problem. As the marine biologists sought to introduce smaller fish into the exhibit to fill out the natural ecosystem, it was like ringing the dinner bell. As soon as the small fish were introduced into the tank, the bigger fish treated them like a meal, and the biologists could not keep small fish in the tank because they would constantly get eaten!

One enterprising individual thought of a creative solution to their problem. They took a number of small fish and put them in the water, within a glass bell jar that they then suspended into the water of the exhibit tank. Within minutes the large fish in the tank would take a run at the small fish, expecting to get a meal. Instead, what they got was a snout full of hard glass. They smashed their sensitive snouts against the sides of the glass jar and were denied their prize. Over time, the number of strikes by the large fish was reduced to zero as the large fish in the aquarium came to learn that they could not eat the small fish. It became clear to them that their inability to eat these small fish was a condition of their life and that, if they tried, it would only cause them discomfort. They learned to become helpless. After *a period of time when no strikes were recorded by big fish on the glass jar, the aquarium handlers took the bell jar out of the exhibit and poured the small fish directly into the big tank. The problem was solved as the large fish continued to believe that they could not eat the small fish, and this belief was reflected in their behavior. Indeed, the large fish in the tank would starve themselves to death even though they were surrounded by a plentiful food supply. Their behavior is based on a false belief, but the consequence of that belief is as powerful as if the small fish were still protected by the walls of the glass bell jar.*

(Visit PerformancePrime.com to learn more about Dr. Jacques Dallaire and *Performance Thinking*.)

What are the results you want in your life? Is it possible that like the elephant and the large fish you have limiting beliefs keeping you from achieving what you want? Is there an unlimited supply of little fish available to you, but you believe you cannot have them, so you may not even see them in front of you? You bet there are! We all swim in those waters.

> *It is necessary for us to think our own thoughts,*
> *instead of having our thoughts think us.*

How do we change our belief system to get the results we want? While it is necessary to distinguish our beliefs, it is also necessary for us (our *Soul Selves*) to create and think our own thoughts instead of having our thoughts (*The Voice*) think us. Is it possible? Yes, it is. However, it requires practice, commitment and an understanding that you can easily slip back, without any notice, into listening to *The Voice*. Training the mind is a lot like strengthening a muscle, the more time you spend strengthening it, the stronger it becomes. A strong mind, led by the powerful commander of the *Soul Self* will produce incredible results.

There is only room for one commander at a time and *The Voice* is always standing nearby, ready to jump in and take control!

Our beliefs are firmly rooted in our minds; some say they are rooted in our bodies. Dr. Candace Pert is an internationally recognized pharmacologist who has published over 250 scientific articles and books, such as *Molecules of Emotion: The Scientific Basis Behind Mind-Body Medicine.* She states that our memories, our beliefs and our emotions are all contained inside our bodies, not just our minds. That is why it is often so difficult to change a belief, because much like a drug addict whose body is craving the drug, our bodies are craving the emotions, habits and beliefs that we have had all of our lives.

Dr. Bruce Lipton shares his fascinating research in his books, *The Biology of Belief—Unleashing the Power of Consciousness, Matter & Miracles* and *The Wisdom of Your Cells—How Your Beliefs Control Your Biology.* Dr. Lipton discusses *Epigenetics*, the field of study that explores how our genes and DNA do not control our biology, but rather, DNA is controlled by signals from outside the cell, including the energetic messages emanating from our thoughts.

Neuroplasticity of the brain is also a fairly new field of research. In *Train Your Mind, Change Your Brain: How a New Science Reveals Our Extraordinary Potential to Transform Ourselves,* author Sharon Begley looks at how we literally change (rewire) our brains by changing our minds (our thoughts). Experiments have shown that the brain is capable of altering its structure and function and even of generating new neurons, a power we retain well into old age. The brain can adapt, heal and renew itself after trauma, compensate for disabilities, rewire itself to overcome dyslexia and break cycles of depression and OCD (Obsessive-Compulsive Disorder). There is so much incredible evidence of how our thoughts can change our brains, change our beliefs, change our bodies, change our emotions and ultimately, change the results in our lives.

Hypnosis, visual imagery and Neurolinguistic Programming (NLP) all are excellent ways to reprogram our minds. One thing that is necessary in changing any mind is quieting *The Voice* in our heads. I call it *being in the present moment*, some call it *meditation*, others call it *mindfulness*. Let me remind you that not only can you reprogram your body and mind in this zone, but this is also the place that taps into *Universal Knowledge* or our *Soul Self*, making it possible to see the past, present, or future through remote viewing or connect with a deceased loved one. Being in this zone allows us to dowse energy fields, find water underground, diagnose the ailments of others, as well as send out healing prayers. Being in this *present moment* allows us to send out the necessary strings of vibrating energy, through our desires and our emotions, and have the things we want come back to us in the form of *matter*.

When I first learned some of this information, I had the opportunity to test its validity. I had planned a weekend trip with my mother to Las Vegas, to see a show, eat some good food, gamble a little and have some fun. My mother, Marion, is a fun and wonderful person to spend time with.

My flight left Boston and I was to change airplanes in Salt Lake City, Utah and take another airplane to Las Vegas. I was unhappy that I would have to spend over three hours in Salt Lake City before the flight left for Vegas. I had such a *desire* to not sit in the airport and I wonder if I unconsciously sent out the strings of energy for this to occur. A sick passenger was on the flight and we had to make an emergency landing in Iowa to get this passenger to a hospital. We spent well over three hours on the ground in Iowa before resuming our flight to Salt Lake.

I was not happy! I realized that I would now miss the flight from Salt Lake to Las Vegas and I would have to wait until the following day to fly to Vegas!

However, I remembered thinking, "Maybe I can change my thoughts and have a different result." I purposely spent the entire flight from Iowa to Salt Lake City visualizing, with full gratitude and excitement, *as if it had already occurred*, the following:

I landed in Salt Lake City, got off the jet bridge and saw the sign that the Las Vegas flight had been delayed by an hour. The departure gate for the Las Vegas flight was the gate next to my arrival flight from Boston. I handed my boarding pass to the Delta Airlines representative and I was delighted to see a first class ticket come out of her machine and I was upgraded to first class. I sat in my seat, arrived safely in Las Vegas, and my mother was waiting for me in the baggage claim area.

It was very difficult to repeat this story over and over in my mind. *The Voice* kept jumping in and telling me that it was ridiculous and that I wouldn't see my mother until the next day. However, I didn't listen to it and kept concentrating my thoughts and emotions on the above scenario. Over an hour later our plane landed in Salt Lake City. Looking at my watch, it was clear that unless there was *divine intervention*, the flight to Las Vegas would have already departed.

When I got off the airplane I looked up at the monitor. The flight to Las Vegas had not yet left! It was delayed for whatever reason and they changed its departure gate, to the gate next to where I was standing! They were doing their final boarding, I walked over to the gate, gave the gate agent my boarding pass and up popped a first class ticket from the machine! I enjoyed the flight and, when I landed, Mom was there to meet me in the baggage claim area.

I often wonder if I created that future or if I predicted the future. Knowing that time is an illusion and that we can create anything, I feel like I created it. It was one of the most extraordinary feelings I have ever felt.

In racing, they say that your car goes where your eyes go. The driver who cannot tear his eyes away from the wall as he spins out of control will meet that wall; the driver who looks down the track as he feels his tires break free will regain control of his vehicle.

~ Garth Stein, The Art of Racing in the Rain

My good friend is American Le Mans Series, champion race car driver, David Brabham. David is the youngest son of three-time Formula One world champion Sir Jack Brabham. David and I often exchange books and talk about what is possible for human beings. Often, David comes into the kitchen while I'm cooking, gives me a big hug and we catch up on what new cool stuff we have each learned. On this particular day, I told him about my amazing flight to Las Vegas. David then told me he had a dream, to win the 24 Hours of Le Mans, the most famous sports car race in the world. He would be one of three drivers working with Team Peugeot. 24 Hours of Le Mans is a tough race; the drivers take turns driving a car that averages 140 miles per hour (225 km/h) and can reach a top speed of 248 mph (399 km/h) on the Mulsanne Straight. Racing is a tough and dangerous sport and my friend David was going to compete in this race the following month.

David, always up for one of my experiments, joined me in a visual imagery session, similar to how I envisioned my flight to Las Vegas. He and I sat outside, behind my kitchen, closed our eyes and pictured exactly how the race was going to go. David told me in great detail everything he wanted, how the race was going to start, who his main competition would be, when he would take the lead and how he would win the race. He included every bit of detail possible and we both sat and pictured, with full excitement, gratitude and desire, how this race was going to turn out. (By the way, I do believe that when two or more people picture the same image and feelings, we increase the vibrations we are sending out by several times). I also had David imagine that he was in the Winner's Circle, receiving his trophy, getting adorned with a huge wreath of flowers and spraying a bottle of champagne, celebrating his victory as thousands of fans watched.

The 2009, 24 Hours of Le Mans fell on June 13 and 14th. I did not have to cook for this race, so I sat at home watching it on television. I slept on the couch that night, so I could keep an eye on how David was doing. I was fascinated to witness David taking the lead, just how he described he would in our visualization. And then the miraculous happened: at 3:00 in the afternoon, my friend David Brabham won the race! I cried tears of happiness when I watched him in the Winner's Circle receiving his trophy, with his wreath of flowers, spraying champagne and celebrating his victory with his teammates.

I want to remind you that although I have had the most extraordinary experiences in my life and have had miraculous, awe-inspiring results, *The Voice* is never far to quickly take control of the ship and effectively makes me forget these things. *The Voice* can make things that are really big deals, like communicating with the dead, doing remote viewing and now producing miraculous results seem like no big deal. No matter what miracles I have experienced, my mind is usually worried, thinking about what food I should eat or not eat, not wanting to exercise, worried about finances and wondering if I will ever have a boyfriend. It is absurd, isn't it? But that's how it works.

Part of the game of life is to forget who we really are.

There are a few words of advice I have to offer you so that you don't forget who you really are and so the big things that you experience can fuel you into desiring and achieving more extraordinary results.

1. Share this knowledge with others. You can share this book or any of the information contained in these pages. Most people have experienced something incredible in their lives that they cannot explain and you will get to remember who you are when you have many conversations about the topics within *We Don't Die*.

2. Continue your learning. Read some of the books or watch some of the movies that I have included in this book. Or, just do a search on the Internet and follow the links your intuition takes you to. The more you learn, the more time you spend remembering who you really are.

3. Do remote viewing, as often as you can, with another person or even with a magazine you haven't looked at. Doing so will keep you mystified and intrigued about your abilities.

4. Have daily reminders sent to you via email or pull a daily card out of a motivational deck. Everyday, I receive a *Note from the Universe*, from author Mike Dooley (TUT.com) and a daily inspiration called *I Believe God Wants You to Know*, from the author of *Conversations with God*, Neale Donald Walsch. (NealeDonaldWalsch.com). I also have an application for my cell phone called *Osho Zen Tarot*, that allows me to virtually pull a card and receive a profound bit of wisdom any time I need it. You can do this on your computer as well at Osho.com.

5. Become part of a group. There are associations and groups for whatever you are interested in. When you are part of a group, your *Soul Self* gets the opportunity to drive your energy vehicle while you leave *The Voice* in the back seat!

6. Become part of the *We Don't Die* family. It is free and you can belong to an amazing group of people who all share the desire to remember who they really are and who want to produce amazing results during the time they have on Planet Earth. Join at: WeDontDie.com/JoinOurFamily.html.

HOMEWORK ASSIGNMENT

1. Look at yourself as a big fish swimming in a tank filled with lots of little fish. Look at the dreams you want to have fulfilled and then write down the reasons why you do not already have them. Pick the five biggest negative beliefs that you have about yourself and write them down. Next, write down evidence that each one of those beliefs is *absolutely true*.

Even though you may know that the beliefs are not true, you still need to complete this exercise and write them down. The act of writing will cause some of the beliefs to start breaking apart in your subconscious mind.

2. Begin to see yourself through the eyes of the people that are in your life. You are not who *The Voice* tells you that you are. There is only one

of you who will try to convince yourself of the negative beliefs. Listen to what the people in your life say about you, for that is really who you are. They can see you swimming in the water with all kinds of little fish around you to eat. Open your eyes to what they see and be responsible for being that person in the world.

You are not who you think you are.
Who you are is who the people in your life
tell you that you are.

Chapter 14

10 Daily Habits to Super Charge Your Life

We can choose to function at a lower level of awareness and simply exist, caring for our possessions, eating, drinking, sleeping, and managing in the world as pawns of the elements, or we can soar to new and higher levels of awareness, allowing ourselves to transcend our environment and literally create a world of our own—a world of real magic.

~ Wayne Dyer, motivational speaker and author, b. 1940

The time has now come, my friend, for you to start having the life of your dreams, better than anything you could have ever imagined. You are an eternal soul, here on Earth having a human experience. You are a walking miracle, living in an amazing, high performance energy vehicle. It is your time to shine, your time to have all the amazing experiences you wanted to have when you waited in line to come to Planet Earth. Your life and the things around are about to be transformed into *Heaven on Earth*. You have more power than you can possibly know and I am ready to help you start having the results that you want.

Creation—A Sioux Indian Story

The Creator gathered all of Creation and said, "I want to hide something from the humans until they are ready for it. It is the realization that they create their own reality."

The eagle said, "Give it to me, I will take it to the moon."

The Creator said, "No. One day they will go there and find it."

The salmon said, "I will bury it on the bottom of the ocean."

"No. They will go there too."

The buffalo said, "I will bury it on the Great Plains."

The Creator said, "They will cut into the skin of the Earth and find it even there."

Grandmother Mole, who lives in the breast of Mother Earth, and who has no physical eyes but sees with spiritual eyes, said, "Put it inside of them."

And the Creator said, "It is done."

Throughout this book, we have uncovered thoughts, beliefs and views of reality. You have seen that they are all just illusions of the mind. Out before you is a world in which you can have anything, anything at all. You are an artist and you have an empty canvas in front of you.

The question is, what do you want? What do you want to paint on that canvas? You may start by looking back at your childhood and some of the dreams you had then, before *The Voice* took over and told you that you could not have them. You may know some of the dreams you desire and you may also be ready to create some new dreams. So often in life we are driven to do things that we feel we must do, based on what *The Voice* says or what other people think we should do. I am asking you now to see what your *Soul Self* wants. What are the things that give you the most joy, what makes you the happiest and what gives you the biggest sense of fulfillment?

The immediate answers may be things like, "I want more money,"

"I want to be in a relationship," or "I want a different job." While those answers are fine, I do believe there is something beneath them, something you really want, that having those things represent. So let's *drill down* beneath the surface to find what is really the most important to you.

Get your notebook out for this exercise. I know you may want many, many things. That is normal and certainly everything you wish for is possible. However, for this exercise I want you to pick one thing, then later, you can go back and work this exercise for every item on your list. Let's begin.

1. On your piece of paper write down one thing that you really want. For this example, I am going to pick money, as I believe that it is something that many people can relate to. So, mark a number one in your notebook and next to it write: *money.*

2. Let's start drilling down and find out what the reason is that you want this money. I want you to take a paragraph or a page or two and write out the reason you want money. It could go something like this:

> *I am normally a happy person but I hate struggling with money. I know I have a roof over my head, always have food on the table, the kids are doing okay, but every month there seem to be more bills than money to pay them. I get the credit card statements in the mail and it seems as though I can only pay the minimum payment. I find myself thinking of ways I can earn more money to pay the bills or if there is something I can take out of our life to save money. I don't seem as though I am as fun as I used to be, and even my kids notice. I used to have time to listen to them and play with them, and it seems like this money worry is taking up all my time. Life just isn't as fun as it used to be, I don't even enjoy the time with my wife like I used to. There are just too many demands and struggles. I'd like peace for a change.*

As you may observe in this example, while it looks like this person wants money, can you drill down and see what this person is really after? Sounds like he believes that by having money, he would get the things he really wants: time to be with his family, fun, play, joy and peace.

Take a few minutes and write your story of what you think you really want. How would your life be if you had those things? Would you feel satisfied, happy, joyful, excited, peaceful, confident, successful, or perhaps fulfilled? If you have trouble coming up with this answer it may be helpful to talk to someone else about it. Drill down together and see what you come up with.

Can you see that perhaps you might have been chasing the wrong thing? You may be spending day and night so stressed over how to create more money when really what you want is to have some fun and joy in your life. As we discussed earlier, desire is the very first thing we need to accomplish any goal. How much desire can you have for actual money, meaning the paper and the coins? That doesn't sound very exciting at all, does it? No wonder most people don't achieve their dreams. They are chasing after the wrong goal.

If your word or words have something to do with a feeling, emotion, or a way of being, you are in luck! I have the perfect recipe for you to produce a great result in that area. You may be thinking, "Great, I'll get happiness, but I will still be broke and have debt." Here's the good news, *"You can have it all!"*

In Napoleon Hill's book *Think and Grow Rich*, he says you must have the following to achieve a goal:

a. Burning desire

b. A plan to make it happen

c. A friend who has what you want

d. Don't listen to negative people

Burning desire

Simply stated, that whatever you want, you must really, really want it. State it in such a way that it is so incredible, that you absolutely must have it. Desire is the number one fuel for both your conscious and your subconscious mind to help you make your dream a reality.

The Plan

I wish it was as simple as having a dream, closing our eyes, feeling good thoughts and the goal will come true. It is not. While all those things are parts of achieving a goal, it is not all of it. You must take physical action to make the dream a reality. To take action, you first need a plan. Write out the goal and the things that would need to happen for that goal to be fulfilled. There will be action steps to take. In attracting a soul mate, for example, you would need a plan of how you might meet this person. The plan would involve dating and you'd need to plan how you will find the people to date. The book, *The Magic Lamp*, by Keith Ellis may help. It is all about goal setting and action steps.

A Supportive Friend

This supportive friend must be a person that already has what you want. For instance, if you want to start a business, your support friend would be a successful business owner. There is a shift that happens in the brain when you have people in your life that have success in the area of your dream. My small business had not been very profitable and caused me stress, worry and more than a few bounced checks. Think of my delight when a wonderful, new friend came into my life who also happened to be a successful business owner who had made millions of dollars. Within six months of our friendship my small business became profitable again!

You get to be a supportive friend to that person too. As it turns out, I have skills and results in areas that my wealthy new friend does not have. Friends get to be gifts to each other.

Who Not to Listen To

It is so important to have a supportive friend while taking steps to achieve your goal, especially when the people in your life think you are crazy for doing what you are doing. Every person has been on their own journey and sees life from their experiences. They may not be ready to hear that they are an eternal soul having a human experience! In fact, they may think you are crazy. In 2002, I wouldn't have believed any of the words that I am now writing. I just wasn't ready. The people in your life may not be ready, either. If they make you feel bad about what you are doing or tell you that the dreams that you have aren't valid, don't listen to them. Still love them, though, because from their point of view, they love you and don't want to see you fail.

One more word of caution here. Don't tell people who aren't supportive friends too much about what you are up to and what your dreams are. Studies have proven that if you tell people the big plans you have, they can get excited for you, start celebrating with you, then you subconsciously feel that you have already achieved that goal and you may stop working toward it. I did it myself; for many years I spoke of writing a book and felt the satisfaction of being an author, even though I hadn't started writing. Thank you, Mom, for telling me to stop talking about it and get writing!

The Recipe for Success

As I am a chef, I think it is important to compare the wonderful results of having your dream come true to a decadent chocolate cake. If you would prefer a vanilla or a strawberry cake (my supportive friend prefers strawberry) then imagine that.

To have a cake become a delicious masterpiece, it needs ingredients. Flour, sugar, salt, eggs, baking powder, butter and unsweetened chocolate all go into this cake. Any one of the above ingredients on its own is not very exciting. But mixed together, they have the possibility of becoming a masterpiece.

Ingredients are important in cake baking, but in addition, you need to know how much of each ingredient you must use, in what order to mix them, how long to stir the mixture, how to oil the pan so the cake does not stick, and what temperature and how to long to bake the cake. You may not know, but all the dry ingredients and all the wet ingredients get mixed separately before being combined to make cake batter.

Can you imagine the mess if you didn't know how much of each ingredient you needed and how to mix the batter? However, given the proper procedure, these ingredients can be made into an award-winning, delicious, chocolate cake!

The masterpiece you are about to create is not a chocolate cake but *Your Life*. You are now about to be given the recipe to help you have the results you want in your life. We are going to polish your high performance vehicle on the inside and outside, so it radiates with powerful strings of vibrating energy. Your vehicle will be charged so full of energy, it will look like a car that just received an extremely high powered set of headlights. It will send out light forty feet or more into the darkness, unlike how we've been traveling, with mud on the headlights or worse yet, one light burned out, not glowing too much at all.

People who soar are those who refuse to sit back, sigh, and wish things would change. They neither complain of their lot nor passively dream of some distant ship coming in. Rather, they visualize in their minds that they are not quitters; they will not allow life's circumstances to push them down and hold them under.

~ Charles Swindoll, writer and clergyman, b.1934

10 DAILY HABITS TO SUPER CHARGE YOUR LIFE

Morning: Wake Up Your Soul Self

Think Your Own Thoughts

Be Present

Eat Healthy Foods and Exercise

Make a Difference for Another

Take One Action Toward Your Dream

Do Something that Makes You Feel Good

Laugh / Remote View / Try Something New (Your Choice)

Have Integrity and Be Responsible

Evening: Gratitude Exercise

EXTRA CREDIT: Do One Thing You Fear

We are what we repeatedly do.
Excellence, then, is not an act, but a habit.

~ Aristotle

We are about to super charge your energy vehicle, so that you radiate the necessary, highest strings of vibrating energy, attached to your desires, so they come back to you in the form of results. Your strong, positive emotions and intentions will cause strong energy vibrations.

Feeling strong emotions will also allow you to feel motivated, confident and courageous, allowing you to take more action toward turning your dreams into realities.

Your thoughts are made up of content and energy, like invisible radio waves. It is very important to monitor your thoughts. The stronger you think and feel about something, the more energy you give to it. This applies to positive and negative thoughts.

Feel your desire fully for things. Feel the joy of having the desires fulfilled. Remember, suffering is caused by unfilled expectations. Detach from a specific expectation and allow for wonderful, unexpected surprises. Let the universe give you a couple of gifts for a change!

Do not give up feeling desire if you think you have failed in getting what you want. You must practice feeling the desire as intensely as before. Your energy will be weak if you do not fully experience your desires and good-feeling emotions.

10 DAILY HABITS TO SUPER CHARGE YOUR LIFE:

You will first need a notebook or journal that you can keep by your bed. As results start occurring, it is good to see when you started and how quickly you started producing them. You will be doing your journaling only five minutes in the morning when you first wake up and five minutes at night, just before you go to bed. Your mind is most susceptible to receiving new information in the morning and at night. On occasion, if you cannot complete the journal work in the morning, do it when you can.

1. Morning—Wake Up Your Soul Self

Good morning! Most days *The Voice* is in the driver's seat when we wake up. We want to put *The Voice* in the backseat so you can start your day vibrating as much good-feeling energy as possible.

Open your journal. Write the date and A.M. on the paper. Write down, MY DESIRES and, in just a few sentences, write your desires down, being sure to *feel* how much you want them. They should be easy to think of because these are the things you want badly. Next, write down MY SUCCESSES and list those things that you are proud of in your life. They can be big things or little things. *Feel* how successful you are as you write them. Next, write down WHAT PEOPLE LOVE ABOUT ME and take the next several lines to write all those great attributes that people (including yourself) love about you. *Feel good about yourself, you are those things.*

Then, take a glance at the desires you wrote. This magnificent person is worthy of having those desires fulfilled and certainly does have enough successes to have them happen! Feel confident that your desires are on their way to coming true and that *you are worth it.*

Waking up your *Soul Self* will only take five to ten minutes and you can fit it all on one page of your journal.

2. Think Your Own Thoughts

The Voice is going to be eager to be in the driver's seat all day long! It's important to watch your thinking. Notice when *The Voice* is driving. Usually, these are times when you have fear, worry, or negative self-talk. First, you must catch *The Voice* talking. It is not who you really are. Then, put your own thoughts in, filled with the confidence, wisdom, and trust that you can make anything happen. Remember, you are a soul here having a human experience. You have an incredible power that lies within you. Return *The Voice* to the backseat. Also remember to watch your words. The words you speak have real power. Don't complain, don't gossip, don't speak poorly of others, and intentionally speak positive words.

3. Be In the Present Moment

It is critical that on a daily basis you rest your mind and allow it to get in touch with the bank of Universal Knowledge. This is the same place you go to when you remote view. The best way to access it is to be in the present moment. Be *thought-free* for at least five minutes. It is helpful to be present as much as you can during the day. Not only will it increase the energy your vehicle is creating, but it will allow you to come up with new ideas and it feels good. Whatever it is you are doing, give it full attention without thinking. For instance, as you listen to music, be there 100% with the music, don't think. Any time you see a stop sign while you are traveling, let it serve as a reminder to stop your thinking and be in the present moment.

4. Eat Healthy Foods and Exercise

A finely-tuned body emits a very high level of result producing vibrations. The better you take care of your vehicle, the more results you will produce. Drink water, take vitamins, get plenty of rest, eat more whole, organic, healthy foods and exercise your body, preferably doing something you love to do. I often enjoy taking a walk in nature while being present or I put on my headphones and some dance music! Even when I am in a bad mood, dancing forces me to feel good. We are trying to feel good all day, so you might want to try that!

5. Make a Difference for Another

Several years ago, my sister Heidi offered to help me paint and refurnish my small business, to make it more attractive to customers. The plan was for me to meet her at my shop on a specific night after returning from a vacation. On the specific night, I arrived with my work clothes on, not looking forward to painting throughout the night. Imagine my surprise when I walked into the shop and Heidi had transformed it into a beautiful, modern-looking coffee shop. She had done all the work during the week I was on vacation! That was the best surprise I've ever had, no one has ever made a difference like she has.

The people in our lives are put there for two reasons. One, they allow an opportunity for your soul to grow, as you made a soul contract with this person before you came to Earth. Make sure you learn the lesson you are supposed to learn. Two, they may be one of your guides to get back on track or help you fulfill your desires. Pay special attention to the words and actions of people, they may contain a special message just for you.

During the day, make a difference for another person. This will guarantee that you talk to people on a daily basis (*The Voice* would rather you be alone). Make a difference for that person, either help them with something or share the difference that they have made for you. Give them a sincere compliment. While you speak with them, be loving toward them, envision them being someone you love and really appreciate. They will feel it, you will boost your energy and you both will be left feeling good. Please note, you must actually talk to a person today. However, it is perfectly okay to text or email people in addition, letting them know how special they are to you.

> *I've learned that people will forget what you said,*
> *people will forget what you did,*
> *but people will never forget how you made them feel.*
> ~ Maya Angelou

6. Take One Action Toward Your Dream

The power of the Universe is surely behind you in fulfilling your dreams and will do its best to have the things you want be real in your life. However, it has to know you are serious about your desires. The only way it can know you are serious, is if you work toward your dreams as well.

Take at least one step toward the thing you want and it will take a step closer to you. Taking action is the key to fulfilling your desires. I am not alone in this thinking. Read the below quotes. So, what is the one thing you are going to do today?

> *You are never given a dream without also being given*
> *the power to make it true.*
> *You may have to work for it, however.*
> ~ Richard Bach

> *We should be taught not to wait for inspiration to*
> *start a thing. Action always generates inspiration.*
> *Inspiration seldom generates action.*
> ~ Frank Tibolt

Take the first step in faith.
You don't have to see the whole staircase,
just take the first step.

~ Dr. Martin Luther King

7. Do Something that Makes You Feel Good

Your feelings and your emotions are what super charge your results. We spend so much time doing things for other people and being responsible, don't we? Yes, it's important to keep doing those things, but I want you to do something for yourself today. It can be big or little, but it must be something that makes you feel good. Call a friend, go for a walk, see a movie, take a bubble bath, go to the batting cage and hit a few balls, you get the idea.

8. Laugh, Remote View, or Try Something New

What soap is to the body, laughter is to the soul.

~ Yiddish Proverb

You can pick which one of these three you wish to do today. If you pick *laughter*, you must purposefully set out to laugh. Watch a comedy, find a funny video online, read something humorous, or call a friend that you always laugh with. At the end of the day, you cannot just remember that you laughed a little and call this part of the homework complete. No, you must plan for laughter!

Remote viewing will allow you to remember who you really are. There is nothing like it to connect you to your Soul Self. You will have more results in your life more quickly, because confidence and courage develop after each remote viewing session. You realize you are much more than your body, you realize you can never really fail and you will take more action in the areas that are important to you.

Trying something new allows you to have new experiences, new results and extra soul growth. Plus, doing new things is fun, especially if you do them with people you care about. Remember what Einstein said: *"Insanity is doing the same thing over and over and expecting different results."* Try something new today!

9. Have Integrity and Be Responsible

The *integrity* I speak of to super charge your life is this: do the things you know you should do, even if no one is looking. Only you know what you need to do. Have integrity with little things like *brush your teeth before going to bed*, or *returning phone calls* and big things like *be honest, do your best* and *be committed to people (and even to yourself)*. Integrity gives you power, courage and confidence. It all sends some pretty serious, heavy duty strings of vibration out into the universe, too. Only you know what you should or should not do.

> *Every person, all the events of your life are there*
> *because you have drawn them there.*
> *What you choose to do with them is up to you.*
>
> ~ Richard Bach

When I say *be responsible*, I mean be responsible for your entire life, *everything and everyone*. Remember you are an eternal soul that picked this life, these people and these circumstances. Do not be a victim and do not complain. Find the soul growth in each interaction you have and be responsible that you created it.

10. Evening: Gratitude Exercise

Miracle Log—Go to the back of your journal and list all the really great things that have happened in your life, things that have occurred like miracles: meeting your spouse, having a chance encounter with someone who changed your life, anything that you feel is out of the ordinary. Pay daily attention to the great things and great people that come into your life. Keep a list of these things in the back of your journal. Add to that list daily, whenever something really great happens in your life or when you fulfill a goal. (You can also refer to this list whenever you might be feeling a bit down to remind yourself of who you really are.)

Just before you go to bed at night, take a look at the words you wrote in your journal from the morning exercise. Allow yourself to feel those feelings of desire, success and love. Then, think back on your day, think about all the good things that happened and the accomplishments you've had. Think about the people for whom you have made a difference and the miracles that resulted.

Write the date and *P.M.* on the top of the page. Take five minutes or more and write down the things you are grateful for. They should include things you are generally grateful for (like your family, the good things you have in your life) and then write the things specifically from today that you are grateful for. Finally, you will write down that you are grateful for your desires becoming real (even though they haven't happened yet). Be grateful as if they already have happened. You must feel like these things you want have already happened and are real for you. Write with as much detail as you can that you are so incredibly happy and grateful for them happening. For instance, if you want a promotion you'd write, "I am so grateful I received the promotion. I love my job, I love the difference I get to make with my employees, I am grateful for the friendship I have with my boss and how we believe in each other and our dreams for the company. I am grateful that I now have extra time to spend with my family and extra money that allowed us to take that fabulous trip to Hawaii."

Be grateful, as if your desires have already been fulfilled. Gratitude is the number one emotion responsible for you emitting huge amounts of high vibration strings of energy. Make sure you feel the gratitude as you write. When you go to bed at night, your energy vehicle will continue to produce the vibrations as you sleep. Plus, you'll probably have some great dreams!

EXTRA CREDIT: DO ONE THING YOU FEAR TODAY

I know how often fear stops us. Sometimes I am afraid of little things! I don't want to have a conversation with a person or I don't want to do something I have to do. What is ridiculous is that when we actually do the thing we are afraid of, we do not feel fear. I can spend a week being afraid to make a call to a person, yet when I am on the phone, I am in the present moment with that person and it is not scary. Unless it is a life or death situation, fear is a waste of our time.

Some say FEAR stands for *False Evidence Appearing Real.* The great results you wish to have often take courage to accomplish and that means being afraid and taking action anyway. Do you remember being afraid to do something and yet you pushed yourself through it? Would you have had the same result if you let your fear win?

I have a friend that convinces himself that when he feels fearful about something it is really excitement he is feeling. If you think about it, fear and excitement produce the exact same physical sensations. He takes action when he is afraid! You know what? He is a millionaire several times over and he is happy.

Remember, there is no fear in the present moment, only in the anticipation of doing the thing you fear.

> *The secret to achieving your wildest dreams is to search for what makes you afraid and then go do it.*
>
> ~ Jennifer Gresham, scientist, poet & optimist

(There is a Daily Checklist to carry around with you that you may print at WeDontDie.com/checklist.html.)

Emergency Roadside Assistance

As much as we want to stay positive, be happy and enjoy good feelings, things come up. *The Voice* will jump into the driver's seat without you even being aware that there was a *driver change*! You may be filled with fear, worry, guilt, regret, jealously, anger, or sadness, or feel like a failure. What is important, is to:

1. First recognize that it is *The Voice* who is in command now. Not your *Soul Self*.

2. Be in the present moment and simply *be* with the feelings that you are experiencing. Notice how they feel in your body. They will persist if you try to make them go away, so take a few deep breaths and let them be. Stay present and keep your mind quiet.

3. Choose an activity below to cause yourself to begin generating good-feeling emotions that will charge your energy field with positive strings of vibrating energy.

Make a list of what you are grateful for in life—write at least 50 things.

Look at your journal. Read the successes and the miracles and what people love about you.

Be out in nature. Don't take anything for granted. See each bird, tree or flower as a miracle.

Call a friend and be a friend.

Do some remote viewing to reconnect with who you really are.

Put on some music that makes you feel good.

Move your body to get your heart beating. Go for a walk or dance.

Open this book to a random chapter, or read something that inspires you.

Do something you love to do.

Find something humorous to watch or read.

Write in your journal—get the thoughts onto paper so new thoughts may arise.

Pray or bless someone or something. Focus your attention outside yourself.

Look for the soul growth in what is happening. Be accountable that you made it this way.

Learn something new and stimulate your mind.

Do something for another person, move the focus off of you.

Make a list of all your successes and what people love about you.

The Possums and the Stick

By Travis Lane Jenkins

I can't remember exactly how old I was, but I was in my mid-twenties. I hadn't found any real level of success, in fact, I was struggling in my first few years as a business owner.

I was spending time with my father at his house, on a large piece of property in Texas. On our way back from a walk, my father noticed that there was a small family of baby possums stuck inside a trash can that was standing straight up so the possums could not get out.

My dad hated possums, called them varmints and felt like they were nothing more than rats. We grew up on a farm and it was normal for him to shoot varmints on site. But when I called after my father, I noticed that he had found a stick and put it inside the trash can on an angle so that it stuck all the way out of the top.

My father and I never talked about why he did that for the family of small baby possums, I guess because I already knew the reason. The stick was their chance to get themselves out of that situation. He provided the opportunity and the rest was up to them.

All my life my dad's had a hard time showing affection or even giving me a pat on the back for a job well done. This was the first time that I ever saw the depth of humanity in my father.

I thought about the stick and the possums over and over for the next several weeks. Over time I came to realize that my father gave me a stick as a younger man. He gave me strength, integrity, skills, taught me leadership and how to recognize opportunities.

It has taken me 20 years to see that he gave me all he could and, unfortunately, I've spent the majority of that time wanting things that he couldn't give me. Now with age, wisdom, and understanding I am making peace with it.

(After he realized the *stick* his father had given him, Travis Lane Jenkins has gone on using those skills to find opportunities and has now generated over 70 million dollars in his business.)

The one thing worse than a quitter is a person who is afraid to begin.

~ Anonymous

My friend, I have given you all that I know to give. You will always have my support for anything you need in life and I welcome your emails: Sandra@SandraChamplain.com

You have been given the stick that will allow you to leave the trash can and find an amazing new world with new results. You know that you are a big fish swimming in waters with lots of opportunities that perhaps you have not seen before. You are a mighty elephant who does not have to be stopped by a small stake and a chain holding you to the ground.

Our spirits are eternal and live way beyond the life of the used car we call our bodies.

~ Maureen Hancock, Medium

EPILOGUE

A ship in a harbor is safe,
but that is not what ships are built for.

~ William Shedd, American theologian, b.1820

You are the commander of your ship. Your *Soul Self* determines the destination and your sails are full of your desires, positive emotions, powerful thoughts and gratitude.

In the past you may have felt like a ship without a rudder, unable to steer yourself to the magnificent destinations of your dreams. You may have existed in fear, constantly being tossed and turned by the mighty ocean waves of life.

However, you have now received your rudder, that will guide and direct you to places more spectacular than you could have ever dreamed. It is your time to venture out of the safe harbor and into the wondrous seas of life. You are more powerful than the mightiest ship in the oceans.

Twenty years from now you will be more disappointed by the
things you didn't do than by the things you did do. So throw
off the bowlines. Sail away from safe harbor. Catch the trade
winds in your sails. Explore. Dream. Discover.

~ Mark Twain

When the moment comes for you to *cross the bridge*, have no regrets. Know that you have lived, you have loved, and you have traveled courageously in the direction of your dreams.

Row, row, row your boat,
Gently down the stream.
Merrily, merrily, merrily, merrily,
Life is but a dream.

10 DAILY HABITS TO SUPER-CHARGE YOUR LIFE

Morning: Wake Up Your Soul Self

Think Your Own Thoughts

Be in the Present Moment

Eat Healthy and Exercise

Make a Difference for Another

Take an Action Toward Your Desire

Do Something that Makes You Feel Good

Have Integrity and Be Responsible

Laugh, Remote View, or Try Something New

Evening: Gratitude Exercise

EXTRA CREDIT: Do One Thing You Fear

EMERGENCY ASSISTANCE

Recognize that *The Voice* is in command, not your *Soul Self*. Take a few deep breaths and get into the present moment. Quiet your mind and notice the experience in your body. Choose an activity below to cause yourself to begin generating good-feeling emotions that will charge your energy field with positive strings of vibrating energy.

Make a list of what you are grateful for in life—write at least 50 things.

Look at your journal. Read the successes and the miracles and what people love about you.

Go outside in nature. Be present and look at life that everything is a miracle.

Call a friend and be a friend.

Do some remote viewing to reconnect with who you really are.

Put on some music that makes you feel good.

Move your body to get your heart beating. Go for a walk or dance.

Open this book to a random chapter, or read something that inspires you.

Do something you love to do.

Find something humorous to watch or read.

Write in your journal: get the thoughts onto paper so new thoughts may arise.

Pray or bless someone or something and focus your attention outside yourself.

Look for the soul growth that is happening. Be accountable that you made it this way.

Learn something new and stimulate your mind.

Do something for another person, getting the focus off of you.

Make a list of all your successes and what people love about you.

ACKNOWLEDGMENTS

Thank you Kristen Moeller, David Hancock, Scott Frishman and the gang at Imbue Press and Morgan James Publishing for turning my dream into a reality. An extra special thank you to Rick Frishman for creating Author 101 University and giving me the tools, the connections and most importantly, the belief in myself that I am an author and that my words matter.

Hobie Hobart and Kathi Dunn at Dunn + Associates, you guided me through the writing process and created a magnificent cover. Hannah Ryan, you edited my words masterfully. Dorie McClelland of Spring Book Design, you gave warmth to the words with your layout.

To my coaches and mentors, thank you for giving me your all and giving me the foundation to have this book be realized. Ellen Snortland, Brendon Burchard, Tom Antion, Dov Baron, Clint Arthur, Stefanie Hartman, Peter Hoppenfeld, Gary Goldstein, Greg Habstritt, Jeff Walker, Craig Duswalt, Aurora Winter, Alex Carroll and Wendy Lipton-Dibner, I thank you from the bottom of my heart.

Thank you to all the incredible program leaders and fellow participants in Landmark Education and Cultural Architecture that caused me to be more powerful and happier than I've ever known myself to be. Greg Hartmann, you have supported me throughout it all, both as a friend and as a coach and I am so grateful that you always stand for me having the best life ever. Paul D. Nunn, your guidance has made me take action, to fulfill the purpose you told me I had in this life.

Sharon Songal and the crew at Kent Coffee & Chocolate Company, thank you for running the business as your own, so that I may have the time to write. Jill Zinzi, Chucha Cavalleiro, and Darlene Decker I know we all experienced deep, personal grief and I appreciate all that you have given to make a difference in my life and the lives of others.

Chef Duane Larson, David Brabham, Reggie Murphy, Carol Ann Mueller, Vanessa Weikart, Randy Doyle, Holly Connell, Chris Torres, Christian Galan, Donnie Wilson, Mark and Anita Plowman, and all my friends in the American Le Mans and Grand-Am Series of automobile racing, thank you for all of your support and friendship.

Nance Murray, you were the one to introduce me to this new world of the miraculous; thank you for not giving up on me. Dr. Annemarie Leyden, Joannie Luongo, and Laura Atchison, you are the most incredible friends, ever! Michael Coller, your friendship has been immeasurable. I am so grateful for you, as we both traveled through the loss of our parents together. Nancy Lucio, my longest and dearest friend, you have stuck by me through all of the good and all of the tough times and I love you dearly for that. Travis Lane Jenkins, I am honored to be your friend. You called me a rockstar and saw something in me that I didn't see in myself, which paved the way for me taking actions I had never dreamed of taking. Thank you.

To all of my father's friends and loved ones in Florida, especially the gang at Spruce Creek Fly-In, you played an essential role and I deeply appreciate your generosity. To the doctors and the staff at The Feline Hospital, your compassion has meant the world to me and you have taught me so much about the difference our furry friends make in our lives.

Heidi, Steve and Karen, my wonderful siblings, I love you and I thank you for being the most important part of this process. Our journey of losing Dad caused me to explore the world of grief. Thousands have received healing because of you and many more will have access to this important information.

Donna Champlain, my aunt, my housemate, but most importantly, my friend, I thank you for supporting me and caring for me on my journey, especially through all the time I sat on the couch night after night, typing. We shared a lot of grief together with the deaths in our family and I am so grateful we have had each other. I love you, Donna.

Marion Champlain, my wonderful mother, you have always taught me to believe in myself and taught me that it is okay to fail, that failure just means, "It is time to do something else." I thank you for supporting me, believing in me and most importantly, loving me.

Betsy Champlain, my most wonderful grandmother, thank you for making me promise that I would write this book so that the world could heal from my story. I kept my promise, Grammy. I miss you terribly but know that you are often by my side even though I cannot see you.

John Champlain, my dad, losing you in 2010 was the most painful thing that I've ever experienced. I am grateful for being able to spend the last months of your life with you. We shared so many laughs and deep conversations, and I am so grateful to learn how to be generous and inspiring from you. I do realize that although times were tough, you gave your life so that ultimately this book could be written and lives would be saved. I love you, Dad.

To the reader, I thank you for spending your valuable time with the words within this book. I hope they provide hope, faith and comfort to you and I encourage you to go powerfully in the direction of your dreams. Make this life count.

RECOMMENDED READING

Allen, James. *As a Man Thinketh.* White Plains: Peter Pauper, 1900.

Amen, Daniel G. *Making a Good Brain Great: The Amen Clinic Program for Achieving and Sustaining Optimal Mental Performance.* New York: Harmony, 2005.

Arthur, Clint. *The Last Year of Your Life: A Personal Exploration Experience.* Las Vegas, NV: Clint Arthur, I.C.S., 2010.

Baron, Dov. *Don't Read This—Your Ego Won't like It.* Burnaby, BC: Baron Mastery Institute, 2009.

Begley, Sharon. *Train Your Mind, Change Your Brain: How a New Science Reveals Our Extraordinary Potential to Transform Ourselves.* New York: Ballantine, 2007.

Bertoldi, Concetta. *Do Dead People Watch You Shower? And Other Questions You've Been All but Dying to Ask a Medium.* New York: Harper, 2008.

Burchard, Brendon. *Life's Golden Ticket: An Inspirational Novel.* San Francisco: HarperCollins, 2007.

Butler, Tom, and Lisa Butler. *There Is No Death and There Are No Dead: Evidence of Survival and Spirit Communication through Voices and Images from Those on the Other Side.* Reno, NV: AA-EVP Pub, 2003.

Clark, Glenn. *The Man Who Tapped the Secrets of the Universe*: University of Science and Philosophy, 1946.

Coelho, Paulo. *Aleph.* New York: Alfred A. Knopf, 2011.

Dallaire, Jacques. *Performance Thinking.* Concord, NC: Dallaire Consulting LLC, 2012.

Hawkins, David R. *Power vs. Force: The Hidden Determinants of Human Behavior*. Carlsbad, CA: Hay House, 2002.

Hill, Napoleon. *Think and Grow Rich*. Cleveland, Ohio: The Ralston Publishing Co, 1953.

Kübler-Ross, Elisabeth, and David Kessler. *On Grief and Grieving: Finding the Meaning of Grief through the Five Stages of Loss*. London: Simon & Schuster, 2005.

Moody, Raymond A. *Life After Life: The Investigation of a Phenomenon—Survival of Bodily Death*. Harrisburg, PA: Stackpole, 1976.

Ring, Kenneth. *Life at Death: A Scientific Investigation of the Near-Death Experience*. New York: Coward, McCann & Geoghegan, 1980.

Rinpoche, Sogyal. *The Tibetan Book of Living and Dying*: Berkeley, CA: Audio Literature, 1993.

Schwartz, Gary E., and William Simon. *The Afterlife Experiments: Breakthrough Scientific Evidence of Life After Death*. New York: Simon & Schuster, 2003.

Stein, Garth. *The Art of Racing in the Rain: A Novel*. New York: Harper, 2008.

Targ, Russell. *Limitless Mind: A Guide to Remote Viewing and Transformation of Consciousness*. New World Library, 2004.

ABOUT THE AUTHOR

Sandra Champlain is a top graduate of the Culinary Institute of America. She owns The Kent Coffee and Chocolate Company in Connecticut and travels with world-class race car teams providing hospitality in the American Le Mans and Grand-Am series.

Her fear of dying and skepticism led her on a 15-year journey to discover the undeniable proof of life after death. She is the author of *The Law of Chocolate* and *How to Survive Grief*.

Sandra is a highly respected speaker, author, and entrepreneur committed to making a difference in the lives of others. She lives in Byfield, Massachusetts, with her aunt, Donna, and her kitty, Millie.

For more information about Sandra, please visit
SandraChamplain.com

NOTES

NOTES

CPSIA information can be obtained
at www.ICGtesting.com
Printed in the USA
BVHW031445100319
542256BV00002B/76/P

9 781614 483823